THE ULTIMATE QUESTION
AND ANSWER BOOK

BASEBALL

HarperCollins books may be purchased for educational, business, or sales promotional use. For information, please write: Special Markets Department, HarperCollins Publishers, 10 East 53rd Street, New York, NY 10022.

Produced for HarperCollins by:

Hydra Publishing
129 Main Street
Irvington, NY 10533
www.hylaspublishing.com

FIRST EDITION

Library of Congress Cataloging-in-Publication Data

Fischer, David, 1963-
  Smithsonian Q & A : Baseball : the ultimate question and answer book / David Fischer. -- 1st ed.
      p. cm.
  Includes bibliographical references and index.
  ISBN: 978-0-06-089125-1
  ISBN-10: 0-06-089125-4
  1. Baseball--Miscellanea. I. Smithsonian Institution. II. Title. III. Title: Smithsonian Q and A. IV. Title: Smithsonian question and answer. V. Title: Baseball.

  GV873.F49 2007
  796.357--dc22

                                        2007060873

07 08 09 10   QW   10 9 8 7 6 5 4 3 2 1

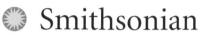

Smithsonian

Q&A

THE ULTIMATE QUESTION
AND ANSWER BOOK

BASEBALL

David Fischer

Collins
An Imprint of HarperCollinsPublishers

BASEBALL

Contents

1   **The National Pastime**

5   **Chapter 1:** Baseball's Early Days

23   **Chapter 2:** Babe Ruth and the Golden Age

41   **Chapter 3:** The Hitters

61   **Chapter 4:** The Pitchers

81   **Chapter 5:** Streaks and Feats

99   **Chapter 6:** Legends, Myths, and Lore

READY REFERENCE
114   Baseball Milestones
118   Most Valuable Player Winners
120   Hall of Famers

Possessing a rocket arm and a ferocious swing, the Angels' Vladimir Guerrero is one of the game's brightest stars.

Baseball has become a global game, with players such as Japan's Hideki Matsui now playing for the New York Yankees.

125 Chapter 7: Customs, Rituals, and Traditions

137 Chapter 8: The Business of Baseball

151 Chapter 9: The War Years

163 Chapter 10: The Changing Game

175 Chapter 11: Trailblazers, Heroes, and Icons

189 Chapter 12: The Ballpark Experience

204 Glossary
208 Further Reading
210 At the Smithsonian
212 Index
218 Acknowledgments/Picture Credits

An autographed baseball is a treasured keepsake for many fans.

THE NATIONAL PASTIME

It is easy to start an argument among baseball fans. All you need do, for example, is tell a Yankees follower that Leo Durocher was a far better manager than Casey Stengel. Or that Willie Mays can run rings around Mickey Mantle. You can get some mighty sharp retorts, too, when trying to name the greatest ball team of all time. Although you would be hard-pressed to top the New York Yankees of 1927. For this was a team that had everything—speed, crushing power, and a marvelous defense. As Casey would say: "You could look it up."

Baseball has been called America's national pastime since the Civil War. It is a uniquely American game and it has spawned more celebrity athletes, unforgettable games, and distinctive jargon than any other sport.

Success in baseball is most often measured by statistics. Today's most ardent stat scientists spend hundreds of hours coming up with new ways to capture the game in numbers. But the numbers and totals that major league players strive to reach each season have changed little

Left: To many fans, spending a summer evening at a venerable ballpark such as Boston's Fenway is nothing short of perfection.

Below: Pittsburgh's new PNC Park pays homage to its baseball history with a statue of Pirates Hall of Famer Honus Wagner keeping watch outside.

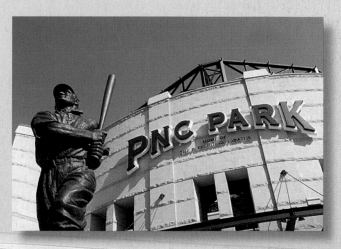

over the decades. For batters: a .300 batting average, 100 runs batted in, 30 home runs, and 30 stolen bases. For starting pitchers: The elusive 20-win season remains the benchmark.

Baseball and its numbers have been inseparable ever since the game's birth. Henry Chadwick, a 19th-century writer, howled endlessly about which statistics mattered and which did not, arousing the curious-minded fan to see for him (or her) self. Over the next 150 years, almost every baseball fan has been drawn to the game by its statistics, whether through newspaper box scores, the back of baseball cards, sports almanacs, or fantasy leagues.

More than any other sports fans, baseball fans have a personal memory book, a treasury of meaningful events and unforgettable feats, moments in which a game was spectacularly won (or lost) against all odds, a brave warrior was crowned champion, or an unspeakable human error cost a team the entire season. It is a common repository. The fan who would think nothing of paying scalpers' prices for a ticket to the World Series and the one who would rather spend it at the theater both remember certain compelling moments in baseball history: Bobby Thomson's "Shot Heard 'Round the World." Roger Maris hitting 61 in '61. Nolan Ryan pitching the seventh no-hitter of his career (at age 44). The night a slugger with a big mouth, Reggie Jackson, did indeed become the straw that stirs the drink.

Over the years, these shared moments and personalities evolve into a kind of canon of baseball history. Babe Ruth allegedly pointing at the center-field bleachers in Chicago's Wrigley Field before belting a

long home run to that exact spot is part of the canon. The night Cal Ripken broke Lou Gehrig's "unbreakable" record for consecutive games played is also included. So is Jackie Robinson, the first black player in modern major league history. Bigoted players and fans insulted him, but he answered their taunts with a .297 batting average and the first-ever Rookie of the Year award. And yes, so is the achingly sad death of Roberto Clemente, who died in a plane crash while delivering supplies to earthquake victims in Nicaragua in 1972.

Players' attitudes have changed. Fans' attitudes have changed. Rules have changed. Motives have changed. Franchises have moved across the country. Free-agent heroes have come and gone, selling their services to the highest bidder. Old loyalties have been shaken, uprooted and forgotten. Well, the times, indeed, have changed.

Still, baseball will manage to prevail, despite television saturation, and the destruction of the illusion that owners always think first of their fans and players, and that players always think first of their fans.

To be sure, baseball is bigger than any one player, any labor contract, or any club owner. The beauty of the game, the thrill of a great performance, can make us forget the other stuff. Sometimes all it takes is one crack of the bat or one spectacular catch. And as we approach the second decade of the 21st century, it is not gambling or free agency that we think about—it is the game and the players, and the anticipation of going to the ballpark and seeing something you've never seen before.

More than 76 million people attended major league games in the United States and Canada in 2006, establishing a single-season attendance record for the third consecutive season. If there is still a doubt that baseball is not our country's national pastime, remember the last two words of our national anthem: "Play ball!"

Left: Perennial all-star, Yankees shortstop Derek Jeter is one of those rare players who has spent his entire career with one team.

Right: Not even the grim realities of World War I could deter these soldiers from enjoying an impromptu game of baseball. Many professional ballplayers also served their country with valor in wartime.

CHAPTER 1

BASEBALL'S EARLY DAYS

Throughout history children and adults have played games that involve hitting a ball with a stick and running from one base to another. Baseball as we know it today evolved in part from the British games of cricket and rounders, which came to New England with the earliest colonists.

Still immensely popular overseas, cricket is played between two 11-person teams. There are two wickets, one at each end of a long field. A wicket consists of three sticks 28 inches high. A batter, called a striker, stands in front of a wicket. A bowler (similar to a baseball pitcher) throws the ball at a wicket. If the striker hits the ball, he runs back and forth between the wickets. Each time he reaches a wicket he scores a run for his team. If the striker misses the ball and the ball hits the wicket, the striker is out.

In rounders, which was played mostly by children in the schoolyards, the striker hits a pitched ball, runs counterclockwise around four posts—similar in concept to bases—and can be "out" if the ball is caught before it hits the ground.

As cricket and rounders migrated throughout the Northeast, many uniquely American variations grew out of these two British games, including old cat, barn ball, round ball, town ball, and a game played in parks in New York City in the early 1840s called base ball.

Above: A friendly game of cricket is played in Hoboken, New Jersey, in October 1859. Baseball evolved in part from the British games of cricket and rounders, which came to New England with the earliest colonists.

Left: Fielders' gloves have been used since the 1870s. Back then they were no more than a thin piece of leather that covered and protected the palm of the hand.

Getting Organized

Q: **What were base-ball's first written rules?**

A: On September 23, 1845, in a public park in Manhattan, Alexander Joy Cartwright, a 25-year-old bank teller and volunteer fireman from New York City, helped write a list of rules for the game of "base ball" that he and his friends played.

The rules for their game, a loose version of rounders, included:

- The bases shall be from "home" to second base, forty-two paces; from first to third base, forty-two paces, equidistant.
- The ball must be pitched, not thrown, for the bat.
- A ball knocked out of the field, or outside the range of the first and third base, is foul.
- A player running the bases shall be out if the ball is in the hands of an adversary on the base, or the runner is touched with it before he makes his base; it being understood, however, that in no instance is a ball to be thrown at him.
- Players must take their strike in regular turn.

The game as played by Cartwright and his associates nudged baseball away from

Alexander Cartwright, founder of the Knickerbocker Base Ball Club of New York, in 1860. Fifteen years earlier, he had written the first set of standard rules for baseball.

its British roots by placing the batter at home plate, instead of several feet away toward first base, as in rounders. In rounders, an entire team had to be retired to end an inning, but Cartwright's rules reduced the outs needed to complete an inning to three. Runners were tagged out or thrown out; previously the ball had been thrown at the runner for an out. Other rules were changed or added through the years. By the early 1900s, baseball was being played practically the same way it is today.

Q: **What was the first organized baseball team ever?**

A: After putting down rules in September 1845, Cartwright and about 25 friends formed the Knickerbocker Base Ball Club of New York. The Knickerbockers fashioned their own uniforms: white flannel shirts and blue wool pants with a straw hat, and began playing games in public parks in New York and New Jersey.

As other ball clubs began to formally adopt the Knickerbocker rules, organized games became common. Within a few years baseball was being played all over the East Coast.

Q: **Where did the Knickerbockers play their first game?**

A: The first organized baseball game played by Cartwright's rules was held on June 19, 1846, at the Elysian Fields, a grassy picnic area overlooking the Hudson River in Hoboken, New Jersey. With Cartwright as umpire, the New York Base Ball Club beat the Knickerbockers at their own game, 23–1, in four innings.

Due to the fact that there were very few suitable fields in Manhattan, the Knickerbockers made the Elysian Fields their permanent home, and as new teams were organized, they journeyed to Hoboken for games that attracted large gatherings of spectators. By the end of the decade several other clubs were using the grounds as well.

Q: **How long before the first league was formed?**

A: By 1858 the Knickerbockers and 24 other teams from the New York City area that played by the same rules formed the National Association of Base Ball Players (NABBP). By the middle of the 1860s about 60 teams belonged to this organization, which had been created to regulate the game. One of the association's main rules was that all players must be amateurs. But as more teams were formed, the demand for good players grew, and some teams began paying top players to play for them.

One of the early baseball games played at the Elysian Fields in Hoboken, New Jersey. This was the 1840s home of Alexander Cartwright's Knickerbocker Base Ball Club.

Birth of a Game

Q: Who is commonly—and incorrectly—credited as the man who invented baseball?

A: Baseball was not invented. Baseball evolved.

For many years it was believed that a student named Abner Doubleday created baseball in 1839 in Cooperstown, a small town in rural upstate New York.

According to legend, Doubleday tweaked the rules of the game of town ball and established rules for a new game that he called baseball. It was said that he laid out a diamond-shaped field in Elihu Phinney's Cooperstown cow pasture, thus creating the first baseball field. For a long time this story was accepted as the origin of baseball, and for this reason the town of Cooperstown was chosen as the site of the National Baseball Hall of Fame and Museum. In fact, the story says that Doubleday Field, where the annual Hall of Fame Game is held each summer, was built on the site of that very same cow pasture where Doubleday allegedly created the baseball field.

Doubleday was a heroic Civil War general at the Battle of Gettysburg, and he later became an influential writer and stirring

Abner Doubleday, the legendary creator of baseball, in 1861. Even if Doubleday did not invent baseball, the Union general did distinguish himself at the Battle of Gettysburg.

orator—but he is most certainly not the inventor of baseball. Doubleday could not have been in Cooperstown in 1839; his military records show he was at West Point. No matter, said a special baseball commission appointed in 1905 to determine the origins of the great American pastime. The members of the Mills Commission wanted to find evidence that baseball was an American creation, in no way associated to the similar game from Great Britain called rounders.

Q: How did Henry Chadwick help champion the game?

A: In the late 1850s stories about baseball games began appearing regularly in newspapers. Sportswriter Henry Chadwick helped make baseball popular by writing many articles and books about it. He wrote manuals on how to play and edited early baseball guides. He published the original rulebook in 1858 and served as chairman of the first rules committee. Born in England, Chadwick relied on his cricket background to promote baseball in America and was considered the most knowledgeable source of the day.

In 1868 Chadwick published a history of baseball that greatly helped to popularize the game throughout the United States. Chadwick also published the idea—later proved to be at least partially true—that baseball evolved from the British games of rounders and cricket. It was this idea that led to the search for baseball's origins, which eventually gave birth to the Abner Doubleday myth.

Q: When did the first box score appear in newspapers?

A: Sportswriter Henry Chadwick compiled an early box score, published in the *New York Clipper* in the summer of 1859. The game was played between two Brooklyn, New York, teams, the Stars and the Excelsiors. The Stars won 17–12, scoring 10 runs in the top of the ninth inning.

The makeup of Chadwick's original box score—so called for the old newspaper custom of placing the data in a boxed-off section on the page—consisted of five columns devoted to each player's runs, hits, putouts, assists, and errors. Also included were a line score (an inning-by-inning accounting of runs), the umpire, and time of game. Chadwick's was the first box score as we know it today, an offshoot of British variations that appeared prior to 1859.

Chadwick's box score creation appeared regularly in newspapers after the organization of the National League in 1876. As the game's popularity grew, the box score became an integral device for reporting data comprehensively in a condensed space. The creation of the newspaper box score also allowed readers to measure one player's performance against another's in a fair and statistical fashion. According to pioneering baseball executive Branch Rickey, the box score is "the mortar of which baseball is held together."

Stories about baseball games began appearing regularly in newspapers in the 1850s. Sportswriter Henry Chadwick of the *New York Clipper*, seen here in 1888, helped make baseball even more popular by writing many articles and books about it.

> "[I] was struck with the idea that base ball was just the game for a national sport for Americans and . . . that from this game of ball a powerful lever might be made by which our people could be lifted into a position of more devotion to physical exercise and healthful out-door recreation than they had, hitherto, been noted for."
>
> —*Henry Chadwick, from his book* The Game of Base Ball: How to Learn It, How to Play It, and How to Teach It

America's Pastime

Q: How did the Civil War affect baseball?

A: Despite the political tumult causing a divided America, baseball's popularity actually grew during the Civil War (1861–65) as both Union and Confederate soldiers played the game in their camps as a morale booster whenever they could find the time.

The Civil War was the first time that baseball would bring people together during a national crisis. Soldiers from both sides, often far from home, could bond by sharing common interests such as baseball. The games served as an emotional escape to relieve stress and ease boredom. Baseball games also created an esprit de corps among the men, because both officers and enlisted men played on a level playing field, with soldiers earning their baseball stripes with athletic success, not by their military rank or family connections.

The large numbers of young males now learning and playing the game caused baseball to begin morphing from a sport once played by gentlemen in straw hats into a recreational pastime for folks of every race, religion, and social background.

After the battles ceased and the war came to an end, thousands of young men returned home to the North and South to spread the gospel of baseball. The resulting widespread knowledge of the game's rules and strategies brought attention to its simple charms and presaged baseball's first golden age, in the 1880s.

Union prisoners play baseball at Salisbury, North Carolina, in this 1863 lithograph by Otto Boetticher, a Union soldier and artist from New York who was held prisoner at the Confederate prison at Salisbury in 1862.

Q: Who were baseball's earliest folk heroes?

A: In the 1860s, newspapers and magazines about baseball were helping to make national heroes of some of the players. In addition to developing individual skills, the early amateur players added something more to the game—aggressiveness. In 1865 Eddie Cuthbert of the Philadelphia Keystones startled the fans by making the first sliding steal of a base. He did it by dropping to the seat of his pants and thrusting both legs forward. In 1869 another player, Bob Addy of the Rockford (Illinois) Forest Citys, was even more daring. He slid headfirst, riding on his stomach.

The game was becoming faster, and more exciting. Baseball was making great strides, but it was still only a beginning. By the 1880s baseball was so ingrained in the American culture that poems and popular songs were being written about it. Some players even inspired songs about themselves.

Mike "King" Kelly was a big star in the early days of professional baseball. His speed was legendary. On a base-stealing attempt Kelly would begin his dive into second base about 10 feet from the bag, often prompting second basemen to jump out of harm's way. In Chicago, where he starred from 1880 to 1886, the crowds loved to cry, "Slide, Kelly, slide!" as he began his approach to second. This battle cry became the title of a popular song of the era:

Slide, Kelly, slide!
Your running's a disgrace!
Slide, Kelly, slide!
Stay there, hold your base!
If someone doesn't steal ya,
And your batting doesn't fail ya,
They'll take you to Australia,
Slide, Kelly, slide!

But the most famous work of all, Ernest Lawrence Thayer's "Casey at the Bat," was published in the *San Francisco Examiner* on June 3, 1888. Reading and hearing the poem has brought joy to generations of Americans, if none to Mudville.

Thayer, who had been editor of the *Harvard Lampoon* in college before going to work for the *Examiner's* founder, William Randolph Hearst, originally published "Casey" anonymously. The poem that brought American baseball to verse was an instant hit, and a fictional ballplayer named Casey became a new American folk hero.

By the summer of 1889, people began flocking to vaudeville shows at Wallack's Theater in New York City to hear actor DeWolf Hopper recite Thayer's poem. Hopper claimed to have delivered the piece on stage more than 10,000 times. Most everyone has heard or read at least part of "Casey at the Bat," which is subtitled, "A Ballad of the Republic, Sung in the Year 1888." The final verse of the poem is a classic.

Oh, somewhere in this favored land
    the sun is shining bright;
The band is playing somewhere,
    and somewhere hearts are light,
And somewhere men are laughing,
    and somewhere children shout;
But there is no joy in Mudville
    —mighty Casey has struck out.

William Randolph Hearst, seen here in 1904, first published Ernest Lawrence Thayer's poem "Casey at the Bat" in the *San Francisco Examiner*, on June 3, 1888.

It's a Living

Q: Who was the "Father of Professional Baseball"?

A: That honor goes to Harry Wright, a former cricket player who played outfield on Alexander Cartwright's Knickerbocker team. By 1867 Wright had moved to the baseball hotbed of Cincinnati, to serve as player-manager of the newly formed Cincinnati Red Stockings.

With the Red Stockings, Wright was an outfielder, a pitcher, and a manager. The first manager to use coaching signals during games, he molded the Red Stockings into a terrific team by emphasizing teamwork and strategy. On the mound, he perfected the change-up—a slower pitch thrown to surprise batters looking for a fastball. Wright introduced the pants and stockings that are still a standard part of baseball uniforms, and he also came up with the idea of playing extra innings to decide the outcome of a tie game.

The Red Stockings under Wright's leadership did well drawing fans, but after the novelty wore off the team had trouble competing with the more established Cincinnati Buckeyes. The Buckeyes were officially an amateur team, as were all teams of the time. Some Buckeyes players, however, were receiving salaries from the team under the table. In 1868 Wright decided to openly offer salaries to the best baseball players he could find.

Q: What was the first professional baseball team?

A: By 1869 Wright had signed nine players to contracts at an average annual salary of $950 to play for his Cincinnati Red Stockings, and the first baseball team composed completely of "admitted" professional players was formed. The Red Stockings played their initial game on March 15, 1869, routing Antioch College, 41–7.

Wright figured that if people would pay one dollar to attend the theater they would gladly pay half that amount to watch a baseball game. He was right. The Red Stockings (who still play in Cincinnati but are now known simply as the Reds) soon had other professional teams to compete against. They traveled to Brooklyn, Philadelphia, and Washington, D.C., to play before enthusiastic crowds. Clearly, word of mouth was spreading.

The Red Stockings finished the year with 51 wins, no losses, and one tie. Their success made other cities want professional teams of their own. Wright and his fellow pros had proven that Americans enjoyed watching professionals play.

Harry Wright, known as the Father of Professional Baseball, in the late 1880s. Wright organized the first professional baseball team, the Cincinnati Red Stockings, in 1869.

New York Mutuals, Troy (New York) Haymakers, Fort Wayne (Indiana) Kekiongas, Cleveland Forest Cities, Washington (D.C.) Nationals, and the Rockford (Illinois) Forest Cities. In those days, athletic clubs in small cities could form pro teams, unlike today, where only major metropolises play host to teams.

Some of the clubs lasted only a short time in the original National Association. In baseball's early days, teams sometimes disbanded in the middle of a season or were transformed into other franchises with the exchange of little more than a handshake between the owners or organizers.

The National Association did introduce important changes to the game, such as fielders' gloves and called strikes by umpires—until then, batters did not have to swing unless they wanted to. Trick pitches such as curveballs and change-ups were commonplace, but pitchers still threw underhand.

The National Association, however, may have tried to grow too big too quickly. Two teams were added in 1872; by 1875 there were 13. Fan support was not yet strong enough to keep all of them in business. In 1875, after five seasons, the league collapsed. Yet, a true major league was soon to be formed.

The nine players of the Cincinnati Red Stockings Base Ball Club, the first professional team, earned an average annual salary of $950.

Q: What was the first professional baseball league?

A: During the winter of 1870, Wright and his associates on other teams broke away from the National Association of Base Ball Players, which still claimed to be for amateurs only. In March of 1871 they formed a new organization and called it the National Association of Professional Base Ball Players. This was the first major pro league.

The National Association had 10 teams its first season: the Philadelphia Athletics, Chicago White Stockings, Boston Red Stockings, Washington (D.C.) Olympics,

The National Game

Q: What cities made up the original National League?

A: In 1876 Chicago businessman William A. Hulbert and seven other owners formed the National League of Professional Baseball Clubs. Eventually, the new organization simply called itself the National League.

This new National League consisted of teams in Boston, Chicago, Cincinnati, Hartford, Louisville, New York, Philadelphia, and St. Louis. The league decided to include only teams from cities with more than 75,000 people. Ticket prices were set at 50 cents, and no games were played on Sundays. Alcohol and gambling, common at baseball games until now, were barred.

Q: Who won the first National League game?

A: The first official National League baseball game was played on April 22, 1876, with the visiting Boston Red Stockings scoring two runs in the ninth ining to defeat the Philadelphia Athletics, 6–5. Boston's Jim O'Rourke got the first National League hit, and Joe Borden became the league's first winning pitcher.

The National League took bold steps to help professional baseball thrive: rule changes now allowed batters three strikes for an out or four balls for a walk; pitchers were encouraged to throw overhand; and for the first time fans could buy food and beverages at the ballpark.

> **Notable NL Firsts**
> • First Home Run: Ross Barnes, Chicago White Stockings, May 2, 1876.
> • First Grand Slam: Roger Connor, Troy Trojans, September 10, 1881.
> • First No-Hitter: George Bradley, St. Louis Brown Stockings, July 15, 1876.
> • First Perfect Game: John Richmond, Worcester Ruby Legs, June 12, 1880.

Q: Who was the National League's first big drawing card?

A: Albert Goodwill Spalding was the best pitcher of the 1870s and would become the first professional to win 200 games. Spalding led the Boston Red Stockings to four straight National Association championships. He won 54 games in

Albert Spalding was the best pitcher of the 1870s and the first professional to win 200 games. He became an influential force in sports business after his playing career ended.

1875—including 24 in a row—and earned enough newspaper headlines to become the most famous pitcher in America. In 1876 Spalding left Boston to pitch for the Chicago White Stockings in the new National League. He won 47 games that year, leading Chicago to the championship.

In the middle of the next season Spalding gave up pitching. His arm was overworked, and he had bigger things in mind for baseball. He devoted himself to becoming a full-time business executive and promoter of the game.

Q: Which of the original National League teams remain?

A: Though the National League started with eight teams located in cities capable of supplying plenty of fan support and media attention, the league did struggle with internal problems during its first few years.

The Mutuals of New York and the Athletics of Philadelphia, once eliminated from pennant contention, refused to make road trips. The Cincinnati Reds broke the rules by selling beer at games, and Hulbert tried to expel the team from the league. A gambling scandal involving players on the Louisville Grays caused that team to fold.

In fact, of the original eight teams, only Boston (now the Atlanta Braves), Chicago, and Cincinnati are still in the National League today.

Q: Did other leagues compete with the National League?

A: Several rival leagues hoping to challenge the National League came and went between 1877 and 1892. The American Association, formed in 1882, was the most successful. For a time, the six clubs of the American Association attracted more paying customers than the National League by charging 25 cents admission (NL admission was still 50 cents), playing games on Sundays, and selling beer. The "Beer and Whiskey League," as it was known, folded after the 1891 season, but it was fun while it lasted.

Then, in 1893, a former college baseball player and sportswriter-turned-entrepreneur by the name of Byron Bancroft "Ban" Johnson took over a struggling minor league called the Western League. Under Johnson's leadership the league became a financial success, and by 1899 it had changed its name to the American League.

Ban Johnson (left), founder and first president of the American League, attending a World Series game at the Polo Grounds in New York.

> "I ask all living professional baseball players to join me in raising our hats to the memory of William A. Hulbert, the man who saved the game."
>
> — ALBERT SPALDING, WRITING AFTER HULBERT'S DEATH, AT THE AGE OF 49, IN APRIL 1882

American Staying Power

Q: Which teams made up the original American League?

A: Ban Johnson's new American League began play in 1901 with eight teams: the Baltimore Orioles, Boston Pilgrims, Chicago White Stockings, Cleveland Spiders, Detroit Tigers, Milwaukee Brewers, Philadelphia Athletics, and Washington Senators. When Orioles manager John McGraw said a team in Philadelphia would be "a white elephant," meaning a money loser, Philadelphia owner Connie Mack replied by making the white elephant the team's symbol.

Persuading Mack to take command of the newly formed Philadelphia club by promising him a one-quarter ownership in the franchise was Johnson's shrewdest move. Connie Mack, whose real name was Cornelius McGillicuddy, guided his Philadelphia A's to five World Series. He managed in the major leagues for 53 seasons and retired in 1950, at age 87, with the record for most wins by a manager (3,731).

Q: What was key to the American League's survival?

A: The American League survived because it played by the rules—that is, the American League played baseball with the accepted rules already agreed upon by the National League. Between 1877 and 1892, when new leagues came and went, the rules of the game were changing nearly

every year. This was confusing to fans. For example, the number of balls it took to draw a walk changed from nine, to eight, to seven, to six, then went back to seven, down to five, and finally, in 1889, to four, where it remains today.

Johnson was keenly aware that playing by the rules would be a main factor of American League stability, and he was just the person to make it happen. He was one of baseball's most influential men for more than 25 years. He served on baseball's three-man National Commission, which ran the sport until the appointment of the first commissioner in 1920. He also played a major role in elevating the power of umpires, helping to keep what was a rowdy game under control, and thus enhancing its reputation and popularity among the public.

Thanks to Johnson's efforts, combined with player raids and a leadership void in the NL, the American League was soon considered equal to the National League. In fact, all eight original franchises are alive today, despite moves and expansion contortions. Milwaukee became the St. Louis Browns in 1902, who then became the Baltimore

Above right: These members of the National Commission, made up of (left to right) NL president Harry Pulliam, Cincinnati owner August Herrmann, AL president Ban Johnson, and J. E. Bruce (the group's secretary), ran major league baseball until 1920.

Below: No man led a major league baseball team for more years, 50, than Philadelphia's Connie Mack, whose real name was Cornelius McGillicuddy.

Orioles in 1954. The original Orioles became the New York Highlanders (later the Yankees) in 1903. And the Philadelphia Athletics moved to Kansas City in 1955, and eventually Oakland in 1968.

Notable AL Firsts

- First Winning Pitcher: Roy Patterson, Chicago, April 24, 1901.
- First Home Run: Erve Beck, Cleveland Indians, April 25, 1901.
- First Grand Slam: Herm McFarland, Chicago White Sox, May 1, 1901.
- First No-Hitter: Jim Callahan, Chicago White Sox, September 20, 1902.
- First Perfect Game: Cy Young, Boston Red Sox, May 5, 1904.

Q: How did the American League jump-start baseball's popularity?

A: American League owners offered National League stars more money in the hopes of luring them to switch leagues. As a result, more than a hundred National League players jumped over to the new American League team, which was quite often in the same city, including future Hall of Famers "Wee Willie" Keeler and Denton True "Cy" Young.

These regional rivalries naturally sparked debate among baseball fans in the nation's largest cities. Whereas talk of the day had once centered on religion or politics, the majority of Americans were now wrapped up in baseball.

By the early 1900s major league baseball was exploding in popularity. There were no other pro sports to compete with it. Baseball mania seized America as new heroes emerged as icons to a cheering public.

Q: Who was the American League's first hitting superstar?

A: Napoleon Lajoie (la-jo-ay) was a graceful second baseman and the first great American League hitter of the early 1900s. He hit .300 or better in 16 of his 21 major league seasons, and he batted over .350 ten times. His lifetime average is .338, and he accumulated more than 3,000 hits.

In 1901 he left the Philadelphia Phillies to join the rival Athletics of the brand-new American League, where he won the Triple Crown with a .422 batting average, 14 home runs, and 125 RBIs. In late 1904 he was named player-manager of the Cleveland Blues, who soon changed their name to the Naps in his honor.

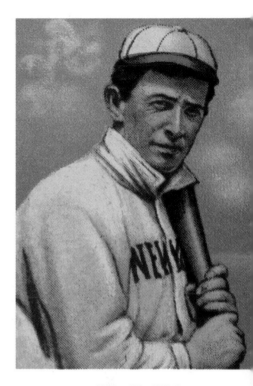

William "Wee Willie" Keeler, a future Hall of Famer, was one of the more than 100 National League stars who jumped over to the American League for more money in 1901.

"Baseball is the very symbol, the outward and visible expression of the drive and push and rush and struggle of the raging, tearing, booming nineteenth century."

—MARK TWAIN, *1889*

Solid Foundations

Q: Which team was the first 20th-century baseball dynasty?

A: The Chicago Cubs, winners of three straight National League championships between 1906 and 1908. The Cubs were led by that fabled double-play combination of shortstop Joe Tinker, second baseman Johnny Evers, and first baseman–manager Frank Chance, the only players to enter the Hall of Fame together as a unit. But these Cubs were built on pitching, and the formidable rotation of Mordecai "Three-Finger" Brown, Ed Reulbach, Orval Overall, and John Pfiester won 232 of the amazing 322 wins the Cubs amassed in those three unforgettable seasons.

The Cubs won a major-league record 116 games in 1906, finishing a distant 20 games ahead of the second-place New York Giants. But then, to the astonishment of everyone, they lost in the World Series, four games to two, to the Chicago White Sox in the first and only all-Chicago World Series. Known as the "Hitless Wonders," the Sox batted just .230 that season, with just seven home runs.

Despite the upset, the Cubs stormed back with 107 wins in 1907 and finished 17 games ahead of the Pittsburgh Pirates. The Cubs then won the World Series by sweeping the Detroit Tigers in four straight games, stealing 16 bases in the process. The next year, the Cubs once again crushed the Tigers in the Series, four games to one this time, winning so convincingly that only 6,210 fans, the smallest crowd in World Series history, showed up at Detroit's Bennett Park to watch the fifth and final game.

It was, as it turns out, the last World Series the Cubs have ever won.

Q: What is the oldest ballpark still in use?

A: The 1912 season saw the debut of Fenway Park, the unique and charming home field of the Boston Red Sox. The Red Sox were scheduled to open Fenway Park, so named because it was built in the Fenway section of Boston, on April 18, 1912, against the New York Highlanders (who would change their name to the Yankees in 1913).

The Fenway Park grand opening was overshadowed by tragedy and delayed by rain. On April 15, 1912, three days before the scheduled opener, the ocean liner *Titanic* sank in the Atlantic Ocean. More than 1,500 people died.

Tris Speaker, the Hall of Fame center fielder with the Boston Red Sox, in 1911. When Fenway Park opened the next season, Speaker drove in the winning run in the first game ever played there.

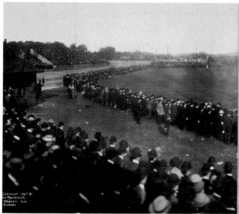

WORLD'S CHAMPIONSHIP SERIES
CHICAGO vs DETROIT
Bennett Park, Oct 12, 1907

Left: The Chicago Cubs play the Detroit Tigers at Bennett Park in the deciding fifth game of the 1907 World Series. Mordecai "Three Finger" Brown wrapped up the Series for Chicago with a 2–0 victory.

Johnny Evers of the Chicago Cubs in 1911. The second baseman teamed with shortstop Joe Tinker and first baseman Frank Chance to form a fabled double-play combination.

Understandably, the catastrophe was front-page news for many days.

On April 18 the scheduled opener was rained out. The rain continued on April 19. Finally, on Saturday, April 20, Fenway Park hosted its first major league baseball game. Some 27,000 fans were in attendance.

The Highlanders entered the game with a five-game losing streak. New York scored three runs in the top of the first inning off Red Sox spitball ace (the spitball was still legal) Buck O'Brien. The Sox rallied to tie the score, and the game eventually went into extra innings with the score tied 6–6. In the bottom of the 11th inning, Boston center fielder Tris Speaker ended the 3-hour, 20-minute marathon with an RBI single. Boston won the game 7–6.

Today Fenway Park is the oldest ballpark in the major leagues. Although the stadium still looks much as it did when it opened, it is worth noting that the fabled Green Monster—the 37-foot-high left-field wall—was not built until 1934. Before then, left field ended with a steep 10-foot embankment where fans were allowed to sit. That ridge was known as "Duffy's Cliff" after Red Sox left fielder Duffy Lewis. Fans today can sit in seats atop the Monster.

Squashing the Competition

Q: When was the Federal League established?

A: Baseball had become such profitable business by 1914 that a third league, the eight-team Federal League, declared itself a major league and began buying star ballplayers from the National and American leagues.

Chicago Cubs shortstop Joe Tinker and pitcher Mordecai "Three Finger" Brown were two of the first to jump to the new league. Walter "The Big Train" Johnson (so nicknamed because that's what his fastball sounded like), the Washington Senators' star pitcher, nearly signed with the upstart league, but at the last moment the American League owners chipped in to pay for his salary increase.

On April 13, 1914, one day before major league baseball's opening day, the Federal League launched its inaugural season as the Baltimore Terrapins beat the Buffalo Feds 3–2, in front of 27,140 fans. American League and National League officials took notice of the large crowd. Some Federal League players shined. Benny Kauff paced the league with a .370 batting average for the Indianapolis Hoosiers, who captured the Federal League flag in 1914. (The Hoosiers became the Newark Peps in 1915, the only major league pennant-winner to move to a new city the next year.)

The Federal League, hounded by lawsuits from the other two leagues, soon began losing money. Fans, their curiosity satisfied, returned to watching the established American and National league teams. A year later, the Federal league folded.

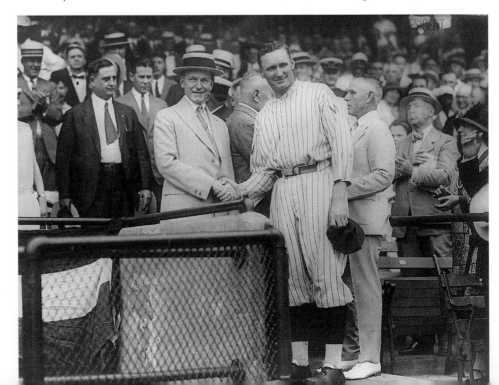

Walter Johnson of the Washington Senators shaking hands with President Calvin Coolidge at Griffith Stadium. American League owners had chipped in to help pay for Johnson's salary increase for the 1914 season.

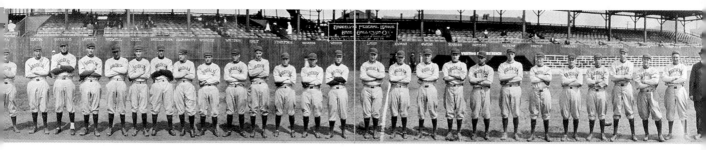

Q: How was the Federal League lawsuit settled?

A: The first major battle for the public's sporting dollars was settled on December 22, 1915, in Cincinnati, when an agreement was negotiated between the Federal League and the major leagues. In exchange for its surrender, the National and American league owners paid each of the Federal League owners $600,000, an enormous sum in those days. With the signing of baseball's peace treaty, economic security and financial prosperity—at least for the owners—would soon return to major league baseball.

The American and National league owners agreed to forgive those players that had jumped to the rival Federal League and allowed them to be reinstated and placed in a pool of players made eligible for a special draft. Teams were then allowed to buy back those players, causing a scramble for the best players to sell their services to the highest bidder.

Two Federal League owners were allowed to purchase existing major league teams. Charles Weeghman, who had been owner of the Chicago Whales, took over the Chicago Cubs of the National League. Philip Ball of the St. Louis Terriers took control of the St. Louis Browns of the American League. The conditions of these sales later became clear when the players from the Federal League clubs in Chicago and St. Louis were required to join the respective clubs in the National and American leagues.

Q: Did all Federal League teams abide by the settlement?

A: The Baltimore franchise refused to drop the Federal League's legal claim against organized baseball as being in violation of antitrust laws of fair business practices that was brought before Judge Kenesaw Mountain Landis—the man who would become the game's first commissioner by the end of the decade.

Baltimore pursued the lawsuit all the way to the U.S. Supreme Court. The result was a 1922 decision by Justice Oliver Wendell Holmes that gave the major leagues the ability to operate without competition.

No rival baseball league has since competed against the American and National leagues.

Members of the Federal League Brooklyn Tip-Tops at their Washington Park grounds in 1914. The next year the Federal League would fold after just two seasons, and no rival circuit has since competed against the American and National leagues.

CHAPTER 2

BABE RUTH AND THE GOLDEN AGE

Babe Ruth hit his first home run on May 6, 1915, off New York Yankees pitcher Jack Warhop. Five years later, in 1920, he was sold to the Yankees, where he became an outfielder and gained fame as "The Sultan of Swat" and "The Bambino" for his power hitting. He was the first batter to slug 30, 40, 50, and 60 home runs in a season, and when he belted his 700th career homer in 1934 it was a record that many thought would stand for all time.

Ruth changed the very way the game was played. He ushered out the age of the singles hitters and helped transform baseball into a power-hitting game. His hitting exploits were so legendary, it is sometimes forgotten that he began his career in 1914 as a pitcher for the Boston Red Sox, and a pretty good one at that.

The Babe retired in 1935, and the following year he was chosen among the first players elected to the National Baseball Hall of Fame, along with Honus Wagner, Christy Mathewson, Walter Johnson, and Ty Cobb.

To fully grasp how the power hitting of baseball's biggest star created a new style of play, saved the game from taint, and ushered in baseball's golden age, it is important to first look back at how baseball was played at the turn of the century.

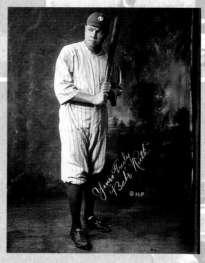

Above: Babe Ruth, whose home runs traveled higher and farther than anyone had ever thought imaginable.

Left: Yankee Stadium, with a capacity of 38,000, opened in April 1923, as the largest baseball park in the United States. Attendance for opening day was 70,000, and by 1937 the building was expanded to hold that many.

The Dead Ball Era

Q: What was the "Dead Ball Era"?

A: During the years between 1900 and 1919 baseball was dominated by great pitchers, such as Cy Young, Walter Johnson, and Grover Cleveland Alexander. Solid pitching and speed on the base paths were the mark of the great teams of the era. During those years players like Frank "Home Run" Baker, who hit 10 to 12 homers in a season, led the league. Runs were manufactured through bunting and stealing.

This period was known as the "Dead Ball Era." In those days, the baseball was soft and loosely wound, and therefore did not travel very far even when batters managed to hit it. Not that there were not some great hitters during those years—Ty Cobb, Joe Jackson, and Honus Wagner all had career batting averages well over .300—but the pitchers of the day had a clear advantage.

Q: Who were the best hitters during the Dead Ball Era?

A: The Detroit Tigers center fielder Ty Cobb was the American League's biggest star during the dead-ball era. He finished his career with an astounding 4,189 hits, and his lifetime .367 batting average is the highest in major league history. Cobb batted .400 or better three times, including a .420 season in 1911. His 12 batting titles—including 9 in a row—are a record, and his total of 892 stolen bases stood as the benchmark for 50 years.

Cobb described baseball as "an unrelenting war of nerves" and played the game like a ticking time bomb. He sought every advantage, physical and mental, to intimidate and defeat his opponents. Cobb went so far as to sharpen his metal spikes and slide into bases with his feet high in the air. "He got meaner than the devil himself," said teammate Davy Jones.

The Tigers roared from 1907 to 1909, winning three consecutive pennants, but lost in the World Series every time. Cobb won the Triple Crown in 1909, leading the league in batting average, home runs, and RBIs. He also led the league in stolen bases that year.

Cobb became Detroit's player-manager in 1921 and guided the club through 1926, when he suddenly retired amid

Ty Cobb of the Detroit Tigers in 1915, the year he hit .369 to lead all American League batters for a record ninth year in a row. He also stole 96 bases, a record that would stand for 47 years.

triples, doubles, and stolen bases. He led the league in stolen bases five times, hence his nickname, "The Flying Dutchman."

Q: How did equipment improvements and rules changes mark the end of the Dead Ball Era?

A: Pitchers at this time were allowed to smear the ball with dirt or tobacco juice. They were allowed to scuff, sandpaper, or spit on the ball. Because of these tactics the ball moved in an unpredictable manner and was difficult to see as it crossed the plate. One unfortunate side effect of this was that several players were hit and injured by these pitches. In 1920 Ray Chapman of the Cleveland Indians was hit with a pitch that crushed his skull and later killed him. Chapman claimed he never saw the ball coming.

Eventually, rules were adopted that changed the way the game was played. The spitball was outlawed, although some pitchers who depended on the pitch in order to continue their careers were exempted from the rule. All other foreign substances on the ball were banned. If a ball was dirty, the umpire removed it from play, replacing it with a clean ball. The yarn within the ball itself was also wound more tightly, making it livelier when hit. A clean, tightly wound baseball now crossed the plate, and batters could see it better and hit it farther.

The era of the pitcher was ending, and the era of the home-run hitter was about to begin. But first baseball had to weather its darkest moment.

Honus Wagner of the Pittsburgh Pirates is considered one of the best shortstops in baseball history. He led the National League in batting eight times during the early 1900s.

accusations of having fixed a game back in 1919. Baseball commissioner Kenesaw Mountain Landis cleared Cobb, and Cobb returned to baseball to play for Connie Mack's Philadelphia Athletics. Cobb played two more seasons, and then retired in 1928, batting .323 in his final year.

Over in the National League, Honus Wagner was among the best players in the early 1900s, and arguably the best shortstop in major league history. He starred for the Pittsburgh Pirates from 1900 to 1917. Wagner was the NL batting champ eight times, between 1900 and 1911. His lifetime batting average is .327, and his 3,420 hits put him sixth on the all-time list. He ranks among the career leaders in

The Black Sox Scandal

Charles Comiskey was a star first baseman in the 1880s, but his penny-pinching ways as owner of the Chicago White Sox led to a disastrous player revolt in 1919.

Q: Who was Charles Comiskey, and how did he influence the game?

A: For nearly half a century, Charles Comiskey was one of baseball's most powerful and influential figures. As a player, he revolutionized the position of first baseman. He was the first player to position himself away from the bag, allowing him to field ground balls hit to the right side of the infield much more effectively.

As a manager, Comiskey led the St. Louis Browns to four consecutive pennants from 1885 to 1888, but his greatest claim to fame came during his years as an executive. In 1901 he was instrumental in the formation of the American League, along with Ban Johnson. From 1901 to 1931 Comiskey was the owner and president of the Chicago White Sox, and during that time his club won four pennants. One of those four winning teams was the infamous 1919 "Black Sox."

Q: What events led to the "Black Sox Scandal"?

A: World War I ended in November of 1918. Major League Baseball, sensing increasing postwar interest in the national pastime, chose to make the World Series a best-of-nine affair. The Series would be remembered, though, as the darkest moment in baseball history.

The Chicago White Sox, appearing in the World Series for the second time in three years, were the heavy favorites against the Cincinnati Reds. The White Sox players, however, hated their owner Charles Comiskey, because he was a notorious cheapskate, among other things. The talented group of players felt they were terribly underpaid. Their uniforms were filthy because of Comiskey's order to cut down the laundry bill. In 1917 Comiskey promised the club a bonus for winning the pennant. All they got was a case of cheap champagne.

Tiring of Comiskey's penny-pinching, eight players allegedly decided to accept money from gamblers to "fix" (purposely lose) the World Series. In the bottom of the first inning of Game One, Chicago's 29-game winner, Eddie Cicotte, hit the Cincinnati leadoff batter with a pitch. Supposedly, Cicotte's pitch was more than an errant toss. It was a signal to bettors that a few members of the White Sox planned to "fix" the Series so the gamblers could boost their winnings.

Competing at less than full effort, the Sox played uninspired baseball. The Sox lost Game One and Game Two, won

was awry. Baseball's three-man National Commission was told of those fears but did not take action.

Q: How did the Sox conspiracy become public?

A: On September 28, 1920, eight White Sox players were indicted and charged with complicity in a conspiracy with gamblers to fix the 1919 World Series. They were pitchers Cicotte and Claude "Lefty" Williams, center fielder Hap Felsch, shortstop Swede Risberg, first baseman Chick Gandil, third baseman Buck Weaver, reserve infielder Fred McMullin, and left fielder Joe Jackson.

The indictments were based on evidence obtained for the Cook County (Illinois) grand jury by White Sox owner Comiskey and after Cicotte and Jackson made open confessions about how they were "double-crossed" by the gamblers.

The specific charge against the eight players was "conspiracy to commit an illegal act," which was punishable by five years' imprisonment or a fine up to $10,000. As soon as news of the indictments became public, Comiskey suspended the seven players (Gandil had since retired), almost certainly forfeiting his chances to win the 1920 AL pennant.

Left: Chicago White Sox pitcher Ed Cicotte warming up in 1917. When Cicotte hit the first batter of the 1919 World Series, gamblers knew that the fix was in.

Below: Shoeless Joe Jackson and seven other members of the 1919 White Sox were indicted by a Chicago grand jury for throwing the World Series to the Reds.

Game Three, and were shut out in Games Four and Five. Chicago manager Kid Gleason was suspicious of his players, though they did rally to win Games Six and Seven. The Reds, however, clinched the Series in Game Eight.

During the Series, and especially after, rumors swirled that a few of the Sox had taken money in exchange for not playing their best, so that the underdog Reds would win. Newspaper reporter Ring Lardner also suspected something

" My God! Think of my children. "

—*EDDIE CICOTTE, STAR PITCHER OF THE WHITE SOX, TO THE CHICAGO GRAND JURY*

Comiskey's letter notifying the seven players of their suspensions read in part:

"You are hereby notified of your indefinite suspension as a member of the Chicago American Baseball Club. Your suspension is brought about by information which has just come to me directly involving you and each of you in the baseball scandal resulting from the world's series of 1919.

If you are innocent of any wrongdoing you and each of you will be reinstated; if you are guilty you will be retired from organized baseball for the rest of your lives if I can accomplish it. Until there is a finality to this investigation it is due to the public that I take this action, even though it costs Chicago the pennant."

Baseball suffered its worst setback to date. Owners feared the game was in danger of being destroyed. They needed to turn to someone who would clean things up.

Q: Why did baseball name a commissioner?

A: Baseball team owners and league officials were concerned. Gambling was widespread, and they wanted to give baseball an honest image. The owners grew so worried that fans would lose faith in the game's integrity that they hired a federal judge named Kenesaw Mountain Landis to become baseball's first commissioner.

Baseball owners were already familiar with Judge Landis when they turned to him in 1920 to restore the good name of baseball to fans around the country. The U.S. District Court judge, named for a famous Civil War battle, had earned the admiration of the major league owners when he refused to rule on a lawsuit brought against the owners by the rival Federal League, in 1915.

When Landis became baseball's first commissioner in 1920, he replaced the three-man National Commission that had ruled baseball since 1903 under the leadership of American League founder Ban Johnson. In light of what came to be called the "Black Sox scandal," the commission was weakening and strong leadership was needed to put the game back on its feet.

Kenesaw Mountain Landis in 1907. He was appointed baseball's first commissioner in 1920. His Hall of Fame plaque reads: "His integrity and leadership established baseball in the respect, esteem and affection of the American people."

Within his first year as commissioner Landis had banned a total of 15 players. He uncovered bribery, thrown games, betting plots, and other schemes that showed just how widespread corruption had become in professional baseball. He held the office of commissioner until his death in 1944. He dealt out strict punishment to players, owners, gamblers, and umpires, though his rulings were notoriously inconsistent. Baseball has had eight commissioners since Landis, but none who wielded so much power.

Q: What became of the White Sox players involved in the 1919 World Series scandal?

A: On August 2, 1921, eight White Sox players were found innocent because of a lack of evidence. The confessions of Joe Jackson, Eddie Cicotte, and Claude Williams were reported missing and were never heard by the jurors.

The players had allegedly been promised between $5,000 and $10,000 by local gamblers to throw the Series, but never collected all the money. Though acquitted in a court of law, it made no matter to Judge Landis.

Immediately after the verdict, Landis banned all eight White Sox players from baseball for life. They were Cicotte, Williams, Felsch, Risberg, Gandil, Weaver, McMullin, and Jackson. None of them ever returned to the game in any capacity, although Cicotte, Risberg, and Jackson continued to play baseball for some years in outlaw leagues or on semipro teams.

Joe Jackson actually led all regular batters in the Series with a .375 average. Because of his involvement in the scandal, "Shoeless Joe," as he was known, whose .356 career batting average ranks third best in baseball history, is not in the Baseball Hall of Fame. Jackson later owned and operated a liquor store. He died in Greenville, South Carolina, at age 62 in 1951.

Judge Kenesaw Mountain Landis (rear left) interviewing Swede Risberg (rear center) and Chick Gandil (next to Risberg), two of the eight White Sox players who allegedly conspired to intentionally lose the 1919 World Series.

" Say it ain't so, Joe. "

—A YOUNG BOY, AS QUOTED BY A REPORTER

The Sultan of Swat

Q: How did Babe Ruth help save baseball?

A: Major League Baseball was reeling from the Black Sox scandal. The fans had lost faith in the national pastime. All of the goodwill baseball had accumulated and the future of the game itself appeared uncertain. It took Babe Ruth and his incredible home run stroke to restore the nation's trust in the game.

Babe Ruth hitting his record-setting 60th home run of the 1927 season against the Washington Senators at Yankee Stadium. Ruth hit more homers than any team in the league that season.

When Babe Ruth whacked 29 home runs in 1919, setting a new single-season record, it stunned the baseball world. The next-highest home run total that year was twelve. In 1920, the Babe knocked 54 out of the park in a year in which nobody else hit more than 19. In 1921, he smacked a whopping 59 homers. Ruth's single-season record of 60 homers in 1927 would remain the benchmark for 34 years until Roger Maris came along.

To understand just how unique Ruth's home run production was during his greatest seasons, consider this: In 1920 and again in 1927 Ruth single-handedly hit more homers than any

team in the league (54 in 1920, 60 in 1927). In all, Babe led the American League in home runs 12 times, including six consecutive seasons, from 1926 through 1931, when he averaged more than 50 home runs a year.

Ruth hit baseballs higher and farther than anyone had ever imagined possible. He changed the way the game was played, making the home run the dominant aspect of the sport. Fans flocked to every American League ballpark to watch the Babe knock one out of the yard. Because of his amazing talent and his larger-than-life personality, he commanded more newsprint in the 1920s than any other celebrity in the United States.

Ruth became the first nationally known baseball star. Even people who were not baseball fans knew his name. His fame soon spread to Europe and the Far East. When the game needed him most, Ruth emerged into international fame, defining a new American hero: The professional athlete.

Q: Why is Yankee Stadium called "The House That Ruth Built"?

A: The arrival of Babe Ruth in New York City in 1920 caused the turnstiles to spin like never before at the Polo Grounds, which the Yankees had shared with the New York Giants since 1913. In 1920, Ruth's first season with the Yankees, they became the first major league team to draw more than one million fans (officially 1,289,422) in a single season. As landlord, the Giants were not happy playing second fiddle to the guests, and

notified the Yankees to vacate the premises as soon as possible. In February 1921, the Yankees purchased 10 acres of property from the estate of William Waldorf Astor in the South Bronx, directly across the Harlem River from the Polo Grounds.

Yankees owners Jacob Ruppert and Tillinghast Huston announced the construction of baseball's first triple-decked structure. With an eventual capacity of over 70,000, it would also be the first structure to be called a "stadium." The new stadium would favor left-handed power hitters with a right-field foul pole only 295 feet from home plate. Incredibly, the stadium was built in only 284 working days and at a price of $2.5 million.

Because it was widely recognized that Ruth's tremendous drawing power had made the new stadium possible, it would become known as "The House That Ruth Built." At the Yankee Stadium inaugural on April 18, 1923, a throng of 74,200 gleeful fans witnessed Ruth fittingly christen the new ballpark in the Bronx by slamming the first home run in Yankee Stadium history—a three-run shot off Howard Ehmke to help Bob Shawkey and the Yankees capture a 4–1 victory over the Red Sox, Ruth's former team.

Q: Why did the Red Sox sell Babe Ruth to the Yankees?

A: During the 1918 season Red Sox manager Ed Barrow decided to play Ruth in the outfield on the days he did not pitch. Ruth hit 11 homers in only 317 at

Yankee Stadium on the day it opened in 1923. More than 74,000 fans packed themselves inside to watch Babe Ruth fittingly christen the place by hitting the first home run there.

" **Let's see someone top that.** "

—*Babe Ruth after hitting his famous 60th home run against Tom Zachary of the Washington Senators at Yankee Stadium*

Harry Frazee (center), Boston Red Sox owner, with players at Chicago's Comiskey Park in 1917. Frazee would sell Babe Ruth to the Yankees in January 1920 and change the course of history for both teams.

bats to lead the league. Ruth moved to the outfield and pitched even less in 1919. That season, Ruth set a single-season home run record with 29. But even Ruth's homers could not lift the Red Sox out of the second division; the team finished in sixth place.

Red Sox owner Harry Frazee, a theatrical producer, was riddled with debt. Seeking solutions, he cast an eye on his floundering ball club. In the off-season, he sold Ruth to the Yankees for $125,000 and a $300,000 loan. The unexpected deal has haunted Boston baseball fans ever since.

Frazee said that he had sold Ruth to the Yankees because he thought it was an "injustice" to keep him with the Red Sox, who were "fast becoming a one-man

team." Ruth, who had two years more to run on his Boston contract that called for a salary of $10,000 a year, had announced that he would refuse to play for Boston unless his salary was doubled.

"I am not surprised," Ruth said upon being told that he was sold to New York. "When I made my demand on the Red Sox for $20,000 a year, I had an idea they would choose to sell me rather than pay the increase, and I knew the Yankees were the most probable purchasers in that event."

At Ruth's demand, the Yankees immediately doubled his salary to the then unheard of amount of $20,000 a year. No athlete had ever been paid so much. But the Babe was worth every penny. He led the Yankees to seven World Series in 12 years.

Q: Just how good a pitcher was Babe Ruth?

A: Before he was a slugger, Babe Ruth was a terrific pitcher. Ruth was so talented that had he remained a pitcher for his entire career, he possibly would have made it into the Hall of Fame for his skill on the mound. He pitched for the Boston Red Sox from 1914 to 1919, posting a record of 89 wins and only 46 losses.

Ruth debuted for the Red Sox on July 11, 1914, and defeated the Cleveland Indians, 4–3. Over the next three seasons Ruth won 65 games and became the most dominant left-handed pitcher in baseball. In 1916, only his second full season in the majors, Ruth won 23 games and led the American League with a 1.75 earned run average. He faced Walter Johnson, widely considered the best pitcher of the day, eight times. Ruth won six times, three by 1–0 shutouts, including one game decided by his own home run.

In World Series play, Babe's earned run average was a minuscule 0.87. In 1916 the Red Sox faced the Brooklyn Dodgers, who were then known as the Robins, in the World Series. The second game of the Series, played in Boston, was a pitchers' duel between Brooklyn's Sherry Smith

and Ruth. Ruth's performance in this game cemented his reputation as a great pitcher. He hurled 13 innings of shutout ball, setting a Series single-game record, as the Red Sox won in the bottom of the 14th inning, 2–1.

Two years later Ruth helped the Red Sox to another World Series title, this time over the Chicago Cubs. Ruth, who won 13 games during the regular season, outdueled the Cubs' 22-game winner, Hippo Vaughn, in Game One, 1–0. Ruth's complete-game shutout added to his 13 scoreless innings in the 1916 World Series, gave him 22 consecutive scoreless innings pitched in the Series. By the end of this Series, his record had reached 29 straight, a mark that would stand for more than 40 years.

The 1918 World Series, however, gained immortality for an entirely different reason. The Red Sox would not win another World Series for 86 years.

Babe Ruth made his mark pitching in Boston before becoming a slugger in New York. His valuable left arm helped the Red Sox win the World Series in 1916 and 1918.

> " So what? I had a better year than he did. "
>
> —BABE RUTH, UPON SIGNING AN $80,000 CONTRACT IN 1930, WHICH WAS MORE MONEY THAN PRESIDENT HERBERT HOOVER WAS PAID

Building Blocks

Q: Which team dominated the American League before the Yankees?

A: Connie Mack's Philadelphia Athletics won six of the first 14 American League pennants, including four flags in five years from 1910 to 1914. The A's also captured the World Series in 1910, 1911, and 1913.

In the 1910 Series, left-hander Eddie Plank had a sore arm and was unable to pitch, so Mack went with just two starters: Jack Coombs and Charles "Chief" Bender, so-called because his mother was a Chippewa Indian. Both were aces. Bender's 23–5 record was the highest winning percentage in the American League that season, but team-mate Coombs was even more impressive. The 27-year-old pitched 13 shutouts (still an AL record) while compiling a 31–9 record.

The Athletics toppled the mighty Chicago Cubs, winners of four National League titles in five years, four games to one. The A's scored an average of seven runs a game. Bender won the opener, and Coombs won the other three. The A's had earned their first world championship and in the process used only two pitchers, Bender and Coombs, to work 45 $^2/_3$ innings.

The Athletics defeated the New York Giants in the 1911 World Series four games to two, in a Series that belonged to Philadelphia third baseman Frank Baker. In Game Two, Baker belted a game-winning home run. In Game Three, with one out in the ninth inning and New York leading 1–0, Baker walloped a game-tying homer off Christy Mathewson. The A's went on to win, 3–2, in the 11th inning. Suddenly the A's were up two games to one in the Series and Frank Baker had a new nickname: "Home Run."

In 1913 the A's won the AL pennant by six and a half games over the Washington Senators, and then beat John McGraw's Giants again, four games to one. Mack used just 12 players in the entire Series: two catchers besides the position players and three pitchers: Bender, Plank, and 21-year-old "Bullet" Joe Bush. Again the star at the plate was Baker, hitting .450 with one home run and seven runs batted in to lead all batters.

The Athletics had lost only four games in the three previous World Series, but they were victims of a shocking upset when Boston's "Miracle Braves" swept them in 1914. The losses went to Plank, Bush, Bob Shawkey, and, after six straight Series victories, to Bender.

Q: Which two players helped expand baseball's popularity westward?

A: The highlight of the 1922 season came in St. Louis, Missouri, where a pair of future Hall of Famers put on a great hitting display.

Frank Baker of the Philadelphia Athletics acquired his nickname "Home Run" after hitting two clutch round-trippers in the 1911 World Series against the New York Giants.

The St. Louis Browns of the American League and the St. Louis Cardinals of the National League occupied the same stadium, Sportsman's Park. The Browns had left-handed hitting George Sisler, a slick-fielding first baseman. The Cardinals boasted right-handed hitting second baseman Rogers Hornsby, considered one of the best ever at his position.

How dazzling was Sisler's 1922 performance? His teammate, left fielder Ken Williams, led the AL in home runs and runs batted in. Williams also became the first 30–30 player (30 homers, 30 stolen bases) in major league history. Despite his feats, Williams did not receive a single vote for Most Valuable Player. Sisler was simply too spectacular. He batted an astounding .420 and led the major leagues in stolen bases with 51. Sisler's 41-game hit streak helped the Browns come within one game of overtaking the Yankees for the pennant.

This was the second time Sisler had batted over .400—he won the batting title in 1920 with a .407 average, collecting an incredible 257 hits, a record for most hits in a season that stood for 83 years until surpassed by Seattle's Ichiro Suzuki, in 2004.

When the Browns hit the road, Cardinals fans came to Sportsman's Park to cheer for Rogers Hornsby, one the greatest right-handed hitters ever. (Rogers was his mother's maiden name.) The Rajah, as he was known, won baseball's Triple Crown in 1922, leading the National League in batting average (.401), RBIs (152), and home runs (42). Only Babe Ruth had ever smacked as many homers in a single season.

In the 1920s Hornsby was the dominant player in the National League. From 1920 to 1925 he won six straight batting titles, a league record. His batting average in the years 1921 to 1925 averaged over .400. His .424 average in 1924 still ranks as the highest single-season average of the modern age. Hornsby capped his incredible run with another Triple Crown in 1925, becoming the player-manager of the Cardinals and batting .403 with 39 home runs and 143 RBIs. He was voted the league's Most Valuable Player. The following year Hornsby guided the Cardinals to their first World Series triumph, and St. Louis's love affair with baseball was consummated.

Left: George Sisler, who played for the University of Michigan from 1912 to 1915, went on to hit an astounding .420 for the St. Louis Browns in 1922.

Below: The outstanding right-handed batter Rogers Hornsby, a Triple Crown winner in 1922, is often overlooked when the discussion turns to the greatest baseball players of all time.

“ He's the nearest thing to a perfect ballplayer. He can do everything—hit, hit with power, field, run, and throw. ”

—TY COBB ON GEORGE SISLER

Storming the Airwaves

Q: When was the first radio broadcast of a major league game?

A: The first Major League Baseball game ever broadcast on radio occurred on August 5, 1921, by radio station KDKA in Pittsburgh. The first-place Pirates beat the last-place Philadelphia Phillies, 8–5, at Forbes Field. But the game itself was of little note. The real action was taking place in a field-level box seat just behind home plate, where Harold Arlin, a 26-year-old Westinghouse engineer, was making history as the game's first live play-by-play announcer.

KDKA had become the nation's first commercial radio station just a year before, and Arlin had announced over the air that Warren Harding was the winner of the 1920 presidential election.

But it was a baseball broadcast that made history. Surrounded by equipment that looked something like a ham radio kit, Arlin described the action into a converted telephone. Sure, there were glitches. The transmitter carrying the radio signal sometimes did not work, and sometimes the crowd noise would drown out Arlin's voice.

"Our guys at KDKA didn't even think that baseball would last on radio," said Arlin later. "Quite frankly, we didn't know what the reaction would be, whether we'd be talking into a total vacuum or whether somebody would actually hear us."

Enough people were listening that the following year, the entire World Series was broadcast by station WJZ in Newark, New Jersey, with the sports-writer Grantland Rice calling the plays.

Legendary sportswriter Grantland Rice (second from left) visiting the White House in 1922, the same year he was at the microphone to call the first World Series ever broadcast over the radio airwaves. Also pictured are President Warren Harding, Ring Lardner, and Henry P. Fletcher.

Q: When was the first television broadcast of a major league game?

A: The first Major League Baseball game ever televised was broadcast on August 26, 1939, when the Cincinnati Reds played a doubleheader against the Brooklyn Dodgers at Ebbets Field. The Reds won the opener, 5–2, and the Dodgers triumphed in the nightcap, 6–1.

The game was carried by W2XBS, an experimental station in the Empire State Building, in Manhattan. Two cameras were used. One camera was placed near the visiting dugout, in foul territory on the third-base side, for a view from behind the right-handed batter's position. The other camera was located high behind home plate, in a second-tier grandstand box, affording a bird's eye view of the entire field.

Only about 400 people in New York had TV sets to watch the game. Using the video-sound channels of the National Broadcasting Company, television set owners from as far away as 50 miles could watch Bucky Walters pitch a two-hitter for his 21st win and hear the roar of the crowd after Dolph Camilli hit his 22nd homer.

This was not the first time baseball was caught by the prying eyes of the camera. Three months earlier, NBC had produced a test broadcast of a college game between Columbia and Princeton at Baker Field in New York City. To those who viewed both games on their television, however, it was apparent that considerable technical progress had been made.

"At times," wrote Roscoe McGowen, "it was possible to catch a fleeting glimpse of the ball as it sped from the pitcher's hand toward home plate."

Forty-six years later the television coverage of baseball was so refined that fans at home knew instantly from a videotape replay that an umpire's call was wrong. The mistake led to the St. Louis Cardinals' losing a World Series game and ultimately the Series itself, in 1985.

Ebbets Field in Brooklyn, New York, was the site of the first televised major league game, in 1939. Viewers watched the Dodgers split a doubleheader against the Cincinnati Reds.

Let There Be Light

Q: When was the major league's first night game?

A: By the 1930s owners were like carnival barkers, willing to try almost any promotion to lure fans to the ballpark. The most innovative promoter in the game was Cincinnati Reds general manager Larry MacPhail. In 1935 he erected light towers at Crosley Field, and on May 24, in a game against the Philadelphia Phillies, Crosley played host to a crowd in excess of 20,000 Cincinnati fans at the first night game in the major leagues.

It was also the first game under the lights for practically all the players. After President Franklin D. Roosevelt flipped the switch from the White House in Washington, D.C., to turn on the lights, most players found that they were able to pick up the ball in the night sky. The

Reds won, 2–1, as neither side made an error. (Two long flies were dropped by Philadelphia outfielders, but the official scorer ruled both as hits.)

Philadelphia manager Jimmy Wilson said the floodlights had nothing to do with the low runs-scored total.

"[The] pitchers just had all their stuff working, that's all," he said. "You can see that ball coming up to the plate just as well under those lights as you can in daytime."

Three years later, when MacPhail was running the Brooklyn Dodgers, he made Ebbets Field the second lighted ballpark in the major leagues. Brooklyn's first home night game was June 15, 1938, against Cincinnati. Reds pitcher Johnny Vander Meer celebrated the occasion by pitching his second consecutive no-hitter, something no one else has ever accomplished.

Cincinnati's Crosley Field during Major League Baseball's first night game, in 1935. President Franklin D. Roosevelt flipped the switch from the White House to turn on the lights.

Q: Which stadium was the longest holdout before installing lights?

A: Night games proved to be a success, making it easier for fans working during the day to get out to the stadium. It also meant ballpark hot dogs for dinner!

By 1941, eleven of the sixteen major league clubs had installed lights. The last holdout, the Chicago Cubs, would wait 47 more years before they put in lights. Other owners, who enjoyed the additional revenue generated by night games, looked at the Cubs' P. K. Wrigley as a hopeless traditionalist. Cubs fans, however, seemed to relish their reputation as the last of the electric light holdouts.

Finally, after 72 years as the site of baseball games played only in the daylight, the Cubs lit up Wrigley Field on August 8, 1988. A 91-year-old Chicago fan flipped the switch that turned on 540 lights divided into six light banks on the park's roof. But the game became a historical footnote when rain forced a postponement after the Cubs had played just three and a half innings against the Philadelphia Phillies.

"Maybe," a fan said, "the Cubs will play better in the dark."

The next night, the Cubs recorded a 6–4 victory over the New York Mets in the first official night game played at Wrigley Field.

A night game at Chicago's Wrigley Field in 1996. The light stands had been erected in 1988, and the friendly confines became the last major league park to get lights.

"Night baseball is all right, if the fans want it, but I'd rather play in the daytime."
—JIMMY WILSON, PHILADELPHIA PHILLIES MANAGER, AFTER THE FIRST MAJOR LEAGUE NIGHT GAME

CHAPTER 3

THE HITTERS

The great Boston Red Sox slugger Ted Williams once said that hitting a baseball is the most difficult skill in all of sports to master. A batter must hit a round ball with a round bat squarely. The batter has barely one second from the time the ball is pitched until it reaches the plate. Even top major league players who maintain a .300 batting average make an out 70 percent of the time. The very best hitters bat about .330 or higher, but batting .400 (four hits per ten at-bats) for an entire season is extremely rare. The last time it happened was more then 65 years ago.

Success in baseball is most often measured by statistics. Major league hitters each season strive to reach such marks as 30 home runs and 100 runs batted in. Only five players in major league history have hit 60 or more home runs, and no major leaguer has ever had 200 runs batted in a single season. Hack Wilson's record of 191 runs batted in with the Chicago Cubs in 1930 is still the benchmark. Still, with each passing season old offensive records are challenged and new chapters of hitting lore are written.

Above: Visitors to Boston's Fenway Park can admire this statue of Ted Williams.

Left: Hack Wilson of the Chicago Cubs strikes a pose during spring training in 1931. The stocky slugger was one of baseball's greatest run producers, setting a record of 191 runs batted in in 1930.

Batter Up!

Q: Other than a hit, how can a batter reach base safely?

A: Other than a hit, there are six ways a batter can reach base safely. They are:

Khalil Greene of the San Diego Padres busts it down the line in a game against the St. Louis Cardinals. Besides getting a hit, there are six other ways Greene could have reached first base safely.

1. **Error:** A batter can reach first base safely because of a defensive misplay of a batted ball that should be properly handled for an out. The most common errors are charged to infielders who boot ground balls or throw wildly to first base.

2. **Base on balls:** A batter can receive a free trip to first base after a pitcher has thrown four balls during one at-bat.

3. **Hit by pitch:** A batter is hit by a pitched ball and is awarded first base.

4. **Dropped third strike:** A batter can run to first base after swinging at strike three if the catcher drops or misses the pitched ball (with first base open or with two outs). A putout is recorded only if the catcher picks up

for getting out the lead runner. This does not count as a hit for the batter.

6. **Catcher's interference:** The umpire calls catcher's interference if a catcher makes contact with a batter or his bat during the swing. The batter is awarded first base and the official scorer gives the catcher an error. Catcher's interference usually occurs because the catcher is squatting too close to the plate and the batter swings at the pitch and hits the catcher's mitt.

Q: Which player got hits for two different teams on the same day?

A: Joel Youngblood made major league history by collecting hits for two different clubs in two different cities on the same day, August 4, 1982.

He began the day as a New York Met, playing in an afternoon contest against the Chicago Cubs at Wrigley Field. Youngblood hit a single off Chicago's Ferguson Jenkins, driving home the winning run in the Mets' 7–4 victory. After the game he was told that the Mets had traded him to the Montreal Expos. Youngblood hopped on an airplane and flew to Philadelphia, where the Expos were playing a night game against the Phillies. He arrived in time to stroke a pinch-hit single off Steve Carlton, another future Hall of Fame pitcher.

After finishing the 1982 season with the Expos, Youngblood moved on to the San Francisco Giants. He retired in 1989 as a member of the Cincinnati Reds.

Steve Carlton pitching for the Philadelphia Phillies. He gave up a hit to Joel Youngblood of the Montreal Expos the same day Youngblood had also registered a hit for the New York Mets.

the ball and tags the batter or throws the ball to first base for the putout. Score it as a strikeout for the batter, and a wild pitch or passed ball for the pitcher and catcher.

5. **Fielder's choice:** A batter reaches first base safely because a fielder chooses to put out a different base runner. An example of this is when a ground ball is hit with a runner on first base, and an infielder attempts a force out at second base of the runner coming from first. The batter is allowed to reach first base in exchange

At-Bat Oddities

Q: Who is the shortest player ever to bat in a major league game?

A: Eddie Gaedel, a diminutive 3-foot, 7-inches, came to the plate for the St. Louis Browns during the second game of a doubleheader against the Detroit Tigers on August 19, 1951. It was part of a publicity stunt by Browns owner Bill Veeck (as in wreck), who was always desperately seeking attention for his last-place team.

Veeck decided to stage a between-games celebration of the 50th anniversary of the American League. Hoping to drum up interest in his moribund franchise, Veeck hired a 65-pound circus little person to provide a big finish. At the end of the proceedings, Gaedel popped out of a giant papier-mâché birthday cake, dressed in a tiny Browns uniform. The crowd roared its approval, yet the greatest promotional stunt in the history of baseball was still to come.

With the Browns due up in the bottom of the first inning of the nightcap, Gaedel bounded out of the dugout, swinging three toy bats. The announcer introduced him as the pinch hitter for the leadoff batter Frank Saucier. That is when umpire Ed Hurley summoned Browns manager Zach Taylor for a meeting. Taylor brought out an official AL contract with Gaedel's signature on it, and waved the paper in the face of the humbled official, who had no choice but to allow Gaedel his turn at bat.

So wearing No. 1/8 (one-eighth), Eddie Gaedel stepped into the batter's box, bent his 43-inch frame into a deep crouch, and created the smallest strike zone in history—about an inch and a half. Detroit pitcher Bob Cain tried to suppress laughter. Gaedel, who was under strict orders from Veeck not to swing, looked at four consecutive balls and trotted to first base, tipping his cap to the crowd along the way. Gaedel was replaced by a pinch runner, Jim Delsing, and exited to raucous cheers.

Eddie Gaedel, a 3-foot-7-inch "stuntman," batting against the Tigers at Sportsman's Park. Inserted as a pinch-hitter by St. Louis Browns owner Bill Veeck and wearing uniform No. 1/8, he walked on four pitches and bowed twice before reaching first base.

Fans and players were hysterically laughing, but AL President William Harridge was not amused. He voided Gaedel's contract the next day, saying it was not in the best interests of baseball. Within two days, the rules were changed to ban special players such as Gaedel from the game.

To this day, though, you can still find Gaedel's name in the *Baseball Encyclopedia*, and his career on-base percentage is a perfect 1.000.

Q: Did a batter once triple into a triple play?

A: Almost. The 1926 Brooklyn Dodgers were known as "The Daffiness Boys." The daffiest of all was Floyd "Babe" Herman, their hard-hitting but soft-thinking rookie first baseman. Herman's wacky behavior was legendary.

Herman came to bat one afternoon with the bases loaded against the Boston Braves. With one out in the seventh inning and the score tied, 1–1, Herman slammed a line drive toward right center field. The runners were not sure if the ball would be caught, so they stayed near their bases. Herman just put his head down and ran. The ball hit the fence, and Hank DeBerry, the runner on third, trotted home. Dazzy Vance, a very slow runner on second base, lumbered toward third and headed for the plate. But when the ball was relayed back toward the infield a problem arose.

Chick Fewster, the runner on first, was sprinting around second base and

Dazzy Vance of the Brooklyn Dodgers in 1925. The following season he was involved in one of the great base-running blunders in baseball history.

heading for third. Right behind him was Herman. "Back! Back!" screamed the Dodgers third–base coach. His shouts were meant for Herman, but Vance was the one who responded. Vance put on the brakes midway to the plate and dove back into third. Fewster dove, too. So did Herman. When the dust cleared, all three men were occupying third base.

Unfortunately, Vance was the only one entitled to be there. Fewster and Herman were immediately tagged out to end the inning. Therefore, officially, Herman had merely doubled into a double play. Sheepishly, Herman pointed out afterward: "Everybody overlooks the fact that the run I knocked in on that play was the winning run."

Teddy Ballgame

Q: Who was the last player to bat over .400 for a season?

A: Ted Williams was the last player to hit over .400 for a season. His batting average for the 1941 season was .406—no major leaguer has batted above .390 over a full season since.

Ted Williams was one of the best pure hitters the game has ever seen. Williams joined the Boston Red Sox when he was 20 years old and stayed for his entire playing career. In 1941, his third year in the big leagues, he came into a doubleheader on the last day of the season with his batting average at .39955. His manager told him he could sit out both games against the Philadelphia Athletics at Shibe Park, and his average would have been rounded up to a perfect .400. But Williams wanted to play in both games. He went on to get six hits in eight at-bats to raise his average six percentage points. He finished at .406 (.4057)

A tall, rangy, left-handed batter, Williams was called "The Splendid Splinter" because of his thin body and splendid hitting: a .344 career batting average and six batting titles. Over his 19-year career, Williams's batting average dipped below .316 only once.

He was a powerful hitter too, smacking 521 homers in his career. He led the American League in homers and runs batted in four times, and is the only AL player to win the Triple Crown twice (leading the league in batting average, RBIs, and home runs), in 1942 and 1947. If he had not missed almost five seasons—

he was a Marine Corps pilot in World War II and in the Korean war—Williams might have broken Babe Ruth's home run record before Hank Aaron did.

Q: How did Williams fare against "The Williams Shift"?

A: By 1946 Williams was the most respected hitter in baseball. On July 14 of that season, he faced a strange-looking defense alignment in the second game of a doubleheader at Fenway against the Cleveland Indians. In the first game, Williams had hit three home runs, driven in eight runs, and scored four times. When Williams came to bat in the nightcap, Cleveland player-manager Lou Boudreau unveiled "The Williams Shift."

The shortstop, Lou Boudreau, played back on the grass midway between first and second. The first baseman positioned himself on the grass near the foul line. The third baseman was on the grass on the right side of second base, and the right and center fielders played as deep as possible. Everyone but the left fielder was shifted to the right side of second base, where Williams most often hit the ball.

After Williams doubled in his first at-bat, the Williams Shift was put into effect for the rest of his plate appearances. He ended up walking twice. But the new-fangled defense was effective one time when Boudreau fielded a sharp ground ball and threw out Williams at first. That Boudreau would devise the unusual defense of six players on the right side

of the diamond, virtually leaving the left side open, indicates the esteem his opponents had for him.

Umpires respected Williams too. He had remarkable 20/10 vision (normal eyesight is 20/20), and seemed never to be fooled by a pitch. His eyesight was so famous that umpires did not like to call strikes on close pitches that Williams let pass. As a result he led the American League in walks eight times and totaled over 2,000 free passes in his career.

In 1957, at age 39, he batted .388, and to cap off his illustrious career, he hit a home run at Fenway Park in his last at-bat, at age 42, on September 28, 1960.

Ted Williams of the Boston Red Sox in 1941, the year he became the last player ever to hit for a .400 average in a single season.

"All I want out of life is that when I walk down the street folks will say: 'There goes the greatest hitter who ever lived.'"

—TED WILLIAMS, WHEN HE FIRST JOINED THE RED SOX IN 1939

"The Shot Heard 'Round the World"

Q: Who slugged baseball's most famous home run?

"The Giants win the pennant!. . ." The most famous home run in baseball history leaves the bat of the New York Giants' Bobby Thomson at the Polo Grounds in 1951.

A: One mighty swing of Bobby Thomson's bat produced "The Shot Heard 'Round the World," a home run that propelled the New York Giants to the National League pennant, on October 3, 1951.

As remarkable as Thomson's home run was, it never could have occurred if not for an equally remarkable stretch run by the Giants. On July 27, 1951, the Giants were in second place, 9½ games behind Brooklyn. As late as August 11 they trailed the National League–leading Dodgers by a whopping 13 games. "The Giants is dead," Dodgers manager Charlie Dressen declared.

But then, on August 12, the Giants began an incredible run. They won 16 games in a row and rolled on from there, eventu-

ally tying the Dodgers at the end of the regular season and forcing a three-game playoff to determine the NL champion.

The Giants won the first game at Ebbets Field in Brooklyn; the Dodgers took the second game at the Polo Grounds in Manhattan. Brooklyn was poised to win the third game and the pennant as it took a 4–1 lead into the bottom of the ninth at the Polo Grounds. But then, Don Newcombe, the Dodgers ace pitcher, began to tire. The first two Giants hitters singled. With one out, Giants first baseman Whitey Lockman doubled, scoring one run and putting men on second and third.

The Dodgers had two pitchers warming up in the bullpen, starter Ralph Branca and rookie reliever Clem Labine. The bullpen coach signaled that Labine was bouncing his curve, so manager Dressen chose to bring Branca into the game to face third baseman Bobby Thomson, who had hit 31 home runs already that year. Giants manager and third-base coach Leo Durocher pulled Thomson aside and reportedly told him, "Bobby, if you've ever hit one, hit one now."

The Giants rookie Willie Mays was on deck, but Dressen chose to pitch to Thomson, who had already homered off Branca to help the Giants win Game One. Thomson stepped to the plate. "I was so nervous my eyeballs were vibrating," Thomson said later. The first pitch was a called strike. On Branca's second pitch, Thomson tagged the ball into the left-field seats, just clearing the high wall at the 315-

foot mark. Perhaps as famous as the shot itself was the radio call by Giants broadcaster Russ Hodges: "There's a long drive, it's gonna be it, I believe . . . THE GIANTS WIN THE PENNANT! THE GIANTS WIN THE PENNANT! THE GIANTS WIN THE PENNANT! THE GIANTS WIN THE PENNANT! Bobby Thomson hits into the lower deck of the left-field stands! The Giants win the pennant and they're going crazy, they're going crazy!"

With that one swing of the bat the never-say-die Giants, seemingly hopelessly beaten, instead won the playoff and the pennant. When Thomson finished dancing around the bases in unbridled glee, he was mobbed by teammates at home plate and thousands of fans who had stormed the field. It was one of the most dramatic home runs in baseball history. In fact, the experts at *The Sporting News* named it baseball's greatest moment, in a 1999 poll.

Ralph Branca of the Brooklyn Dodgers (right), who surrendered the famous shot, pretends to choke Thomson in a ceremony marking the homer's 40th anniversary.

"Ralph Branca turned and started for the clubhouse. The number on his uniform looked huge. Thirteen."

—SPORTSWRITER RED SMITH

Home Run Highlights

Q: Who hit the longest home run ever?

A: While this is impossible to gauge for certain, the longest home run on record was an estimated 565-foot clout hit at old Griffith Stadium in Washington, D.C., on April 17, 1953. Mickey Mantle, a switch-hitter for the New York Yankees, was batting right-handed against left-handed pitcher Chuck Stobbs of the Washington Senators. Mantle hit a rising line drive that nicked the lower right-hand corner of a huge beer sign atop a football scoreboard behind the left-center-field bleachers. The ball left the stadium, carried across a street, and landed in someone's backyard.

After the titanic blast, Yankees publicity director Red Patterson left the press box and walked off the distance to where witnesses say the ball came down. The 565-foot figure was at best a guess, but the homer, and the distance associated with it, captured the imagination of fans, who began calling such shots "tape-measure" home runs.

Mantle and perhaps others probably have hit longer home runs. That's certainly the view of Stobbs, 77, now retired and living in Sarasota, Florida.

"He hit 'em pretty far against a lot of people," said Stobbs. "The only reason they remember this one is because they marked the spot on the beer sign where the ball left the park; but Bucky Harris [the Senators' manager] later made them take the marker down.

"I got Mantle out pretty good later on. I think he was 2 for 25 off me one year, but nobody ever talks about that."

Stobbs had a career record of 107 wins and 130 losses during his 15 seasons from 1947 to 1961. In 1957, after losing his first eleven decisions of the season, Stobbs tried to change his luck. He switched his uniform jersey to No. 13, and fans in attendance at Griffith Stadium on June 21 of that year came with rabbits' feet to help end Stobbs's run of bad fortune. The lucky charms worked for one game, but by season's end Stobbs had become Washington's first 20-game loser since 1916.

New York Yankees outfielder Mickey Mantle blasts a home run in the 1953 World Series against the Dodgers. The Mick awed baseball fans with his tape-measure home runs, including a legendary clout at Washington's Griffith Stadium.

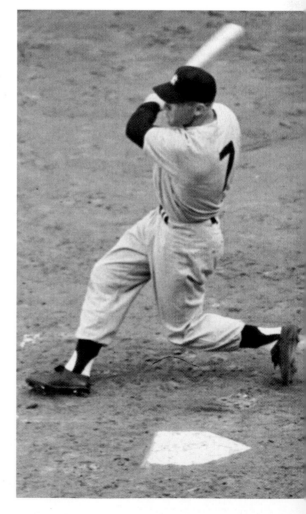

Q: Who is the oldest player to hit a home run?

A: Julio Franco of the New York Mets, at 47 years and 240 days. On April 20, 2006, Franco lined a pinch-hit, two-run homer inside the right-field foul pole at San Diego's Petco Park with one out in the eighth inning off pitcher Scott Linebrink (29 years, 259 days). The homer lifted the Mets to a 7–2 win over the Padres.

"Julio is old and decrepit," said teammate Tom Glavine. "But he can hit."

Franco supplanted Jack Quinn (46 years, 357 days) as the oldest player to go deep. On June 27, 1930, Quinn, a pitcher with the Philadelphia Athletics who took the mound until he was 50, hit one against the St. Louis Browns.

Franco's noteworthy homer was the 171st long fly of his 22-year career. Franco already was the oldest player to hit a grand slam and a pinch-hit homer and have a multihomer game. He was the All-Star Game Most Valuable Player in 1990 and the American League batting champion in 1991.

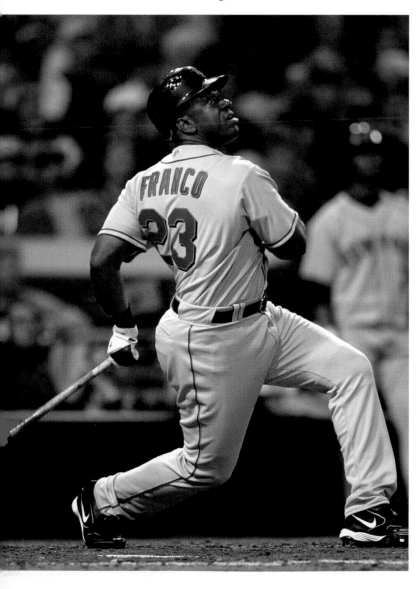

Forty-seven-year-old Julio Franco of the New York Mets became the oldest player in major league history to hit a home run when he connected on this shot against the Padres in 2006.

Longball Legends

Q: Who hit the most grand slam home runs?

A: Among his 493 career home runs, Lou Gehrig hit 23 grand slams (home runs with the bases loaded). Among active players, only Manny Ramirez of the Boston Red Sox has a chance to equal or break the record. Ramirez has hit 20 "grand salamis" through the 2005 season.

For Gehrig, playing on a high-scoring team such as the powerful Yankees of the 1920s and 1930s helped a little in setting the record. But, on closer inspection, most of his 17-year career (1923–39) with New York was spent fourth in the lineup, behind Babe Ruth, who rarely left men on base for the batters behind him.

Gehrig won three home-run titles, despite playing in Ruth's shadow. In 1927, when Ruth hit 60 home runs, Gehrig belted 47. Gehrig was second to Ruth in home runs each season from 1927 to 1931. In 1932 Gehrig hit four home runs in one game, a feat Ruth never matched. When Gehrig retired, he and Ruth sat atop the all-time home run list.

In 1931 Gehrig drove in 184 runs, still the American League record for a single season. He knocked in 165 runs or more four times. Gehrig's lifetime batting average was .340, and he batted .300 or better for 12 straight years, including a league-leading .363 in 1934.

Gehrig is most remembered for his consecutive-games-played streak, which earned him his nickname, The Iron Horse.

Lou Gehrig is a young man making his major league debut with the New York Yankees in this 1923 photo, as he began one of baseball's most storied playing careers.

Q: Who is professional baseball's true home run champion?

A: Henry Aaron is major league baseball's all-time home run king, with 755 career homers, but Sadaharu Oh is the most prolific slugger in professional baseball history. Oh hit 868 home runs during a 22-year career with the Yomiuri Giants of Japan's Central League from 1959 to 1980.

Oh surpassed Aaron's career total when he launched a pitch thrown by Yakult Swallows pitcher Yasumiro Suzuki into the right-field stands of Tokyo's Korakuen Stadium, on September 3, 1977. Oh's 328-foot blast was home run number 756, one more than Aaron hit in his 23-year major league career with Milwaukee and Atlanta. Oh, a 37-year-old first baseman, reached the milestone in his 19th season.

Oh has said he would not have fared as well in American baseball. Japanese parks are generally smaller than those in the United States, and the pitching is not considered to be of equal quality. But Oh achieved his record while playing in considerably shorter seasons of only 140 games.

A left-handed hitter who had an unorthodox, one-footed batting stance, like a flamingo holding the bat, Oh compiled 19 straight seasons of hitting at least 30 home runs. He won back-to-back Triple Crowns in 1973 and 1974, earned five batting championships, and led the Japanese Central League in RBIs 13 times and home runs 15 times. He hit four homers in a single game in 1964, set the Japanese single-season home run record with 55 in 1964 (a record that still stands), and was named Most Valuable Player nine times.

Oh retired in 1980 and has been the manager of the Tokyo Giants ever since.

Sadaharu Oh of the Yomiuri Giants of Japan's Central League taking batting practice in 1977. The following year he would hit his 800th home run, by far the most in the history of Japanese baseball.

" **If he played in the U.S. he'd be a superstar. He'd probably lead the league in home runs and would hit with the best of them.** "

—CLETE BOYER,
THE FIRST AMERICAN PROFESSIONAL
TO BE TRADED TO A JAPANESE LEAGUE, ON SADAHARU OH.

The Designated Hitter

Q: **Who was Major League Baseball's first designated hitter?**

A: Ron Blomberg of the New York Yankees made baseball history when he stepped into the batter's box on Opening Day in 1973. The Yankees were playing the Red Sox in Fenway Park when, in the first inning, Blomberg became the first DH to bat in a major league game. The "designated pinch-hitter" is the 10th man in the lineup, whose only function is to bat for the pitcher.

Blomberg, who faced Boston pitcher Luis Tiant with the bases loaded, drew a walk and forced in a Yankees run. The first major league plate appearance by a designated hitter was not an official at-bat, although Blomberg was credited with a run batted in. The DH rule wasted no time adding offense to the game.

Former major league manager Bobby Bragan is considered the father of the designated hitter. After using the rule for three seasons in the minor leagues, Bragan, then president of the Texas League and a member of baseball's rules committee, put the DH on the panel's agenda for a vote, in January 1973.

National League officials were unanimously against the idea from the start. But American League officials were undecided. From 1970 to 1972 the American League had averaged only 12 million in attendance (less than 75 percent of National League attendance), so Commissioner Bowie Kuhn and AL president Joe Cronin thought the DH would be a quick fix. With Kuhn casting the deciding vote to break the stalemate, the proposal passed as a three-year AL "experiment." At the time Kuhn said, "I hope it works. I would have preferred that both leagues did it. But if it's successful in one, then I hope the National follows suit." No such luck as National League president Chub Feeney summed up the NL's feelings thusly: "We like the game the way it is."

The adoption of the DH rule was a historic action. It was the first major rules change since the spitball was outlawed in 1920. It became the only baseball rule that doesn't apply to both leagues. As a result, the two major leagues now played under different rules for the first time since the American League was organized in 1901.

A DH-like rule was first proposed in 1929 by National League president John Heydler, but the AL then called it "damn foolery."

Interestingly, it cannot be demonstrated that the DH has ever helped AL attendance. But getting rid of this "experiment" will be as hard as instituting a baseball salary cap. Commissioner Bud Selig seems to be against the DH, but AL owners and the Players' Association would have to approve any repeal, and union leaders are not likely to abolish million-dollar jobs currently being held by dues-paying members.

> "It's incredible! I was an answer in Trivial Pursuit. I was a question on Jeopardy. And it all happened because I pulled my hamstring in spring training [all those] years ago."

—*RON BLOMBERG*

Terms and Endearment

Q: What is a "Texas leaguer"?

A: A Texas leaguer is a fly ball that falls just beyond the reach of an infielder and in front of an outfielder for a base hit. Though there are various explanations as to its origin, the term reportedly goes back to the 1800s and a player named Art Sunday, who had been a star hitter for Houston of the Texas League. In 1890 Sunday hit .398 for Toledo of the International League. Many of his hits were short flies that fell safely. Teammates kept referring to them as "Texas League hits." Soon they came to be known by everyone as Texas leaguers.

Bloop hits that safely fall between an infielder and an outfielder, like this one against the Philadelphia Phillies in 2004, are called Texas leaguers.

Texas leaguers, or flares, as players call them today, usually are accidental, but decades ago some hitters became skilled at blooping the ball between the infielders and outfielders.

There is evidence to suggest that these hits, originally called "plunkers," were favored as trick plays in the Texas League because fences generally were far away from the plate and outfielders played deep. Sunday may have been the game's greatest plunker.

Q: What is the "Mendoza line"?

A: Mario Mendoza was a slick-fielding but dreadfully weak-hitting shortstop for the Pittsburgh Pirates, Seattle Mariners, and Texas Rangers from 1974 to 1982. When he hit .198 as a regular for Seattle in 1979, teammates began referring to .200 as the Mendoza line. Soon major league players stopped saying that so-and-so cannot hit his weight; now a feeble hitter had simply passed the Mendoza line.

Mendoza claims the term was invented by former Mariners teammate Tom Paciorek. Paciorek said, "It wasn't my idea. I think it was [former Mariner] Bruce Bochte's. I got the credit, but I don't want it."

Mendoza, whose lifetime average was .215, fell below the Mendoza line in five of his nine seasons. Known as El Aspirador—Spanish for "The Vacuum Cleaner"—he was strictly a glove man. The native of Chihuahua, Mexico, made just 90 errors in 686 games.

In the early 1990s, Mendoza worked as a coach for Class A Palm Springs, a minor league rookie-ball team owned by the California Angels. His job? Hitting instructor.

Q: Which father and son made baseball history together?

A: Ken Griffey Sr. and Ken Griffey Jr. are the only father and son ever to play in the major leagues at the same time. Senior played for the 1975 and

1976 World Series champion Cincinnati Reds, and various other teams, during his 19-year career. Junior made it to the majors in 1989 with the Seattle Mariners, ripping a double in his first at-bat. He also hit a home run in his first at-bat in front of the home crowd.

In 1990 Griffey Senior joined Junior with the Mariners. They became the first father and son to play major league baseball together on the same team when they took the field against the Kansas City Royals on August 31, 1990. Ken Senior started in left field and Ken Junior started in center field for the Mariners, and they singled back to back in their first at-bats. Two weeks later, on September 14, 1990, they became the first father and son to hit back-to-back homers, off California's Kirk McCaskill.

Two years later, father and son combined to achieve yet another milestone. By smacking a home run and being named the MVP of the 1992 All-Star Game, Junior won the same award his father had won 12 years earlier.

Like father, like son. Ken Griffey and Ken Griffey Jr. (right) made major league history in 1989 by becoming the first father and son to play in the major leagues at the same time.

" I surprised myself being in the game for 19 years. I hung around long enough for Junior. "

—*KEN GRIFFEY SENIOR, ANNOUNCING HIS RETIREMENT IN NOVEMBER 1991*

Chin Music

Q: Which player holds the record for being hit by pitches?

A: It is unlikely that Craig Biggio of the Houston Astros ever aspired to be baseball's all-time leader in most times hit by pitch. That is not a milestone that kids dream about during their backyard ball games.

Biggio was drilled on his left elbow by Colorado Rockies pitcher Byung-Hyun Kim on June 29, 2005, marking the 268th time he had been plunked in his career, surpassing Don Baylor's modern black-and-blue mark of 267. Hughie Jennings, with 287, is the all-time HBP leader, but his career began in 1891 and ended in the Dead Ball Era, when the ball was about as hard as a rolled-up pair of socks.

Biggio's unflinching pursuit to become the HBP standard-bearer—by standing and bearing it—belies the fact that he is also approaching the hallowed 3,000 hit mark. Despite having been a human target during his lengthy career, he has never charged the mound. The pesky Biggio irritates opposing pitchers with his willingness to lean into close pitches and get on base any way he can.

At 5 feet, 11 inches, 185 pounds, Biggio is not a big man by baseball standards, but the gritty veteran stands close to the plate—dangerously close. Although he crowds the plate, a pitcher's 90-mile-per-hour fastball does not intimidate him.

"I am up there to get a hit," he says. "I'm not trying to get hit."

Until Baylor and then Biggio overtook him, Montreal Expos second baseman Ron Hunt set the standard for being plunked by pitches. In 1971 pitches hit Hunt 50 times, the most ever in one season.

Scrappy Houston Astros second baseman Craig Biggio has four Gold Glove awards to go along with his record for most times hit by a pitch.

Q: Who is the only batter ever to be killed as a result of a pitched ball?

A: Ray Chapman, a 29-year-old shortstop for the Cleveland Indians, was hit on the head by a pitch thrown by New York Yankees right-hander Carl Mays, on August 16, 1920, and became the only major league player to die as a result of injuries suffered during a game.

Chapman, a career .278 hitter and one of the most

popular players for the pennant-bound Indians, was hit in the head leading off the fifth inning of the Indians-Yankees game at New York's Polo Grounds. Chapman was crouching over the plate in his usual batting stance when a Mays fastball suddenly sailed toward his head. Chapman froze and the ball hit his skull, bouncing toward the mound. Mays retrieved the ball and threw to first, thinking the ball had hit the handle of Chapman's bat.

Mays, a two-time 20-game winner who threw with a submarine delivery, was a known headhunter who had a history of knocking down aggressive hitters. But Mays was reported to be terribly upset over the accident. Miller Huggins, the Yankees manager, thought Chapman was unable to avoid the pitch because the spikes on his left cleat got stick in the dirt.

While other horrible beanings have occurred in the major leagues, some causing career-ending injury, Ray Chapman is the only player to die as a result of a pitched ball. Batting helmets, mandatory since the 1950s, have no doubt saved lives.

Pitcher Carl Mays of the New York Yankees. In 1920 Mays threw a pitch that hit Indians shortstop Ray Chapman in the head. Chapman died the next day. Mays retired in 1929 with a career record of 207–126.

CHAPTER 4

THE PITCHERS

Baseball, among all the sports, is unique because the defense controls the ball. Nothing can happen until the pitcher toes the rubber and goes into his windup. Pitching is the most important part of the game, it is also the instigator of all the action. Games are won and lost on brilliant pitches and hanging mistakes.

Good pitching, it is said, will always beat good hitting. A starting pitcher usually starts about 35 games each season and strives to reach the 20-win mark. In order to do this, he must win in almost two out of every three starts. Truly dominating, so-called power pitchers are capable of striking out 300 batters in a season. The most effective starters pitch about 250 innings, so they must strike out more than one batter each inning to reach this total.

Like the game itself, pitching has evolved over the years. Starting pitchers now throw fewer innings and hand the ball over to relievers. Although there may never be another 30-game winner again, such as Detroit's Denny McLain in 1968, the impact of good pitching in deciding baseball games remains a constant.

Above: Pitchers like Roy Halladay of the Toronto Blue Jays try to keep batters off-balance with an array of fastballs, curves, change-ups, and sliders.

Left: Cy Young with the Cleveland Indians. Easily the greatest turn-of-the-century pitcher, he holds the major league record for victories with 511, and pitching's most coveted award is named after him.

Innovations and Irregularities

Q: **Who was the first pitcher to throw a curveball?**

A: No one really knows for sure, but there are plenty of hitters who would like to get their hands on the man who invented the curveball. According to one legend, 14-year-old Candy Cummings discovered that he could make a clamshell curve when he tossed it through the air by giving it a sharp twist with his right middle finger as he threw it. He wondered if he could do the same thing with a baseball and began to practice. Soon

Cummings discovered he could indeed make the ball curve during its flight.

The 5-foot, 9-inch, 120-pound Cummings used his secret weapon as a pitcher for the Brooklyn Excelsiors in the 1860s. Batters swung wildly, trying to catch up with Cummings's new pitch; most hit nothing but air. "For a long time I was known as the 'boy wonder,'" said Cummings. Traditionalists condemned the curveball as unfair, but Cummings went on to great success throwing it for the New York Mutuals of the National Association from 1872 to 1875, when he was one of the league's top pitchers.

More recent research makes the claim about Cummings being the inventor of the curveball doubtful. The other pitcher receiving credit for the curveball is Fred Goldsmith, who demonstrated the pitch to newspaper reporters in August 1870.

Q: **Do curveballs really curve?**

A: In 1941 *Life* magazine published a strobe-lit photo-graph of a curveball in motion. This was supposed proof that the curve didn't curve and that it was in fact an optical illusion. This

This Baseball Hall of Fame plaque from 1939 honors Candy Cummings as the first pitcher to throw a curveball. However, recent research casts doubt on the claim that Cummings invented the curve.

W. A. "CANDY" CUMMINGS

PITCHED FIRST CURVE BALL IN BASEBALL HISTORY. INVENTED CURVE AS AMATEUR ACE OF BROOKLYN STARS IN 1867. ENDED LONG CAREER AS HARTFORD PITCHER IN NATIONAL LEAGUE'S FIRST YEAR 1876.

fueled (if not started) the curveball controversy, which had proponents on both sides. It did not let up, even after *Life* corrected its error in 1953.

Thanks to a recent book, *The Physics of Baseball,* by Yale physics professor Robert K. Adair, we now have undeniable proof that a curveball does curve on both the horizontal and vertical planes. Hitters always knew this, of course; it was journalists who evidently did not.

On the vertical plane the ball curves downward more than it would simply from gravity because of topspin, which produces greater air pressure above the ball than below it. On the horizontal plane the ball also curves away from the side of the higher air pressure as it spins on its axis like a top.

Any pitcher will tell you that the break on his curveball depends on the speed of the pitch and the amount of spin he puts on it. Most pitchers do not know that it also depends on the density of the air. Former Phillies manager Eddie Sawyer said it best when he was asked in 1950 if a curveball really curves. He replied that if it doesn't, "it would be well to notify a lot of players who were forced to quit the game they love because of this pitch and may now be reached at numerous gas stations, river docks, and mental institutions." That statement, perhaps, provides just as much insight into the curve as one would get in any physics class.

Philadelphia Phillies manager Eddie Sawyer led the "Whiz Kids" team to the National League pennant in 1950, and he had no doubts about a baseball's ability to curve.

Q: Who was the last legal spitball pitcher?

A: Known as "Old Stubblebeard" for his custom of not shaving on the days he pitched, Burleigh Grimes was the last of the legal spitball pitchers. A spitball is basically a pitch where saliva or some other substance is applied to the baseball, giving it an unpredictable movement and rotation when thrown. When the spitball was outlawed in the major leagues in 1920, a handful of pitchers whose livelihoods depended on the pitch were allowed to continue to throw it. Grimes was the last of this group to retire. When he hung up his spikes in 1934, the legal spitball was gone from major league ball.

Over his 19 seasons of throwing the pitch, Grimes picked up 269 lifetime victories hurling for six National League clubs, and then picked up one more win with the Yankees in 1934. Along the way Grimes won NL pennants with the Dodgers in 1920, the Cardinals in 1930 and 1931, and the Cubs in 1932. He won his only World Series in 1931 at the age of 38, going 2–0 with a 2.04 ERA in the Fall Classic for the Cards.

Burleigh Grimes used his spitball to win 19 games for the New York Giants in 1927. The spitball was ruled an illegal pitch seven years earlier, but Grimes was "grandfathered in" and still allowed to throw it.

Q: Has there ever been an ambidextrous pitcher?

A: Tony Mullane, nicknamed "The Apollo of the Box" for his rugged good looks, hurled from both sides during his career in the late 1880s. A native of Ireland, Mullane pitched for several teams from 1881 to 1894, including the Cincinnati Red Stockings, and had a career record of 284–220. Look up Mullane in *The Baseball Encyclopedia* and you will find the unusual notation "BB TB" (Bats Both, Throws Both).

Although he usually pitched right-handed, Mullane would switch arms and pitch left-handed—sometimes in the middle of an at-bat. He did not wear a glove, so he could hide his choice of arm until the last moment. This deception also aided a tricky pickoff move. A fierce competitor who tried to intimidate the opposing batters, Mullane hit so many batters that a rule was passed to award first base to a hit batsman.

The most recent ambidextrous pitcher was Greg Harris, a right-hander who often pitched lefty on the sidelines to entertain his teammates. Hoping to someday pitch both right-handed and left-handed in the same game, Harris owned a special glove with no thumbs designed to be worn on either hand. As a member of the Phillies in 1989, Harris entered a game against the Pittsburgh Pirates as a reliever wearing his special glove.

"What's that?" asked Pirate base runner Andy Van Slyke, who was on third.

"He's amphibious," replied Phillie third baseman Randy Ready.

"Does that mean he can pitch underwater?" asked Van Slyke.

Harris finally got the chance to show off his unusual ability to pitch with either hand, "switch-pitching" once as a member of the Montreal Expos. On September 28, 1995, Harris started off the ninth inning of a game against the Cincinnati Reds pitching righty and retired Reggie Sanders. He then turned around to face the left-handed hitting Hal Morris. Harris walked Morris, stayed a southpaw and got a ground ball out from Eddie Taubensee, then switched back as a righty and retired Bret Boone.

Harris is the only 20th-century pitcher to throw with both hands off a major league mound, and the first ambidextrous pitcher since Elton Chamberlain of the American Association switch-pitched in 1888.

Tony Mullane pitching right-handed for the Cincinnati Red Stockings. Mullane would sometimes switch arms and pitch left-handed in the middle of an at-bat.

"Satch"

Q: Who is professional baseball's winningest pitcher?

A: While there are no definitive records to back it up, Leroy "Satchel" Paige is believed to have won more than 2,000 games. In a career that began in the 1920s and spanned five decades, Paige reportedly pitched in upwards of 2,500 games with several teams, most notably the Pittsburgh Crawfords and the Kansas City Monarchs of the Negro leagues. During his heyday, blacks were not allowed to play in the major or minor leagues.

Paige was a great strikeout pitcher and a showman. Between seasons he barnstormed (traveled with all-star teams) around the United States playing local teams. Sometimes he would have his fielders sit down while he struck out the side. He also played on several Negro league all-star teams that played exhibition games against major league all-stars and acquitted himself nicely.

Legend has it that in 1934 Paige won 104 of the 105 games he started. Following the 1934 season Paige toured with fellow Hall of Fame pitcher Dizzy Dean in a series of mound duels. Paige won four of the six games he pitched against Dean. In one 13-inning matchup in 1934, Paige bested Dean, 1–0, and struck out 17.

"If me and Satch were together in St. Louis," said Dean, "we would clinch the pennant by July and go fishing from then until World Series time." In 1935 Paige beat a team of all-star major leaguers that included Joe DiMaggio, who called Paige "the best I've ever faced and the fastest." Hall of Famer Hack Wilson had this to say about Paige's fastball: "It starts out like a baseball, but when it gets to the plate it looks like a marble." On hearing that, the ever quotable Paige replied, "You must be talking about my slow ball. My fastball looks like a fish egg."

In 1948, the year after baseball integrated, Bill Veeck signed Paige to play for his Cleveland Indians. At 42 (his age was always open to speculation) he was the oldest rookie ever. For the first month of Paige's major league career, Cleveland manager Lou Boudreau used him exclusively in relief. Then, in August 1948, Paige started against the Washington Senators, winning the game 5–3. In his second start he shut out the Chicago White Sox in front of a sellout crowd at Comiskey Park. One week later he shut the White Sox out again, this time before 78,000 people in Cleveland. Paige finished his rookie year of 1948 with a 6–1 record and a 2.48 ERA, helping the Indians win the AL pennant.

When new Cleveland ownership released him after the 1949 season, Veeck picked him up again, this time to pitch for the St. Louis Browns, where he hurled for three more years. In 1954 the Browns released Paige, and he resumed his barnstorming career, pitching around the country until the mid 1960s.

In 1965 the Kansas City Athletics' owner, Charles O. Finley, brought Paige back to the majors for a final game, on September 25. In his farewell performance, Paige pitched three innings against the Boston Red Sox. Although Paige was 59 years old, in those three innings he struck out one batter and gave up just one hit for no runs.

Opposite page: Leroy "Satchel" Paige at spring training for the St. Louis Browns in 1952. Paige was the greatest pitcher in the history of the Negro leagues, and also starred in the majors late in his career.

Win Some, Lose Some

Q: Which major league pitcher lost the most games?

A: Cy Young lost more games than any other pitcher in the history of major league baseball. His 316 losses, accumulated during a 22-year career with the Cleveland Spiders, St. Louis Cardinals, Boston Red Sox, Cleveland Indians, and Boston Braves, are more losses than the win total of 300-game winners Lefty Grove or Early Wynn.

Denton "Cy" (for Cyclone) Young also won more games than any other major league pitcher. His 511 career victories are tops in major league history—and more wins than Tom Seaver and Sandy Koufax combined. Young's record of 511 career victories is one that should stand forever. Even if a pitcher were to come along and win 20 games a year for 20 seasons, he would still be more than 100 victories shy of Young's mark. In addition to the record for career wins and losses, Young also pitched the most innings (7,356) and most complete games (749). His career ERA was 2.63.

Young broke into the big leagues at 23, in 1890, and pitched until 1911, when he was 44. His control was otherworldly for the day, averaging just one and a half walks per nine innings over his career. Five times he won more than 30 games in a season. He is the only pitcher to win 200 games in both the National and American leagues.

He pitched three no-hitters, including the first perfect game in American League history, in 1903.

The annual award for the best pitcher in each league is named for him.

Q: What pitcher gave up the most home runs?

A: Robin Roberts of the Philadelphia Phillies enjoys a place in the Hall of Fame with 286 career victories, but he does not enjoy his all-time record for most home runs allowed. Roberts surrendered 505 homers during his 19 years in the major leagues.

Roberts was a stalwart on the Phillies pitching staff for 14 seasons, dominating National League hitters with a blazing fastball and pinpoint control. In the six years from 1950 to 1955, he won 20 or more games each season and narrowly missed a seventh straight 20-win season in 1956, when he notched 19 victories.

In 1950 he led the Phillies to their first pennant since 1915, and produced his first 20-win season. His 20th victory came on

Because of the way he pitched, Denton True Young earned the nickname of "Cy"— short for cyclone. Here the 42-year-old Young is warming up for the Boston Red Sox during the 1908 season.

Robin Roberts in the final season of his 19-year career, with the Houston Astros in 1966. He won 286 regular-season games despite a penchant for giving up the long ball.

the final day of the season in a 10-inning, pennant-deciding game at Brooklyn. He became the first Phillies pitcher to win 20 games since Grover Cleveland Alexander had done it in 1917. In the 1950 World Series, won by the Yankees in four straight games, Roberts lost his only start, 2–1 in 10 innings.

Roberts's masterful control could sometimes work against him. Batters were unafraid of being hit by a pitched ball, so they dug in and swung from the heels. Consequently he gave up home runs in record numbers. His 46 homers allowed in 1956 stood as the major league mark until 1986, when Bert Blyleven of the Twins allowed 50 dingers. But because he walked batters so seldom—fewer than two free passes per game—most of the homers he served up cost him only single runs.

Young at Heart

Q: Who was the youngest pitcher in major league history?

Joe Nuxhall of the Cincinnati Reds was 15 years old in 1944 when he entered a game and pitched two-thirds of an inning to become the youngest player ever to participate in a major league game.

A: As World War II progressed, major league ball suffered from a noticeable lack of top talent. Many teams welcomed back aging stars. The Cincinnati Reds, going to the other end of the age spectrum, epitomized the difficult search for new talent.

Joe Nuxhall was 15 years old when he took the mound for the Reds, who were losing a 13–0 laugher against the the St. Louis Cardinals, on June 10, 1944. Nuxhall pitched two-thirds of an inning, walked five, gave up two singles, threw a wild pitch, and allowed five more runs to score in the 18-0 rout.

Nuxhall was immediately sent back down to the Reds' minor league system. He did not appear in another major league game for eight years, but then put together a reputable pro career, going 135–117 with a 3.90 ERA, mostly with the Reds. In 1955 he won 17 games and led the league with five shutouts. A two-time National League All-Star, he retired after the 1966 season and has been broadcasting Reds games ever since.

Q: Who is the oldest pitcher to throw a no-hitter?

A: On June 11, 1990, a 43-year-old Nolan Ryan became the oldest major league pitcher ever to throw a no-hitter. The ageless wonder threw another no-hitter the following season at age 44.

Ryan was one of the most intimidating pitchers in the baseball history. He is the all-time strikeout leader with 5,714—over 1,000 more than Roger Clemens (as of 2006), the next nastiest ace. He also pitched a record seven no-hitters—three more than Sandy Koufax, his nearest competitor.

Ryan first no-hitter (May 15, 1973) and his seventh no-hitter (May 1, 1991) were pitched almost 18 years apart. Sandy Alomar was playing second base behind Ryan in the first no-hitter. Ryan struck out Roberto Alomar, Sandy's son, to end the seventh no-hitter. The strikeout came on a 93-mile-per-hour fastball and was Ryan's 16th of the game. Afterward, as usual, the ageless wonder rode an exercise bicycle for a half hour.

A physical fitness marvel, Ryan had a longer career than any pitcher in major league history, and few threw harder. His fastball, called "The Ryan Express," was once clocked at 100.9 miles per hour. The right-hander from Alvin, Texas, pitched for a record 27 big-league seasons, accumulating a lifetime record of 324–292, with four different teams. He was famous for his blistering fastball and nose-to-toes curveball.

Ryan was in his third season in the major leagues when he was a member of the New York Mets team that stunned the Baltimore Orioles to win the 1969 World Series. He struggled early in his career with his control problems, becoming as well known for his wildness as his startling speed. (He ignominiously led the league in walks eight times and is the record-holder for most walks allowed in a career with 2,795.) The impatient Mets traded him to the California Angels after the 1971 season.

With the Angels, Ryan matured as a pitcher and learned to harness his immense power. In eight years with the Angels he led the league in strikeouts seven times, five times exceeding 300 strikeouts. An intimidating presence on the mound, he fanned a modern major league record 383 batters in 1973. That year he became only the fourth pitcher to throw two no-hitters in a single season.

Though wildness would keep Ryan from pitching a perfect game, fans jammed into ballparks to witness his overpowering stuff. He led the league in strikeouts 11 times, including 1989, when he struck out 301 batters—at the age of 42! Ryan fanned 10 or more in a game a

record 209 times, and he put 15 or more down on strikes 26 times.

He played for the Houston Astros from 1980 to 1988 and then the Rangers from 1989 to 1993 as the biggest star in his home state of Texas.

Nolan Ryan of the California Angels unleashing a fastball against Detroit in 1977. Ryan threw seven no-hitters in his career, three more than any other pitcher.

Hurler Dominance

Q: For one week, who was the best pitcher ever?

A: Johnny Vander Meer of the Cincinnati Reds pitched two successive no-hitters within a five-day span in June 1938, a feat that will possibly never be duplicated. Before Vander Meer's stunning achievement, only seven pitchers had ever thrown two or more no-hitters in their careers, and none had ever thrown more than one no-hitter in a single season.

Vander Meer was then a 22-year-old southpaw in his first full major league season. His first no-hitter, a 3–0 victory, was pitched in daylight against the Boston Bees. The second no-hitter was pitched against the Brooklyn Dodgers in the first night game ever played at Ebbets Field. Jesse Owens, the hero of the 1936 Olympics, ran pregame sprints as a sideshow for the record crowd of almost 40,000 fans that jammed the tiny ballpark.

Vander Meer struck out seven Dodgers batters, but he battled his own wildness during the 6–0 win. He had problems finding the strike zone in the bottom of the ninth inning, walking the bases loaded with one out. But with his opportunity at

Cincinnati left-hander Johnny Vander Meer blanked first the Braves and then the Dodgers while racking up his unprecedented and unmatched back-to-back no-hitters.

baseball immortality on the line, Vander Meer took hold of his emotions. He got Ernie Koy to bounce into a force out at the plate and then got Dodgers player-manager Leo "The Lip" Durocher to hit a pop fly to center field for the final out. Despite walking eight batters, Vander Meer became the first pitcher to toss consecutive no-hitters.

Vander Meer began his next start with three hitless innings for a major league record of 21 straight innings without giving up a hit. Vander Meer, who went 15–10 in 1938, pitched for 13 seasons in the major leagues, never completing another no-hitter. His lifetime record was 119 wins and 121 losses.

Q: What is the most legendary pitching performance in an All-Star Game?

A: In 1934, at the Polo Grounds in New York, Carl Hubbell of the Giants used his dazzling screwball to strike out five future Hall of Famers in a row: Babe Ruth, Lou Gehrig, Jimmie Foxx, Al Simmons, and Joe Cronin. Bill Dickey broke the strikeout streak by singling, but Hubbell then fanned Lefty Gomez to end the inning.

"I got every one of them on a screwball," said Hubbell. "I figured they'd hit better fastballs than mine and better curves. If they were going to hit me, it would have to be my best. Oh, I showed them the other pitches, but not where they could get a good swing at them. The third strike on every one of them was a screwball."

Hubbell's dominance over the game's all-time greats is remarkable, yet that was not his most remarkable feat in baseball. Pitching between 1936 and 1937, King Carl recorded 24 consecutive victories and won his second Most Valuable Player award.

In 1984, Hubbell threw out the ceremonial first pitch at Candlestick Park in San Francisco to mark the 50th anniversary of his All-Star Game achievement. Then Hubbell watched as another screwballing lefty, Fernando Valenzuela of the Los Angeles Dodgers, and New York Mets pitcher Dwight "Doc" Gooden, at 19 the youngest All-Star ever, combined to break Hubbell's record with six back-to-back whiffs.

Q: What is the most efficient pitching performance ever?

A: Boston Braves right-hander Red Barrett threw just 58 pitches, an incredible 6.4 pitches per inning, while shutting out the Cincinnati Reds, 2–0, on August 10, 1944. The game, played before 7,783 fans at Crosley Field, lasted 1 hour and 15 minutes.

Barrett allowed two hits, walked none, and struck out none (walks and strikeouts, do not forget, do use up pitches). Most teams toward the end of World War II were patched together, many of the stars having gone overseas, and the box score of Barrett's game contains few well-known names. The best hitter he faced was first baseman Frank McCormick.

His catcher that day in 1944 was Stew Hofferth. The redheaded Barrett "pitched real fast, he didn't wait around," recalled Hofferth. "He was throwing right down the middle and the Reds kept hitting the first pitch—mostly pop-ups and ground balls." Barrett, who had a lifetime record of 69–69 with the Reds, Braves, and St. Louis Cardinals, died in July 1990.

By consecutively striking out five of baseball's most powerful hitters in the 1934 All-Star Game, Carl Hubbell of the New York Giants became the talk of the baseball world.

Big Game Pitchers

Q: What was the "Double No-Hit Game"?

A: On May 2, 1917, at Chicago's Weeghman Park, 3,500 fans witnessed baseball's first double nine-inning no-hitter. Right-hander Fred Toney pitched for the visiting Cincinnati Reds while James "Hippo" Vaughn, a southpaw, was on the mound for the Cubs. Neither pitcher surrendered a hit through nine innings. The Reds won in the 10th inning as Jim Thorpe got the game-winning hit on a swinging bunt. Toney retired the Cubs in order in the bottom of the 10th to preserve his no-hitter.

Q: Who pitched the only no-hitter on Opening Day?

A: In 1940 the 21-year-old Cleveland Indians fireballer Bob Feller became the first major league pitcher to throw an Opening Day no-hitter when he defeated the Chicago White Sox, 1–0, before 14,000 roaring fans at Comiskey Park. Feller struck out eight batters and walked five.

One year after returning from the Navy, Feller tossed his second no-hitter on April 30, 1946, beating the Yankees 1–0. The only run was scored by Feller's battery mate, catcher Frankie Hayes, who hit a home run in the top of the ninth inning.

New York Giants pitcher Red Ames worked nine innings without allowing a hit in the 1909 opener at the Polo Grounds against the Brooklyn Dodgers. But the right-hander surrendered a hit in the 10th inning and lost in the 13th when Brooklyn scored three runs.

Houston Astros pitcher Ken Forsch hurled the earliest calendar no-hitter, beating the Atlanta Braves on April 7, 1979. Bob Forsch (Ken's brother) had pitched his own no-hitter in 1978. The Forsches remain the only brothers to pitch no-hitters in the major leagues.

Q: Which United States senator pitched a perfect game?

A: Jim Bunning of the Philadelphia Phillies, later a Hall of Famer and a United States senator from Kentucky, pitched a perfect game against the New York Mets on June 21, 1964. It was the

Bob Feller of the Cleveland Indians as a 17-year-old in 1936. The Nolan Ryan of his day, Feller threw three no-hitters and twelve one-hitters in an 18-year major-league career.

first regular-season perfect game since 1922 and the first in the National League since 1880.

Splitting his 17-year career between the American League (nine years with Detroit) and National League, Bunning achieved great success as a starting pitcher in each league. He enjoyed his best season in 1957, posting a 20–8 record with a 2.69 ERA for the Tigers. He pitched his first no-hitter on July 20, 1958, against the Boston Red Sox.

Bunning won 118 games in nine years with Detroit. Following the 1963 season he was traded to the Phillies, and during that summer he pitched his second no-hitter, a perfect game, which came at Shea Stadium in New York in the first game of a Father's Day doubleheader. Bunning picked a perfect day for such a feat. Together, he and his wife, Mary, raised nine children and have 35 grandchildren.

Bunning reeled off three straight 19-win seasons for the Phillies in the National League. He went on to win more than 100 games in the NL, becoming, after Cy Young, the second pitcher ever to notch 100 wins and 1,000 strikeouts in both leagues. He was also the first to

Jim Bunning of the Philadelphia Phillies in 1966. His perfect game against the Mets in 1964 was the first "perfecto" thrown in the National League since 1880.

pitch in All-Star Games for both leagues. Bunning retired in 1971, trailing only the immortal Walter Johnson on the all-time strikeout list.

Following his playing career, Bunning managed in the Phillies' minor league system for five years before entering politics. He was elected to the Kentucky state legislature and ran unsuccessfully for governor of that state. Voters from the 4th District of Kentucky elected Bunning to the U.S. House of Representatives in 1986. Twelve years later, in 1998, he was elected to the U.S. Senate, and won a second term in 2004.

Tough Decisions

Q: Who was the first pitcher to throw a no-hitter and lose?

A: The first pitcher to throw a complete game no-hitter and lose was Ken Johnson of the Houston Colt .45s (later the Astros) in 1964. He lost to the Reds, 1–0, when, in the top of the ninth inning, he committed a two-base throwing error on Pete Rose's bunt and Nellie Fox booted a grounder, allowing Rose to score.

Hard luck was nothing new for Johnson, a right-hander whose lifetime record for seven teams was 91–106. "One game against the Phillies, they had a 'Runs For Johnson Night,' and any woman with a run in her stockings got in for free," he recalled of his Colt .45 days. "And then Jim Bunning beat us with a one-hitter."

Steve Barber and Stu Miller of the Baltimore Orioles combined to pitch a no-hitter and yet lost to the Detroit Tigers in 1967. Andy Hawkins of the New York Yankees allowed no hits against the Chicago White Sox in 1990 but lost the game after four runs scored on three errors and two walks in the bottom of the eigth inning.

Since the White Sox won when they set down the Yankees in the top of the ninth, Hawkins had no opportunity to pitch nine innings. Nevertheless, his no-hitter was erased from the record books on September 4, 1991, when baseball's Committee for Statistical Accuracy defined a no-hitter as a complete hitless game of nine innings or more.

The new ruling was quickly enforced when Matt Young of the Red Sox no-hit the Cleveland Indians in April 1992. But the Boston lefty walked seven batters and lost 2–1. Because Cleveland won the game, they did not have to bat in the bottom of the ninth, and Young was denied his official no-hitter.

"A no-hitter is supposed to be where you strike out the last guy and the catcher comes out and jumps in your arms. A loss is a loss," said Young.

Q: Which hard-luck hurler pitched 12 perfect innings and lost?

A: Harvey Haddix of the Pittsburgh Pirates pitched 12 perfect innings on May 26, 1959. Then in the 13th inning, he lost it all.

Haddix retired the first 36 Milwaukee Braves batters in a row. No one in major league history ever had taken a perfect game into extra innings. The trouble was, Haddix's Pirates could not score off Braves starter Lew Burdette, either.

Finally, in the bottom of the 13th inning, the Braves got a man on base via a throwing error, ending Haddix's perfect game. After a sacrifice bunt and an intentional walk, Joe Adcock spoiled Haddix's bid for a no-hitter, a shutout, and a win with one swing of the bat. Adcock drove the ball over the fence for an apparent three-run home run.

Adcock's hit turned out to be just a double, because Hank Aaron, the runner on first, left the base paths before scoring. Adcock passed him and was called out. Officially, the final score was 1–0. Unofficially, Haddix threw the best game ever by a losing pitcher.

"It didn't matter to me whether it was 1–0 or 100–0," Haddix said. "We lost the game, and that's what hurts me most."

Harvey Haddix of the Pirates during one of his 12 perfect innings against the Braves in Milwaukee. He lost in the 13th on an error and a home run, later changed to a double, by Joe Adcock.

Arms Race

Sandy Koufax pitching for the Dodgers in 1957, when the team still played in Brooklyn. The Dodgers moved to Los Angeles after the 1958 season, and Koufax became the dominant pitcher in the major leagues in the mid 1960s.

Q: Which pitcher retired at the top of his game?

A: Los Angeles Dodgers ace pitcher Sandy Koufax retired because of severe arthritis in his throwing arm. The 30-year-old Dodger pitcher had just won 27 games and the Cy Young Award in the 1966 season when he called it quits. The arthritis caused the lefty incredible pain, and he sometimes lost all feeling in his pitching hand. His arm swelled enormously after each game and had to be iced. He had to take countless cortisone shots and did not want to risk permanent damage to his left arm or his health.

Koufax retired from baseball at the top of his profession. From 1962 to 1966, he was the game's most successful left-handed pitcher. During those last five seasons, Koufax won the ERA title five years in a row, was the strikeout king three times, and topped 300 strikeouts in a season three times. Koufax won three Cy Young Awards—when the award was given to just one pitcher from both leagues—and was the National League's Most Valuable Player in 1963. In addition he pitched four no-hitters in four years, including a 1–0 perfect game against the Chicago Cubs in 1965. That season he allowed fewer than six hits per nine innings and struck out 382. Only Nolan Ryan has surpassed his single-season strikeout total.

From 1961 to 1966 Koufax won 129 games and lost only 47. He topped the league in wins three times, with 25 in 1963, 26 in 1965, and 27 in 1966. For his 12-year career, all with the Brooklyn and Los Angeles Dodgers, he was 165–87. He helped the Dodgers win four pennants and three World Series.

When the pain in Koufax's arm became too much, doctors advised him to stop pitching. Upon retiring, he said, "I am leaving the game while I can still comb my hair. I don't regret one minute of the last 12 years, but I think I would regret one minute too many." In 1972, at the age of 36, he became the youngest man ever elected to the National Baseball Hall of Fame.

Q: Why was 1968 called the "Year of the Pitcher"?

A: Perhaps the greatest year for pitchers in baseball history was 1968. Seven pitchers that year had earned run averages under 2.00. Pitchers such as the Los Angeles Dodgers' Don Drysdale, the Detroit Tigers' Denny McLain, and the St. Louis Cardinals' Bob Gibson dominated opposing hitters.

Drysdale pitched six shutouts in a row, McLain won 31 games (the last pitcher to win 30 in a season), and Gibson posted a minuscule earned run average of 1.12, a record for a pitcher with over 300 innings pitched.

Gibson's 1968 season was one of the greatest ever by a major league pitcher. On his way to winning the Cy Young Award and the Most Valuable Player award, he posted a 22–9 record, including 15 straight wins, 13 shutouts, 268 strikeouts, and the lowest earned run average in a season since Walter Johnson's 1.14 ERA in 1913. During one 95-inning stretch Gibson gave up just two runs.

His amazing performance helped the Cardinals back to the World Series for the second straight year. In Game One of the 1968 Series, Gibson beat Detroit's 31-win dynamo, Denny McLain, 4–0, and set a Series record by striking out 17

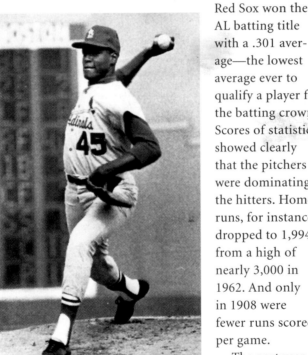

Tigers. His 35 total strikeouts were also a Series record.

The 1968 season was called the "Year of the Pitcher," because hitting stats were at an all-time low. The combined batting average for both leagues was .236, the lowest ever recorded. The entire American League batted only .230, and Carl Yastrzemski of the Boston Red Sox won the AL batting title with a .301 average—the lowest average ever to qualify a player for the batting crown. Scores of statistics showed clearly that the pitchers were dominating the hitters. Home runs, for instance, dropped to 1,994 from a high of nearly 3,000 in 1962. And only in 1908 were fewer runs scored per game.

The next year, the rules changed to help the hitters. The pitcher's mound was lowered and the strike zone was narrowed to give hitters more of a chance against increasingly better pitching. The changes worked. Beginning in 1969 baseball seemed to put an increased emphasis on offense, which eventually led to the tremendous explosion in home runs that we see today.

Bob Gibson of the Cardinals working against the Boston Red Sox in Game Seven of the 1967 World Series. In leading the Cards to the title, he went 3-0, pitching three complete games and recording an ERA of 1.00. He continued his dominance in 1968 en route to being named league MVP.

CHAPTER 5

STREAKS AND FEATS

For a game that pays such close attention to its averages and percentages, baseball sure does celebrate its streaks. There are consecutive-games-played streaks, hitting streaks, home-run-hitting streaks, winning streaks, losing streaks, strikeout streaks, and consecutive-scoreless-innings streaks.

Extraordinary players such as Joe DiMaggio, Cal Ripken Jr., Don Mattingly, Ken Griffey Jr., Carl Hubbell, Tom Seaver, and Orel Hershiser often accomplish these streaks. But just as likely, an otherwise totally ordinary player such as Dale Long, Fernando Tatis, or Anthony Young can achieve an incredible streak.

Oftentimes the streak is determined by good luck, sometimes by bad luck, sometimes by plain old dumb luck, or, sadly, sometimes a streak is determined by no luck at all. In either of these cases, the fans, the media, and the historians all pay close attention whenever baseball's routine is knocked even slightly off kilter.

The game of baseball is also all about consistency—doing the simple things correctly over and over again. Perhaps that is why baseball aficionados have a knack for glomming onto uniquely rare and genuinely amazing feats. There are dramatic one-inning offensive explosions, miracle comebacks by teams seemingly out of pennant contention, and otherworldly two-sport stars such as Bo Jackson and Deion Sanders who rewrite history with their unprecedented legacies.

Above: Fernando Tatis of the St. Louis Cardinals hit two grand slam home runs in the same inning in a 1999 game against the Los Angeles Dodgers.

Left: With this swing, Joe DiMaggio extended his hit streak to 42 consecutive games against the Senators in Washington on June 29, 1941. He would not be stopped for another 15 games.

The Iron Man

Q: Who holds the record for the most consecutive games played?

Cal Ripken Jr. of the Baltimore Orioles was twice named the American League's Most Valuable Player (1983 and 1991). He started in 17 straight All-Star Games. As a shortstop, Ripken hit 319 home runs, which leads all players at that position.

A: Cal Ripken Jr. is modern baseball's iron man, having played in 2,632 consecutive games. The Baltimore Orioles shortstop began his iron-man streak in a game against the Toronto Blue Jays, on May 30, 1982, and defied the odds by playing every game for 16 seasons. He broke Lou Gehrig's record of 2,130 straight games on September 6, 1995. Gehrig's seemingly untouchable record had stood for 56 years.

Ripken surpassed Gehrig's mark at a time when baseball needed him most. An ugly labor dispute had resulted in the cancellation of the previous year's World Series, and strike-weary fans yearning to re-embrace the game exalted Ripken's old-school work ethic. So once the record-breaking game against the California

Angels became official after the top half of the fifth inning, the appreciative crowd at the Orioles' home field at Camden Yards thunderously began to roar Ripken's name, forcing a halt to the contest. Ripken received eight curtain calls during the 20-minute ovation. Teammates pushed the two-time American League Most Valuable Player out of the dugout, and he ran a victory lap around the stadium, shaking and slapping hands with fans. The scoreboard read, "Cal, thank you for saving baseball."

Playing every game for more than 13 seasons certainly is unfathomable to the modern-day player. Yet Ripken had missed only 164 out of a possible 19,395 innings, and he went all-out in every single one of them. Even in the record-setting game, he celebrated by hitting a home run to help the Orioles to a 4–2 win.

"I know that if Lou Gehrig is looking down on tonight's activities," Ripken told the crowd, "he isn't concerned about someone playing one more consecutive game than he did. Instead, he's viewing tonight as just another example of what is good and right about the great American game."

Speaking at a postgame ceremony, Ripken added: "Tonight, I stand here, overwhelmed, as my name is linked with the great and courageous Lou Gehrig. I'm truly humbled to have our names spoken in the same breath. Some may think our strongest connection is because we played many consecutive games. Yet I believe in

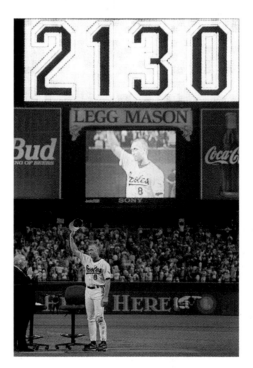

The eyes of Baltimore are on Cal Ripken Jr. as he waves his cap to the fans at Camden Yards after playing in 2,130 consecutive games, tying Lou Gehrig's record, on September 5, 1995. The next night, Ripken would break the record.

my heart that our true link is a common motivation—a love of the game of baseball, a passion for our team, and a desire to compete on the very highest level."

Three years later Ripken unexpectedly asked Baltimore manager Ray Miller to remove him from the Orioles' lineup in the final home game of the season, against the New York Yankees, on September 20, 1998, voluntarily ending his streak of consecutive games at 2,632. (Ryan Minor was his replacement.) It was the 38-year-old Ripken's first game off in 16 seasons. He retired after the 2001 season as one of the best slugging shortstops in history, with 3,184 career hits and 431 home runs.

> **Will this record ever be broken again? Well, I know I sure won't be around to see it if it ever is.**
> —*HALL OF FAME ANNOUNCER ERNIE HARWELL*

Joltin' Joe

Q: Who hit safely in the greatest number of consecutive games?

A: Of all the great batting records that once seemed unapproachable—Babe Ruth's 60 home runs in a season and Hank Aaron's 755 home runs—Joe DiMaggio's hitting streak in 1941 is one of the few that has stood the test of time. "Joltin' Joe" hit safely in 56 games in a row. Pete Rose (1978) and Willie Keeler (1897) are second with 44 games each.

DiMaggio's streak began with a single against the Chicago White Sox on May 15, 1941. Over the next two months, he had at least one base hit in every game in which he played. During that time he had 91 hits and batted .408 with 15 home runs and 55 runs batted in—not a bad season for some players. DiMaggio said he became conscious of the streak when it stretched to 25 straight games on June 10. Newspapermen covering the Yankees had dug up the franchise record for hitting safely in consecutive games, which stood at 33, by Hal Chase, in 1907, when the team was still called the Highlanders. DiMaggio equaled that mark on June 20. The next record to fall was Rogers Hornsby's modern-day National League record. DiMaggio passed that on June 21.

The summer of 1941 belonged to Joe DiMaggio, even though baseball was merely a footnote to world events. As the U.S. drew ever closer to entering World War II, people flocked to radios and newspapers. Soon the entire nation was also checking DiMaggio's performance in the morning papers and getting radio bulletins on every at-bat.

On June 29 DiMaggio equaled George Sisler's single-season mark of 41 consecutive games with a hit, doubling against the Washington Senators in the first game of a doubleheader. He broke Sisler's record in the nightcap with a single. He then passed Willie Keeler's major league record of 44 games, on July 2, and reached 50 games on July 11, pounding out four hits against the St. Louis Browns. On July 16 he got three hits off two Cleveland pitchers, Al Milnar and Joe Krakauskas, marking game number 56. The next night a huge crowd came to the ballpark to see if he could make it 57.

Q: How did the streak finally end?

A: The sensational streak finally ended on July 17, 1941, before 67,468 people in Cleveland's Municipal Stadium. Indians left-hander Al Smith retired DiMaggio on two hard smashes to third baseman Ken Keltner, who made two outstanding plays to rob potential hits. On his third time up DiMaggio walked. Late in the game he came up for the last time, against a knuckleballer, Jim Bagby, with two out and a man on first. He needed a hit to keep the streak going. DiMaggio rapped a Bagby pitch at shortstop Lou Boudreau, who threw to second to force the runner. The impossible streak had ended at 56 games.

An undeterred DiMaggio remained hot. He hit safely in the next 16 games, making his streak 72 out of 73 games. He went on to win the Most Valuable Player award that season, batting .357

The consecutive-game hitting streak of Joe DiMaggio's has been among the most enduring records in sports. Pete Rose of the Cincinnati Reds has come the closest to matching it, hitting in 44 consecutive National League games in 1978.

with 30 homers and a league-leading 125 runs batted in.

DiMaggio was among the game's greatest natural hitters. He could hit for average and hit for power. He had a lifetime batting average of .325 and hit 361 home runs, despite missing three of his prime years while in the armed services in World War II. He had an unusually keen batting eye and rarely struck out. In his entire career he fanned only 369 times.

During his 13-year career DiMaggio led the Yankees to nine World Series titles. He won three MVP awards (1939, 1941, and 1947) and was elected to the Hall of Fame in 1955. Someone once asked DiMaggio why he played so hard day in and day out. He replied, "There might be someone in the park who's never seen me play before."

In 1969, during baseball's Centennial Celebration, he was named the game's greatest living player.

Home Run Hot Streak

Q: What is the record for most consecutive games hitting a home run?

A: On May 28, 1956, Dale Long of the Pittsburgh Pirates went deep against the Brooklyn Dodgers' Carl Erskine at Forbes Field, becoming the first player to hit a home run in eight consecutive games. Don Mattingly of the New York Yankees, in 1987, and Ken Griffey Jr. of the Seattle Mariners, in 1993, later tied the record.

Long's amazing streak started May 19, 1956, against Jim Davis of the Chicago Cubs. The Pirates' first baseman also homered off Milwaukee's Warren Spahn and Ray Crone, St. Louis's Herman Wehmeier and Lindy McDaniel, and Philadelphia's Curt Simmons and Ben Flowers.

Another first baseman, Don Mattingly of the Yankees, equaled Long's 31-year-old record by homering in his eighth consecutive game, on July 18, 1987. Mattingly's shot came off Jose Guzman of the Texas Rangers in Arlington, Texas. The home run was his 10th during the eight-game span. Mattingly, who started his streak July 8 against Minnesota pitcher Mike Smithson, had set the American League record the night before when he connected with a pitch from Texas left-hander Paul Kilgus.

Griffey, 23, duplicated the record set by Long and Mattingly with a 404-foot shot

New York's Don Mattingly waves to the appreciative Yankee Stadium crowd after parking a ball into the bleachers for a home run during the 1993 season. Mattingly hit ten homers during an eight-game stretch in 1987.

off Willie Banks of the Minnesota Twins in the Kingdome on July 28, 1993, for his eighth straight game hitting a home run. Griffey nearly broke the record the next night against the Twins' Scott Erickson, but his long drive to center field smacked off the base of the wall for a double. Then he grounded out and popped out.

Q: What is the most potent offensive production ever by a batter in one inning?

A: Fernando Tatis set a major league record by hitting two grand slams in a single inning against the Los Angeles Dodgers on April 23, 1999. The St. Louis Cardinals third baseman also set a record with eight runs batted in in the inning.

Tatis hit both slams against right-handed pitcher Chan Ho Park. Park is the second pitcher to give up two grand slams in the same inning (Pittsburgh's Bill Phillips did it in 1890), but he is the first ever to serve them both up to the same batter.

Only seven major league *teams* have hit two grand slams in the same inning. The last time it happened was on July 16, 2006, when Cliff Floyd and Carlos Beltran of the New York Mets each hit bases-loaded round-trippers in the sixth inning against the Cubs. The Mets joined the 1890 Cubs, the 1962 Twins, the 1969 Astros, the 1980 Brewers, the 1986 Orioles, and the 1999 Cardinals, when Tatis hit two on his own.

Mostly remembered as being a one-year wonder, Tatis enjoyed a career year with the Cardinals in 1999, finishing the season with a .298 batting average, 34 home runs, 107 runs batted in, and 21 stolen bases. Since then, he struggled with injuries and never approached the form he displayed that season. Tatis last played regularly in the majors in 2003 with the Montreal Expos (now Washington Nationals), but saw time with the Baltimore Orioles in 2006.

He swings, and there it goes: Ken Griffey Jr. of the Seattle Mariners watches the ball rise over the right-field fence for a home run, in 1995. Griffey's career home run total reached 563 in 2006.

24 Up, 27 Down

Q: **Which pitcher holds the record for most consecutive victories?**

A: Carl Hubbell recorded 24 consecutive victories pitching for the New York Giants between 1936 and 1937.

His streak began in 1936, on the way to winning his second National League Most Valuable Player award. He went 26–6, including a streak of 16 straight wins to close the season. The streak continued in 1937, as Hubbell won his sixth successive decision and set the record with his 22nd-straight win, passing former Giants great Rube Marquard, who won 21 in a row in 1911–12. (Marquard had set the major league record for consecutive one-season victories with 19.) Hubbell made an unusual relief appearance and won his 24th in a row thanks to Mel Ott's ninth-inning home run against the Cincinnati Reds, on May 27, 1937.

Most pitchers make a baseball curve by rotating the throwing hand and wrist outward at the end of the delivery. But Hubbell, a left-hander, made a specialty

Carl Hubbell, the New York Giants' "meal ticket." His screwball and remarkable control earned him 253 regular-season wins, including 24 in a row in 1936–37.

of turning his pitching hand inward as he let go of the ball. This gave him a curving pitch called a "screwball." While the pitch was not entirely new, Hubbell put it to use as never before. His screwball and remarkable control earned him 253 regular-season victories. In fact, he was such a reliable winner that the Giants referred to him as their "meal ticket."

But finally, on May 31, 1937, before a Memorial Day crowd of 61,756 at the Polo Grounds, the Brooklyn Dodgers roughed up Hubbell for five runs over four innings in the first game of a doubleheader, handing him his first loss in 25 decisions. Hubbell's 24-game winning streak, the longest in major league history, was over. The pitcher who has come closest to Hubbell's record is the sinker baller Roy Face of the Pittsburgh Pirates, who won 22 consecutive games in 1958–59.

Q: **Which pitcher holds the record for most consecutive losses?**

A: Anthony Young of the New York Mets suffered through a major league-record 27-game losing streak over the 1992–93 seasons. He shattered the igno-minious record of 23 straight losses set by Cliff Curtis of the Boston Braves in 1910 and '11.

Young was a hard-throwing right-hander who ran into bad luck beginning on May 6, 1992. His losing streak did not end until the Mets defeated the Florida Marlins on July 28, 1993. He seemed headed for his 28th straight loss after surrendering a ninth-inning run, giving the Marlins a 4–3 lead. But then outfielder Ryan Thompson singled home the tying run and future Hall of Fame first baseman Eddie Murray doubled home the winning run, in the bottom of the ninth inning, bringing a long-awaited end to Young's losing streak with a 5–4 victory at Shea Stadium.

The victory was the first for Young since April 19, 1992—a span of 74 appearances. After the game he received a bottle of champagne from manager Dallas Green.

"When I finally won, the guys treated me like I had won a World Series!" said Young, who retired in 1996. He played six major league seasons and had a career earned run average of 3.89.

A bubbly New York Mets manager Dallas Green had something to smile about when pitcher Anthony Young finally won a ballgame during the 1993 season.

"Maybe now I'll start a winning streak."

—ANTHONY YOUNG, AFTER BREAKING HIS 27-GAME LOSING STREAK

Goose Eggs and High Cheese

Q: Who pitched the most consecutive shutout innings?

A: Orel Hershiser of the Los Angeles Dodgers pitched a record 59 consecutive shutout innings and led the Dodgers to a World Series championship, in 1988.

Hershiser's 1988 season was one of the best in recent history. On top of the scoreless-inning streak, he went 23–8, with eight shutouts and a 2.26 earned run average. He was the unanimous winner of the National League Cy Young Award, and was named the Most Valuable Player for both the league championship series and the World Series.

Hershiser was fantastic even before his streak began, throwing two consecutive complete games before the streak, which began on August 30, 1988, with four shutout innings to end a game against the Montreal Expos (now the Washington Nationals). Then he threw five successive shutouts, against the Atlanta Braves (twice), Cincinnati Reds, Houston Astros, and San Francisco Giants.

He was still nine innings short of the record of 58 straight scoreless innings, set in

Orel Hershiser was pumped as his scoreless streak reached a record 59 innings a row, in 1988. That year he won the Cy Young Award and led the Dodgers to a world championship.

1968 by Hall of Famer Don Drysdale, a former Dodger. On September 28, 1988, with Drysdale announcing the game as a Dodgers' radio broadcaster, Hershiser pitched 10 scoreless innings against the San Diego Padres in a game the Dodgers would eventually lose in 16 innings. Unofficially, he would extend the streak to 67 innings during the playoffs against the New York Mets.

While setting the major league record during the 59 regular-season innings, Hershiser allowed just 31 hits and 11 walks. He struck out 38. He had one stretch where he threw eight straight complete games and pitched two more complete-game victories over the Oakland Athletics in the World Series.

Hershiser retired after the 2000 season with a career record of 204 wins against 150 losses for a more than respectable .576 winning percentage.

Q: Who struck out the most consecutive batters?

A: Tom Seaver of the New York Mets pitched himself into the record books by striking out 19 San Diego Padres— including the last 10 batters in a row— in a two-hit 2–1 victory at Shea Stadium on April 22, 1970. The performance set a major league record for consecutive strikeouts, and the 19-strikeout game tied the major league mark for a nine-inning

game set by Steve Carlton of the St. Louis Cardinals in 1969. Roger Clemens of the Boston Red Sox broke the record when he struck out 20 Seattle Mariners in 1986 and duplicated it 10 years later against the Detroit Tigers.

Seaver, who was known as "Tom Terrific," was one of the most consistent winners in National League history. The right-hander was Rookie of the Year in 1967 for the Mets and won the Cy Young Award three times. In 1969 he won 25 games and helped the Mets win their first World Series. He won 311 games in his career and was inducted into the Hall of Fame in 1992 with 98.8 percent of the vote, the highest percentage of Hall of Fame votes ever received.

Known as "the Franchise" in New York, Tom Seaver and his powerful pitching turned the Mets from lovable losers into world champions.

" **Blind people come to the park just to listen to him pitch.** "

—*Reggie Jackson, on Tom Seaver*

From Worst to First

Q: Which team staged the greatest single-season comeback?

A: Miracle sports teams? The Boston Braves of 1914 were the first. On July 19, 1914, the Braves began the afternoon in Cincinnati and in the National League cellar. The last-place team had a grim 35–43 record and trailed the first-place New York Giants, who were seeking their fourth pennant in a row, by 11 games.

That afternoon Boston downed the Cincinnati Reds. Afterward, Braves manager George Stallings told his players, "Now we'll catch New York."

Between July 27 and August 6 the Braves reeled off a nine-game winning streak and climbed six spots, from last place to second. Led by pitchers Dick Rudolph (26 wins that season) and Bill James (26 wins), Boston found itself six and a half games behind the Giants.

Rudolph and James were not the only Braves performing miracles. Pitcher Lefty Tyler put together a 23-inning scoreless streak in August. Pitcher George "Iron" Davis, a Harvard law student, pitched a no-hitter. Zany

shortstop Walter "Rabbit" Maranville, who once jumped into a hotel lobby fish tank, leaned into a bases-loaded pitch—with his forehead—to force in the game-winning run in a 1–0 win at Pittsburgh.

By now the Braves had won over their hometown to the extent that Boston Red Sox owner Joe Lannin offered them the use of his newer and more spacious

Walter J. "Rabbit" Maranville of the Boston Braves picked up his nickname because he had large ears and a small body. And he might well have been called Rabbit for his speed on the base paths.

Fenway Park. The Braves moved out of their home field, the South End Grounds, for the remainder of the season.

On September 8 Boston beat the Giants, 8–3, at Fenway to take sole possession of first place. After that the Braves went 25–6, while manager John McGraw's Giants, the National League representative in the past three World Series, went 16–16. The Miracle Braves, 15 games out on July 4, won the pennant by an amazing 10½-game margin.

The Braves had four more miracles remaining. Facing the mighty Philadelphia Athletics, winners of three of the past four World Series, Boston was a big underdog that October. But the Braves had momentum on their side. Not only did Boston upset the A's, but they became the first team to sweep an opponent in four straight games. James and Rudolph were dominant. Each recorded two wins, and the pair combined to allow one earned run in 29 innings.

Q: Which team won the most games in a row?

A: The New York Giants won a record 26 consecutive games in September 1916. Despite that record streak and an earlier 17-game victory streak, John McGraw's squad finished a mediocre fourth place in the National League standings with an 86–66 record.

The Giants were in fourth place, 13½ games out of first, on September 7, when they began the longest winning streak in baseball history. During New York's 26-game run, Mother Nature helped them twice. They had won 12 consecutive home games at the Polo Grounds, but trailing the Cincinnati Reds, 2–0, in the fourth inning on September 15, the Giants were saved when the game was called on account of rain. Three days later the score was tied 1–1 in the eighth inning of the second game of a doubleheader with the Pittsburgh Pirates when the game was called due to darkness. The Giants then won their next 14 in a row, again all played at home, before finally losing, 8–3, to pitcher Lefty Tyler and the Boston Braves in the second game of a double-header, on September 30, 1916. Oddly enough, the 17 straight wins in May were all games played on the road.

Managers John McGraw (right) of the New York Giants and Bucky Harris of the Washington Senators shake hands before the start of the 1924 World Series. Eight years earlier McGraw's Giants won 26 games in a row.

Two-Sport Stars

Q: Who played in Major League Baseball's All-Star Game and the National Football League's Pro Bowl in successive seasons?

A: Bo Jackson of the Kansas City Royals received the Most Valuable Player trophy in the 1989 All-Star Game—the first played with the designated hitter—as he led the Americans to their first repeat victory in 31 years.

Left fielder Jackson, batting leadoff for the first time in his brief major league career, blasted an estimated 448-foot home run over the center field fence at Anaheim Stadium off starter Rick Reuschel. The next batter, Wade Boggs, also homered, the first time in All-Star history that the first two batters in a game had homered. Nolan Ryan, at 42, became the oldest All-Star winning pitcher.

The following year, Jackson, a two-sport star who also played running back for the Los Angeles Raiders, was named to the Pro Bowl, becoming the only athlete ever chosen to play in both the baseball All-Star Game and football's Pro Bowl.

By the time Jackson—the 1985 Heisman Trophy winner as college football's top player—signed his first pro football contract, he had already established himself as an amazingly talented baseball player. He hit massive home runs nearing 500 feet in distance, made impossible throws from the deepest parts of ballparks, and climbed outfield walls to haul in long fly balls and take back home runs.

In 1986 Jackson was the number-one

Bo Jackson pulled double duty by hitting home runs as an outfielder for the Kansas City Royals and scoring touchdowns as a running back for the Los Angeles Raiders from 1987 to 1990.

overall pick in the NFL draft but turned down a lucrative offer from the Tampa Bay Buccaneers. Instead Jackson signed a deal with baseball's Royals and played with one of their minor-league teams. His first full season in the majors was 1987. During that year's All-Star break, in July, Jackson signed a five-year contract to play pro football with the Raiders, calling it a "hobby" to get him through the winter. The agreement called for Jackson to join the Raiders at the end of the baseball season, which would allow him to play in about half the team's 16 NFL games.

During the years that he played both professional sports, from 1987 through 1990, Jackson emerged as one of the most feared hitters in baseball and one of the fastest and most unstoppable running backs in the NFL. A serious hip injury in 1991 ended his football career and cut short his baseball career. Others have played two sports, but no one has shown such ability in both.

Q: **Who hit a major league home run and scored an NFL touchdown in the same week?**

A: In perhaps his signature moment as a two-sport star, Deion Sanders returned a punt 68 yards for a touchdown in the first quarter of his first National Football League game with the Atlanta Falcons, on September 10, 1989. Five days earlier, while playing as a rookie outfielder for the New York Yankees, Sanders had hit a home run in a 12–2 win over the Seattle Mariners. Sanders made history as the first athlete to hit a home run in the major leagues and score a touchdown in the NFL in the same week.

He is also the only athlete to play in a World Series (Atlanta Braves, 1992) and a Super Bowl (San Francisco 49ers, 1995; Dallas Cowboys, '96). During the 1992 World Series, with the Braves, he stole four bases and batted .533, the highest average ever in a six-game series.

The Long and Short of It

Q: What was the fastest baseball game ever played?

A: A baseball game today normally clocks in at around three hours. But in the early days of baseball, games were played much more briskly. The fastest game, by time, in major league history lasted just 51 minutes, as the New York Giants defeated the Philadelphia Phillies, 6–1, at the Polo Grounds on September 28, 1919.

Perhaps the teams were eager to make a quick exit, seeing as the game was the first game of a doubleheader that was played on the last day of the 1919 season. Giants starter Jesse Barnes pitched a five-hitter to gain his 25th victory of the season; Lee Meadows of the Phillies was the losing pitcher.

Q: What was the longest baseball game ever played?

A: One of the great things about baseball is that there is no clock. But some games just do not want to end. The longest game ever, by time, was an extra-inning affair between the Chicago White Sox and the Milwaukee Brewers in 1984. The game lasted an unmanageable eight hours and six minutes before reaching its conclusion.

The game started on May 8 and was suspended in a 3–3 tie after 17 innings. On May 9 the game resumed, and it looked like Milwaukee would win when Ben Oglivie hit a three-run home run in the top of the 21st inning, only to see Chicago strike back with three runs of their own in the bottom of the frame to tie the score at 6–6. Finally, the White Sox won the game, 7–6, in 25 innings when Harold Baines hit a solo homer off losing pitcher Chuck Porter. Tom Seaver, the eighth Sox pitcher used, picked up the victory.

Q: What is the most innings ever played in a major league game?

A: The Brooklyn Dodgers and Boston Braves played a 1–1 tie at Braves Field, going 26 innings, on May 1, 1920. It is the most innings ever played in a major

Jesse Barnes of the New York Giants led all National League pitchers with 25 wins in 1919, including the fastest baseball game ever played.

league game. In the days before lighted stadiums, games could end in ties, such as when games were occasionally called on account of darkness. Such was the case in this contest.

Brooklyn's Leon Cadore and Boston's Joe Oeschger, both right-handers, matched pitches and remarkably went the distance for all 26 innings, though neither got a decision. Brooklyn scored its only run in the fourth inning, and Boston tied the game an inning later. The game remained scoreless for the next 21 innings until the marathon was halted after 3 hours and 50 minutes due to darkness. Cadore allowed 15 hits, five walks, and struck out seven, while Oeschger gave up nine hits and three walks. Although neither team changed pitchers in the game, both changed catchers.

The next season, Oeschger became one of the few pitchers in major league history to record three strikeouts in an inning on just nine pitches.

Harold Baines demonstrates the sweet swing that mercifully ended the longest game in major league history. The game was played over two days.

CHAPTER 6

LEGENDS, MYTHS, AND LORE

Old age, the enemy of every man, comes early in the life of a ballplayer—usually between 35 and 40 years old. New players arrive on the baseball scene every year. Some disappear quickly. Others remain and become a part of the great history of the game. Baseball academics such as those from the Society of American Baseball Research painstakingly mine baseball's folklore, separating fact from fiction, while attempting to set straight the historical canon. In many cases their findings result in a change to the record books. But every once in a while, their work unearths an inaccuracy that the lords of the game can acknowledge only with a simple tip of the cap, for the mark is set in stone and will stand forever—or at least until a player from the next generation goes out and breaks it.

In the meantime fans must be content to admire the exalted lucky men who play the game, and the record-setting performers who don't always receive the accolades due them. Rooting for the home team often involves praying, hope against hope, that a longstanding curse be reversed, or an improbable jinx broken. And when that day finally arrives, even after 86 years, dreams become reality.

Above: The thin air and dry climate at Denver's Coors Field is a welcome atmosphere for hitters, but pitchers there have trouble snapping off a good curveball.

Left: Boston Red Sox players celebrate after beating the St. Louis Cardinals in Game Four to sweep the 2004 World Series.

Rules and Tools

Q: What was "Merkle's Boner"?

A: The race for the National League pennant in 1908 was one of the most exciting pennant races in baseball history. But what is most remembered is not the first one-game playoff in baseball history, but a base-running blunder made by a player two weeks earlier.

The New York Giants and the Chicago Cubs were tied for first place in the NL standings when the two teams met on September 23, 1908, at the Polo Grounds in New York. The score was tied, 1–1, in the bottom of the ninth inning. There were two outs. Giants outfielder "Moose" McCormick was on third base, and 19-year-old rookie first baseman Fred Merkle was on first. A line single into center field by shortstop Al Bridwell scored McCormick with the apparent winning run.

Meanwhile, thousands of spectators had poured onto the field, thinking the Giants had won. In the confusion, Merkle turned around and headed for the dugout without touching second base, which was common practice at the time. Cubs second baseman Johnny Evers realized that he could still get Merkle out, and called for the ball. If he could touch second before Merkle, the Giants' runner would, by rule, be out, and the run would not count.

Evers retrieved a ball and touched second base. Umpire Hank O'Day ruled that Merkle was forced out, and that the run did not count.

With the field awash with people, O'Day suspended play and declared the game a 1–1 tie. The Giants fans swarming on the playing field who realized what had happened threatened the umpire. He had to have police protection to get to his dressing room.

The Giants' management recorded the game as a 2–1 victory and appealed the umpire's decision to the league's president, Harry C. Pulliam, who took several days before finally ruling the game a tie. All of this would not have mattered had the Giants

Fred Merkle's base-running gaffe cost the New York Giants the pennant in 1908. Instead of advancing from first to second on a ninth-inning hit to make sure that a game-winning run from third would count, he headed to the clubhouse.

and Cubs not finished the regular season deadlocked for first place with identical 98-55 records. That meant a one-game playoff was necessary to determine the league champion and the National League representative to the World Series. Unfortunately for Merkle, the Giants lost the game, 4–2, and finished in second place.

Merkle's earlier base-running gaffe was seen as the real cause of the Giants' loss (Giants fans changed Merkle's first name from Fred to "Bonehead"), and he was identified with the base-running blunder for the rest of his career.

Merkle compiled a respectable 16-year career with the Giants, Dodgers, Cubs, and Yankees. He batted .273 and stole 272 bases, including 11 thefts of home. All told, he played in the World Series five times, but never on the winning side.

Q: Why is catchers' gear called the "tools of ignorance"?

A: Catchers' equipment is sometimes called the "tools of ignorance" because catching is such a tough, physical job it would seem that no smart person would want to do it. That phrase has been credited to Bill Dickey, a Hall of Famer who played for the New York Yankees from 1928 to 1946—and was a catcher himself.

The phrase first appeared in print in the *Diamond Jargon* column in the August 1939 issue of *Baseball Magazine*. Dickey is said to have coined the phrase while strapping on the gear and wondering aloud why anyone in their right mind would want to be a catcher in July heat.

"Players call the catcher's armor the 'tools of ignorance,'" said the Hall of Fame catcher Rick Ferrell in the April 6, 1944, issue of *The Sporting News*. "Outfielders contend that no one in their senses would clutter themselves up with a mask, a heavy chest protector, and weigh down their legs with shin guards. All of this when the mercury is trying to climb out of the top of the tube, and those outfielders are off waiting for something to happen."

Bill Dickey, star catcher of the New York Yankees, going after a pop-up in spring training in 1937. Two years later Dickey wondered aloud why anyone would want to wear catching gear in the heat of the summer.

Cobb's Crown

Q: Who really won the 1910 American League batting race?

A: Napoleon "Nap" Lajoie of the Cleveland Indians had already won four (1901–4) American League batting titles when the 1910 baseball season began. Ty Cobb of the Detroit Tigers had also won three AL batting crowns and was aiming for his fourth straight. Cobb was a fiercely competitive and, among his baseball colleagues, a wildly unpopular player.

The Georgia Peach, as Cobb was known, was batting .383 as the season neared an end. On October 9, the last day of the regular season, Cobb decided to protect his narrow lead by sitting out the Tigers' game against the Chicago White Sox; he had sat out the previous day's game as well.

Lajoie, the Indians' second basemen, played both games of a doubleheader against the St. Louis Browns. Jack O'Connor, the manager of the Browns, ordered his rookie third baseman, John "Red" Corriden, to play almost on the edge of the outfield grass when Lajoie batted. Lajoie took advantage of the Browns' gift. In the first game he had four hits in four at-bats, with one triple and three bunt singles. In the second game he had four more bunt singles. At day's end Lajoie had gone eight hits in nine at-bats (he reached base a ninth time on an error), and it appeared he had bunted his way past Cobb with a .384 average. Eight of Cobb's own teammates allegedly sent Lajoie messages of congratulations.

American League president Ban Johnson was furious, suspecting the Browns had conspired to give Lajoie the batting title by ordering Corriden to play so deep in the field. Johnson recalculated the final averages and announced that Cobb's was .384944, while Lajoie's was .384084. Cobb won. The Chalmers Automobile Company, which had promised to award a car to the AL batting champion, gave cars to both players.

Cobb, despite the best efforts of Lajoie and the St. Louis Browns, won his fourth straight batting title. He eventually wound

The record book says Ty Cobb of the Detroit Tigers won his fourth batting title in a row in 1910, but Napoleon Lajoie had every right to cry "Foul" when Cobb was declared the official winner of the crown.

up leading the American League in hitting for nine consecutive years.

In 1981, 20 years after Cobb's death, *The Sporting News* revisited the 1910 AL batting race. The magazine found that in computing Cobb's average, the feisty center fielder was credited twice for one game in which he had two hits. By correcting that error, Cobb's average fell below Lajoie's. The commissioner's committee, however, voted unanimously to leave the record books alone. Cobb remains the officially recognized 1910 AL batting champ.

Ty Cobb, to the consternation of his opponents, and some of his own teammates, was awarded the 1910 batting crown by AL president Ban Johnson.

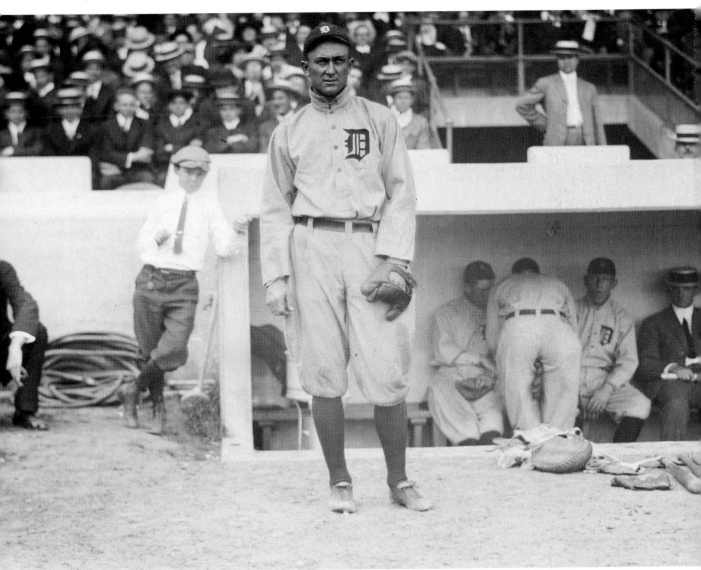

Lucky Man

Q: What did Lou Gehrig really say in his farewell speech?

A: The famous line in Lou Gehrig's "Luckiest Man" speech—"Today I consider myself the luckiest man on the face of this earth"—forever immortalized by screen actor Gary Cooper's stoic portrayal of Gehrig in the 1942 film *The Pride of the Yankees*, actually was spoken at the beginning of the speech, not at the end, as is commonly thought.

Gehrig, the New York Yankees captain, had set a record by playing in 2,130 consecutive games. (Cal Ripken Jr. broke the record in 1995.) On June 1, 1925, Gehrig began his famous streak as a pinch-hitter. It was his first game as a Yankee. The next day, regular first baseman Wally Pipp sat out a game with a headache and Gehrig started in his place. Gehrig's name was written into the Yankees starting lineup for the next 14 years. The streak ended on May 2, 1939, when Gehrig confessed to manager Joe McCarthy in Detroit that he was too tired to play. Gehrig would never play again.

Less than two months later, he was diagnosed with amyotrophic lateral sclerosis (ALS), an incurable neurological

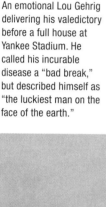

An emotional Lou Gehrig delivering his valedictory before a full house at Yankee Stadium. He called his incurable disease a "bad break," but described himself as "the luckiest man on the face of the earth."

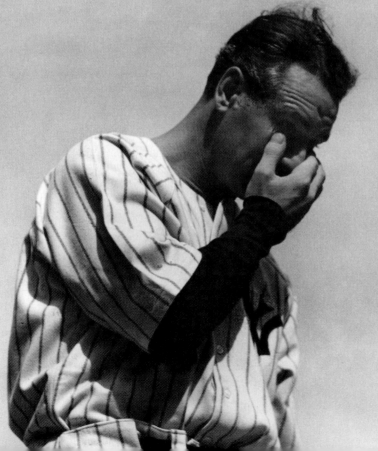

disease. It points up Gehrig's stature, not only in baseball but also in the national spotlight, that ALS would come to be known as "Lou Gehrig's disease."

To express their admiration, the Yankees designated the doubleheader against the Washington Senators as "Lou Gehrig Appreciation Day." On the Fourth July 1939, Gehrig's teammates, past and present, including Babe Ruth and all the members of the superb 1927 team, as well as 61,808 fans, came to honor the man they called "The Iron Horse."

The tribute between games of the doubleheader lasted for more than 40 minutes. It was as if Gehrig, in the words of sports columnist Paul Gallico, was "present at his own funeral." Each of the many dignitaries on the field spoke in glowing terms of their stricken former teammate. Gehrig, never one to seek the spotlight, stood with head bowed, hands placed deep into the rear pockets of his uniform pants, scratching at the turf with his spikes. When it was finally his turn to speak, the Yankee Stadium crowd, sitting in absolute silence, watched as he gingerly approached the microphone. He said simply:

"Fans, for the past two weeks you have been reading about the bad break I got. Yet today I consider myself the luckiest man on the face of this earth. I have been in ballparks for 17 years and have never received anything but kindness and encouragement from you fans.

"Look at these grand men. Which of you wouldn't consider it the highlight of his career just to associate with them for even one day? Sure, I'm lucky. Who wouldn't consider it an honor to have

known Jacob Ruppert? Also, the builder of baseball's greatest empire, Ed Barrow? To have spent six years with that wonderful little fellow, Miller Huggins? Then to have spent the next nine years with that outstanding leader, that smart student of psychology, the best manager in baseball today, Joe McCarthy? Sure, I'm lucky."

He went on to thank many others, including his wife, Eleanor, and his mother-in-law and concluded his stirring speech:

"So I close in saying that I may have had a tough break, but I have an awful lot to live for."

When Gehrig finished speaking, Ruth threw his arms around the big first baseman and hugged him. Gehrig's sincere, humbled words and Ruth's impulsive show of affection brought tears to many pairs of eyes.

At season's end the Yankees retired Gehrig's Number 4, making his the first retired number in major league baseball. (Since then, over one hundred numbers have been retired.) The Hall of Fame, whose building had opened earlier this same year, held a special election for Gehrig, and he was voted into Cooperstown immediately. He died two years later, in 1941.

Babe Ruth hugs former teammate Lou Gehrig at Yankee Stadium on July 4, 1939. Gehrig, the iron man of the Yankees, was almost too moved to speak at the ceremony in his honor.

The Boston Jinx

Q: **What is meant by the "Curse of the Bambino"?**

A: As decades go, the Roaring Twenties jumped out of the starting gate when on January 3, 1920, the Boston Red Sox sold perhaps the best baseball player of all time, Babe Ruth, to the New York Yankees.

In 1920 the Yankees were a 17-year-old team that had never won a pennant. The Red Sox had won four World Series in the past eight seasons. Ruth, only 24, had already led the American League in home runs. In a deal that has haunted Boston baseball fans ever since, Red Sox owner Harry Frazee sold Ruth to New York for a substantial cash payment and a large loan.

The sale of Ruth became the single most important—and infamous—deal in sports history. It dramatically reversed the fortunes of both franchises. The Yankees would win 26 World Series championships by the end of the century, becoming the most successful team in professional sports. The Red Sox did not even play in another World Series until 1946, and the team would not win a World Series for 86 years, often failing in heartbreaking fashion. Many Red Sox fans believed it was Ruth's curse upon them.

Babe Ruth follows through on another mighty hack. The sale of Ruth from Boston to New York changed the World Series fortunes of both cities.

Q: Who popularized the phrase?

A: The phrase became popular following a book by the same title by *Boston Globe* sports columnist Dan Shaughnessy. The book chronicles the classic Bosox debacles, from Johnny Pesky's holding the ball in the seventh game of the 1946 World Series, to Bucky Dent's deflating home run in the deciding game of the 1978 season, to the horrifying dribbler that slithered between Bill Buckner's legs in the 1986 World Series.

Mining such heartbreak led the author Stephen King to give one of publishing's all-time great book-jacket blurbs: "The quintessential New England horror story. Read it and weep."

Q: Did Johnny Pesky hold the ball too long?

A: In a moment's hesitation, Johnny Pesky became another in a long line of World Series goats. The Red Sox shortstop had a league-best 208 hits in 1946, and Boston won the pennant by 12 games. In the World Series against the St. Louis Cardinals, the teams traded wins and were tied after six games.

St. Louis took a 3–1 lead in Game Seven, but Red Sox center fielder Dom DiMaggio tied it up with a two-run double. In the top of the eighth inning, the Cardinals' Enos Slaughter singled. Then, with two outs, Harry (the Hat) Walker lined a clean hit to left center. Slaughter was running with the pitch, and when Leon Culbertson, playing center

field that inning in place of DiMaggio (who had pulled a muscle running out his game-tying double), fielded the ball, Slaughter never stopped running. Pesky caught Culbertson's weak throw with his back to the infield. When he turned to face home, he hesitated before throwing the ball to the plate. Pesky was caught napping by Slaughter's daring sprint, and when he finally made his throw, it was too late. Slaughter's run proved to be the one that won the Series.

"You could almost say it was a dumb play that worked," St. Louis catcher Joe Garagiola said about Slaughter's mad dash. "You know the difference between dumb and smart—the word 'safe.'"

Johnny Pesky, the Boston Red Sox shortstop, in 1952. His hesitation before throwing home in the 1946 World Series allowed the winning run to score.

All-Star Snubs and Flubs

Q: Why did the commissioner remove players who were voted to the 1957 All-Star Game?

A: From 1947 to 1957 fans selected the eight starting position players for both leagues in the All-Star Game. But partisan voting in 1957 brought about the demise of elected All-Star teams, at least for a time. Cincinnati fans stuffed the ballot boxes full of Reds and had apparently elected a starting squad of Johnny Temple at second base, Don Hoak at third, Roy McMillan at shortstop, Frank Robinson in left field, Gus Bell in center, Wally Post in right, and Ed Bailey as catcher. First baseman Stan Musial was the only non-Red elected to the starting lineup.

Before the results were announced, commissioner Ford Frick declared that Bell and Post were disqualified as starters, naming Willie Mays and Hank Aaron in their place. This ballot box stuffing by Cincinnati fans resulted in the major league players, coaches, and managers making the All-Star choices from 1958 to 1969.

In 1970 the new commissioner, Bowie Kuhn, ruled that the selection of starting lineups be returned to the fans. But the flawed balloting system, sponsored by the Gillette Company, named only six players at each position. Detroit's perennial All-Star Al Kaline was not listed on the ballot, nor was Atlanta's Rico Carty, who sported a gaudy .365 batting average at the break, and California's Alex Johnson, the eventual AL batting champion.

The game, played at Cincinnati's Riverfront Stadium, which had opened only two weeks earlier, was the site for a stunning end. The NL scored three runs in the ninth inning to tie the score. In the 12th, Pete Rose thundered head-on into Ray Fosse and sent the Cleveland catcher crashing backward as Rose crossed the plate with the winning run. In the years following, fans would vote Rose as the starter at five different positions, an All-Star Game record.

Q: Was a pitcher really blown off the mound during an All-Star Game?

A: According to legend, Stu Miller was blown off the mound by the wind during the 1961 game (the first of two played that year) at blustery Candlestick Park, in San Francisco. The National League was leading, 3–2, with one out in the ninth inning and Miller pitching to Rocky Colavito with two men on base. When the right-hander took his set position, a fierce gust of wind blasted the 165-pound Miller, causing a slight wobble. The umpire, Stan Landes, called a balk to advance the runners, and the American League tied the score on Ken Boyer's error later in the inning. When the NL won in the 10th inning on Roberto Clemente's game-winning single, Miller was the winning pitcher, but that was not the big news in the nation's sports pages the next day. MILLER BLOWN OFF MOUND was the headline. "I wasn't blown off that mound," said Miller. "I just waved a little."

"I know I balked," Miller explained. "All of a sudden the wind pushed my shoulder forward. My feet didn't move, so I didn't get blown off the mound as the story goes. Each time it gets told, I get blown farther off the mound. [The umpire] was sympathetic. But he told me, 'What can I do? It's the rule.'" After the game umpire Landes was asked if Miller should have been pardoned because the gust was "an act of God." The umpire replied, "If it was an act of God, I blessed him. I gave him the final sacraments. But he still balked."

Pete Rose (14) is hugged by National League teammate Dick Dietz after Rose crashed into AL catcher Ray Fosse to score the winning run in the 1970 All-Star Game. This game returned the All-Star vote to the fans.

The Asterisk

Q: **Did an asterisk really accompany Roger Maris's home run mark in the record book?**

A: No asterisk ever existed in the baseball record book noting that Roger Maris set his single-season home run record in 162 games while Babe Ruth reached his in 154—the records were simply listed separately. But the twin listing itself was controversial, implying to some that Maris's record was somehow inferior to Ruth's.

In 1961 Maris, a 27-year-old outfielder for the New York Yankees, made a run for Ruth's single-season home run record of 60, established in 1927. On July 17, 1961, as it became apparent that Maris would challenge Ruth's record, baseball

Roger Maris watches the flight of his 61st home run off Tracy Stallard of the Red Sox at Yankee Stadium. The shot broke Babe Ruth's record and ignited a controversy, since Maris had 162 games for his mark while Ruth had 154.

commissioner Ford C. Frick announced that Maris would not be recognized as the all-time single-season home run champion unless he broke Ruth's record in 154 games (the number of games on the schedule in Ruth's record-setting year). A home-run record accomplished after the team's 155th game, according to Frick's infamous ruling, would receive second billing to Ruth.

In 1961 Major League Baseball added two new teams to the American League: the Los Angeles Angels (who eventually moved to Anaheim), and the new Washington Senators (who moved to Arlington, Texas, in 1972 and became the Texas Rangers). This marked the first time new teams had joined the big leagues since the AL came into being in 1901. To accommodate the two new teams, the schedule was extended from 154 games to 162 games.

On October 1, the final day of the season, the Yankees were playing the Boston Red Sox in Yankee Stadium. In the fourth inning, the left-handed-hitting Maris connected with a Tracey Stallard fastball and sent it flying over the right-field wall. It was Maris's 61st home run in '61—one more than Ruth hit in 1927—though the milestone homer did not erase Ruth's record. Frick, true to his word, had Maris's accomplishment listed after Ruth's feat in the record books, in effect telling Maris that he was second fiddle to Ruth.

No matter how it was cataloged in the record book, most fans recognized Maris as the true record-holder. In 1991 baseball commissioner Fay Vincent made it official, announcing that a major-league baseball committee on statistical accuracy had voted to remove the distinction, giving the record fully to Maris. He did not live to see the change, having died of cancer at age 51 in 1985.

Maris held the single-season home run record for 37 years—longer than Ruth had held it—until Mark McGwire of the St. Louis Cardinals surpassed the mark with 70 homers in 1998. His record was subsequently broken when the San Francisco Giants' Barry Bonds hit 73 home runs in the 2001 season.

Barry Bonds of the Giants hitting his 73rd home run of the season off Dennis Springer of the Dodgers at Pacific Bell Park in San Francisco on October 7, 2001. Two nights earlier he clouted his 71st and 72nd homers to break Mark McGwire's single-season record.

> As a ballplayer, I would be delighted to do it again. As an individual, I doubt if I could possibly go through it again.
>
> —ROGER MARIS, ON BREAKING BABE RUTH'S RECORD

Sticky Situations

Q: What was the "Pine Tar Game"?

A: It was surely one of baseball's most bizarre and controversial endings. On July 24, 1983, the Kansas City Royals were at Yankee Stadium to play the New York Yankees in just another regular-season game. The Yankees were leading 4–3 with two outs and one man on base in the top of the ninth inning when Royals third baseman George Brett smashed a two-run homer off Yankees relief pitcher Rich "Goose" Gossage, giving the Royals a 5–4 lead. Or so everyone in the stadium thought.

Yankees manager Billy Martin protested to the umpires that Brett had used an illegal bat because it had too much pine tar. (Pine tar is a sticky brown residue batters put on their bats for a better grip.) Baseball rule 1.10 (b) allows a player's bat to have 18 inches of tar from the end of the bat handle.

Without a ruler to measure the pine tar on Brett's bat, the umpires, knowing that home plate measures 17 inches across, placed the bat across home plate. When they saw that the pine tar exceeded 18 inches, home plate umpire Tim McClelland signaled that Brett was out, negating his potential game-winning homer. An enraged Brett sprang from the dugout, his eyes bulging like a madman's, and raced toward McClelland. Umpiring crew chief Joe Brinkman intercepted Brett before he reached McClelland, grabbing him around the neck and restraining him. Royals manager Dick Howser joined the skirmish and was ejected from the game along with Brett.

Said Gossage after the game: "I can sympathize with George, but not that much."

Q: Which team won the "Pine Tar Game"?

A: The home run hit by George Brett was nullified, and the Yankees had won the game 4–3—or so everyone who left the stadium thought. But the Royals protested the umpire's decision, arguing that Brett had no intentional plan to cheat

Nobody complained about the amount of pine tar on George Brett's bat when he singled off California Angels pitcher Tim Fortugno to collect his 3,000th career hit, on September 30, 1992, in Anaheim.

and that he therefore did not violate the spirit of the rules.

After several days consideration, American League president Lee MacPhail upheld the Royals' protest and ruled that the Royals be given back their 5–4 lead. Twenty-five days after it began, on August 18 (an open date for both teams), the "Pine Tar Game" resumed at Yankee Stadium in front of only 1,245 fans, and the Royals won by the same 5–4 score.

Following this incident baseball's rulebook was amended to prevent a similar situation from occurring again. The rule now states that the protest must occur before the bat is used in play.

The late Darryl Kile struggled during his two seasons pitching in the thin air at Denver's Coors Field. He posted a career-best 2.57 earned run average with the Houston Astros in 1997, but his ERA ballooned to 5.20 and 6.61 with Colorado.

Q: Does the thin air at Denver's Coors Field make pitches hang?

A: Any pitcher will tell you that the break on his curveball depends on the speed of the pitch and the amount of spin he puts on it. For pitchers at Coors Field, thin air is only part of the problem. Denver's dry climate also plays a role in making pitches hang.

A ball will tend to curve less at higher altitudes where the air is thinner. At Coors Field in Denver, which is located nearly one mile (5,280 feet) above sea level, balls travel a little faster because there is less resistance in the thinner air. The ball breaks less because it crosses the plate faster and thus has less time to break.

The mile-high altitude of Denver also creates a dry climate, which makes the baseball's outer covering hard and slick. This makes it more difficult for a pitcher to grip the ball, and therefore the ball will not break with the same snap that occurs in more humid conditions closer to sea level.

In 2002 the Rockies began storing their game balls in a humidor to prevent them from drying out in Denver's mile-high, humidity-low climate. Several Rockies' pitchers, who said that the baseballs of prior years were slippery and hard to grip, said that the treated balls felt more like normal ones.

Baseball Milestones

1846 The New York Base Ball Club defeated Alexander Cartwright's Knickerbockers team, 23–1, at the Elysian Fields, in Hoboken, New Jersey, in what most historians believe was the first baseball game ever played. Cartwright, who umpired, had earlier laid out the game's first diamond and established the basic rules of the sport.

1858 All-Star baseball teams from Brooklyn and New York played the first in a series of three games at the Fashion Race Course on Long Island. According to the encyclopedia *Total Baseball*, it was the first time admission (50 cents) was ever charged at a game.

1869 The Cincinnati Red Stockings, the first professional baseball team, played their first game, beating Antioch College, 41–7. The first team to pay all their players, the Red Stockings finished the year undefeated.

1876 In the first major league game played between two National League teams, the Boston Red Stockings beat the Philadelphia Athletics, 6–5. Jim O'Rourke of Boston got the first major league hit and Joe Borden became the league's first winning pitcher.

1878 Frederick Thayer of Massachusetts, captain of the Harvard Baseball Club, received United States Patent No. 200,358 for an invention to reduce cuts and bruises: A wire catcher's mask to be worn during baseball games, strapped over the head and cushioned against the chin.

1886 The first spring training camp is held by the Chicago White Stockings, at Hot Springs, Arkansas. By 1870, the White Stockings and Cincinnati Red Stockings were holding preseason training camp in New Orleans, Louisiana. Soon other teams were taking advantage of the South's warm weather by setting up spring training camps of their own.

1893 Right hander Amos Rusie, considered the hardest-throwing pitcher of the 1800s, won 30 games or more for the New York Giants for a third season in a row. In fact, because of Rusie's overwhelming velocity, the pitcher's mound, which had been 50 feet from home plate, was moved farther away to its current distance of 60 feet 6 inches. Rusie's 50 complete games for the Giants in 1893 are the most by any pitcher since the mound was moved.

1901 In the first official game played between two American League teams, the Chicago White Stockings beat the Cleveland Blues, 8-2, in Chicago. A crowd of over 10,000 people came out to watch the game, which lasted just 1 hour 20 minutes.

1903 Cy Young and Bill Dinneen each pitched two shutouts against the Pittsburgh Pirates to lead the Boston Pilgrims (now the Red Sox) to victory in the first World Series held between the National League and the two-year-old American League. The best-of-nine-game postseason series was the brainchild of Pittsburgh owner Barney Dreyfuss and Boston owner Henry Killilea.

1904 Pitching for the Boston Pilgrims against the Philadelphia Athletics, Cy Young completed the first perfect game in the modern era, with the pitcher's rubber at the current 60 feet 6 inches from home plate.

1910 At age 43, Cy Young of the Cleveland Naps (later renamed the Indians), won his 500th game, defeating the Washington Senators, 5–2, at League Park in the District of Columbia. Young retired in 1911 with 511 victories. Only Walter Johnson of the Senators, with 417, has also won 400 or more games.

1919 Joe Oeschger of the Philadelphia Phillies and Burleigh Grimes of the Brooklyn Dodgers competed in a baseball pitcher's duel for the ages. Each pitcher went 20 innings in a game that ended in a 9–9 tie.

1932 Babe Ruth hit his "called shot" home run into the Wrigley Field bleachers in the fifth inning of Game Three of the World Series. Some historians say Ruth was not pointing to the center-field stands before Charlie Root's two-strike pitch but rather was notifying the Chicago Cubs' bench jockeys that he still had one more pitch to hit. The point is, he hit it, breaking a 4–4 tie and helping the Yankees to a four-game sweep.

1934 Joe Medwick's spikes-up slide into Detroit Tigers third baseman Marv Owen, with the Cardinals leading 11-0 in Game Seven of the World Series, precipitated a riot by fans at Detroit's Navin Field. Medwick was showered with debris when he retook his position, and Commissioner Kenesaw Mountain Landis removed him to quell the disturbance.

1936 Five baseball immortals—Ty Cobb, Babe Ruth, Christy Mathewson, Honus Wagner, and Walter Johnson—were voted charter members of baseball's new Hall of Fame, which opened in 1939 in Cooperstown, New York, where legend has it that the first baseball game was played 100 years before in 1836.

1941 Mickey Owen's passed ball on a third strike to Tommy Henrich in Game Four at Ebbets Field became one of the classic muffs in World Series history. The Brooklyn Dodgers held the lead, 4–3, with two outs in the top of the ninth inning and thought they had evened the Series when the ball got by Owen. The Yankees then rallied with four runs for a 3–1 Series lead and won the title the following day.

1953 The Yankees won their fifth consecutive World Series—no other team besides the 1936–39 and 1998–2001 Yankees has won more than four straight—by defeating the Brooklyn Dodgers, 4–3, in Game Six in the Bronx. Billy Martin singled in the wining run against Clem Labine in the bottom of the ninth inning with his 12th hit of the Series.

Brooklyn's Mickey Owen chases down a foul pop.

1953 The Boston Braves moved to Milwaukee, Wisconsin, changing the major league map for the first time since 1903, when the Baltimore Orioles became the New York Highlanders (now the Yankees). The Braves would move to Atlanta, Georgia, in 1966, and in 1995 the Braves would become the first team to win a World Series in three cities (Boston, 1914; Milwaukee, 1957; Atlanta, 1995).

1954 Willie Mays caught Vic Wertz's 450-foot drive to center field in Game One of the 1954 World Series. The most famous catch in baseball history, it helped the New York Giants sweep the Cleveland Indians.

1956 Don Larsen of the New York Yankees hurled the only perfect game in World Series history, a 2–0 victory over the Brooklyn Dodgers in Game Five at Yankee Stadium. Larsen struck out Dodgers pinch-hitter Dale Mitchell for the 27th and final out.

1958 Major League Baseball reached the West Coast when the Brooklyn Dodgers moved to Los Angeles and the New York Giants transferred to San Francisco.

1960 In the bottom of the ninth inning in the seventh game of the World Series between the Pittsburgh Pirates and the New York Yankees, with the score tied 9–9, the Pirates' light-hitting second baseman Bill Mazeroski hit a walk-off home run against Ralph Terry to give Pittsburgh its first World Series championship since 1925.

1962 The New York Mets are losers for a major league-record 120th time, dropping the season's final game, 5-1, to the Chicago Cubs at Wrigley Field. In an ironic conclusion to a frustrating season, the Mets' Joe Pignatano lined into a triple play in his last major league at-bat.

1965 Rick Monday, an outfielder at Arizona State University, was selected by the Kansas City Athletics as the overall No. 1 pick in baseball's first amateur draft. Monday debuted for the A's in 1966 but played most of his 19-year career with the Chicago Cubs and the Los Angeles Dodgers.

1966 Tony Cloninger of the Atlanta Braves had the best day at the plate of any pitcher in history in the Braves' 17–3 win over the San Francisco Giants at Candlestick Park. Cloninger hit two grand slam home runs and drove in nine runs.

1966 Frank Robinson compiled a triple-crown season and led the Baltimore Orioles to the World Series championship. He batted .316 with 49 home runs and 122 runs batted in, on his way to the American League's Most Valuable Player award, making him the first player to win the award in both leagues. He had won the NL award with the Cincinnati Reds in 1961.

1967 Carl Yastrzemski of the Boston Red Sox won the American League Most Valuable Player award as well as the Triple Crown, leading the league with a .326 average, 44 home runs, and 121 runs batted in. "Yaz" is the last player to win the Triple Crown.

1968 Denny McLain of the Detroit Tigers became the first major leaguer to win 30 games in a season since Dizzy Dean of the St. Louis Cardinals in 1934 when he defeated the Oakland Athletics, 5–4, at Tiger Stadium. He finished the season 31–6 with 280 strikeouts and a 1.96 earned run average.

1968 The National League voted to expand to 12 teams in 1969, adding the Montreal Expos and San Diego Padres. Because the American League had already created two new teams for '69, each league formed two divisions that led to a post season tier of playoff games, eventually called the League Championship Series.

1969 Willie Mays of the San Francisco Giants hit his 600th home run off Mike Corkins of the Padres in a game at Jack Murphy Stadium in San Diego. He became the second to reach that level, after Babe Ruth. Mays finished with 660 home runs, fourth on the all-time list.

1974 Henry Aaron of the Atlanta Braves broke Babe Ruth's record of 714 career home runs with a shot into the left-field bullpen off Dodgers left-hander Al Downing in Atlanta. Aaron finished his career in 1976 with 755 home runs.

A statue of Giants great Willie Mays outside San Francisco's AT&T Park.

1977 Ted Turner, owner of the Atlanta Braves, took over as manager with his team in the midst of a 16-game losing streak, but lost to the Pittsburgh Pirates, 2–1. The next day National League president Chub Feeney ruled that Turner, forever 0–1, had violated a rule against managers having a financial stake in their team, and reinstated Dave Bristol as the skipper.

1982 Rollie Fingers of the Milwaukee Brewers became the first reliever in history to record 300 saves when he pitched the final two innings of a 3–2 victory over the Seattle Mariners at the Kingdome. The premier closer for the Oakland Athletics team that won five division titles and three World Series, he retired in 1985 with 341 saves.

1982 Rickey Henderson of the Oakland Athletics stole his 119th base of the season in the third inning of a 5–4 loss to the host Milwaukee Brewers, breaking Lou Brock's major-league record set with the St. Louis Cardinals in 1974. Henderson finished the year with 130 stolen bases, still the single-season record, and in 1991 broke Brock's career record of 938 steals.

1985 With his hometown crowd cheering, Pete Rose of the Cincinnati Reds lined a single that broke Ty Cobb's record for career hits. Rose's hit was the 4,192nd of his career. He finished his career with 4,256 hits and is still first on the all-time hit list.

1985 Baseball owners and players agreed to expand the postseason championship series in each league from a best-of-five-games format to a best-of-seven.

1986 Roger Clemens of the Boston Red Sox set a major league record by striking out 20 batters in a 3–1 victory over the Seattle Mariners. Clemens struck out 20 for a second time in 1996 against the Detroit Tigers. In 1998 the Chicago Cubs right-hander Kerry Wood, making his fifth major league start at age 20, set a National League record and tied Clemens's major league record for most strikeouts in a game, 20, in a 2–0 one-hitter over the Houston Astros at Wrigley Field.

1988 Jose Canseco of the Oakland Athletics finished the season with 42 home runs and 40 stolen bases, becoming the first player to accomplish this distinctive 40-40 feat. San Francisco's Barry Bonds (1996), Seattle's Alex Rodriguez (1998) and Washington's Alfonso Soriano (2006) are the only other members of this exclusive "40-40" club.

1988 The Columbia Broadcasting System (CBS) won the rights to televise major league baseball games by agreeing to pay the 26 teams $1.1 billion through 1993. The contract leads to an increase in player salaries which contributes to the labor dispute that resulted in the cancellation of the 1994 World Series. The deal was exceeded in 1995 by the $2.5 billion the Fox Network paid for MLB rights from 2001 to 2006.

1989 Saying he believed that Pete Rose had bet on baseball games, including those of the Cincinnati Reds, the team he managed, Commissioner A. Bartlett Giamatti announced an agreement that banned Rose permanently from baseball.

1991 The Minnesota Twins and the Atlanta Braves became the first modern teams to go from last place to first place and meet in the World Series. Minnesota's Jack Morris defeated the Braves, 1–0, in a 10-inning Game Seven.

1992 A Canadian team won a World Series for the first time when 41-year-old Dave Winfield's two-run double off the Atlanta Braves' Charlie Leibrandt with two out in the top of the 11th inning of Game Six at Fulton County Stadium gave the Toronto Blue Jays a 4–3 victory.

1993 Mark Whiten of the St. Louis Cardinals had the best one-game offensive performance in major league baseball history, hitting four home runs and driving in 12 runs in a September 7 game at Riverfront Stadium against the Cincinnati Reds. Whiten's 12 RBIs matched the record set by the Cardinals' Sunny Jim Bottomley in 1924.

1994 Team owners agree to realign the National and American Leagues from two divisions into three divisions each and add a new best-of-five-games playoff series featuring a wild-card team from each league. The expanded playoff system began in 1995 after the 1994 postseason was canceled.

1995 Cal Ripken Jr. played in his 2,131st consecutive game, breaking Lou Gehrig's 56-year-old record.

1998 Locked in a record-setting derby with Sammy Sosa of the Chicago Cubs, Mark McGwire of the St. Louis Cardinals became the first player to hit 70 home runs in a season. Sosa finished with 66. The next year, the pair became the first players ever to hit 60 or more home runs in a season twice.

2001 Barry Bonds of the San Francisco Giants surpassed Mark McGwire's single-season record by hitting his 73rd and final home run of the season off Dennis Springer of the Los Angeles Dodgers at Pacific Bell Park. The next year, Bonds won an unprecedented fifth Most Valuable Player award.

2002 Two wild-card teams met in the World Series for the first time as the Anaheim Angels defeated the San Francisco Giants in seven games.

2004 The Boston Red Sox won the World Series, sweeping St. Louis four games to none, snapping an 86-year title drought.

After 86 years of waiting, another championship banner finally hangs outside Boston's Fenway Park.

Most Valuable Player Winners

American League

Year	Player	Team	Pos.		Year	Player	Team	Pos.
2006	Justin Morneau	Minnesota	1B		1968	Denny McLain	Detroit	P
2005	Alex Rodriguez	New York	3B		1967	Carl Yastrzemski	Boston	OF
2004	Vladimir Guerrero	Anaheim	RF		1966	Frank Robinson	Baltimore	OF
2003	Alex Rodriguez	Texas	SS		1965	Zoilo Versalles	Minnesota	SS
2002	Miguel Tejada	Oakland	SS		1964	Brooks Robinson	Baltimore	3B
2001	Ichiro Suzuki	Seattle	RF		1963	Elston Howard	New York	C
2000	Jason Giambi	Oakland	1B		1962	Mickey Mantle	New York	OF
1999	Ivan Rodriguez	Texas	C		1961	Roger Maris	New York	OF
1998	Juan Gonzalez	Texas	OF		1960	Roger Maris	New York	OF
1997	Ken Griffey Jr.	Seattle	OF		1959	Nellie Fox	Chicago	2B
1996	Juan Gonzalez	Texas	OF		1958	Jackie Jensen	Boston	OF
1995	Mo Vaughn	Boston	1B		1957	Mickey Mantle	New York	OF
1994	Frank Thomas	Chicago	1B		1956	Mickey Mantle	New York	OF
1993	Frank Thomas	Chicago	1B		1955	Yogi Berra	New York	C
1992	Dennis Eckersley	Oakland	P		1954	Yogi Berra	New York	C
1991	Cal Ripken Jr.	Baltimore	SS		1953	Al Rosen	Cleveland	3B
1990	Rickey Henderson	Oakland	OF		1952	Bobby Shantz	Philadelphia	P
1989	Robin Yount	Milwaukee	OF		1951	Yogi Berra	New York	C
1988	Jose Canseco	Oakland	OF		1950	Phil Rizzuto	New York	SS
1987	George Bell	Toronto	OF		1949	Ted Williams	Boston	OF
1986	Roger Clemens	Boston	P		1948	Lou Boudreau	Cleveland	SS
1985	Don Mattingly	New York	1B		1947	Joe DiMaggio	New York	OF
1984	Willie Hernandez	Detroit	P		1946	Ted Williams	Boston	OF
1983	Cal Ripken Jr.	Baltimore	SS		1945	Hal Newhouser	Detroit	P
1982	Robin Yount	Milwaukee	SS		1944	Hal Newhouser	Detroit	P
1981	Rollie Fingers	Milwaukee	P		1943	Spud Chandler	New York	P
1980	George Brett	Kansas City	3B		1942	Joe Gordon	New York	2B
1979	Don Baylor	California	OF		1941	Joe DiMaggio	New York	OF
1978	Jim Rice	Boston	OF		1940	Hank Greenberg	Detoit	OF
1977	Rod Carew	Minnesota	1B		1939	Joe DiMaggio	New York	OF
1976	Thurman Munson	New York	C		1938	Jimmie Foxx	Boston	1B
1975	Fred Lynn	Boston	OF		1937	Charlie Gehringer	Detroit	2B
1974	Jeff Burroughs	Texas	OF		1936	Lou Gehrig	New York	1B
1973	Reggie Jackson	Oakland	OF		1935	Hank Greenberg	Detroit	1B
1972	Richie Allen	Chicago	1B		1934	Mickey Cochrane	Detroit	C
1971	Vida Blue	Oakland	P		1933	Jimmie Foxx	Philadelphia	1B
1970	Boog Powell	Baltimore	1B		1932	Jimmie Foxx	Philadelphia	1B
1969	Harmon Killebrew	Minnesota	1B/3B		1931	Lefty Grove	Philadelphia	P

National League

Year	Player	Team	Pos.
2006	Ryan Howard	Philadelphia	1B
2005	Albert Pujols	St. Louis	1B
2004	Barry Bonds	San Francisco	LF
2003	Barry Bonds	San Francisco	LF
2002	Barry Bonds	San Francisco	LF
2001	Barry Bonds	San Francisco	LF
2000	Jeff Kent	San Francisco	2B
1999	Chipper Jones	Atlanta	3B
1998	Sammy Sosa	Chicago	OF
1997	Larry Walker	Colorado	OF
1996	Ken Caminiti	San Diego	3B
1995	Barry Larkin	Cincinnati	SS
1994	Jeff Bagwell	Houston	1B
1993	Barry Bonds	San Francisco	OF
1992	Barry Bonds	Pittsburgh	OF
1991	Terry Pendleton	Atlanta	3B
1990	Barry Bonds	Pittsburgh	OF
1989	Kevin Mitchell	San Francisco	OF
1988	Kirk Gibson	Los Angeles	OF
1987	Andre Dawson	Chicago	OF
1986	Mike Schmidt	Philadelphia	3B
1985	Willie McGee	St. Louis	OF
1984	Ryne Sandberg	Chicago	2B
1983	Dale Murphy	Atlanta	OF
1982	Dale Murphy	Atlanta	OF
1981	Mike Schmidt	Philadelphia	3B
1980	Mike Schmidt	Philadelphia	OF
1979	Keith Hernandez	St. Louis	1B
	Willie Stargell	Pittsburgh	1B
1978	Dave Parker	Pittsburgh	OF
1977	George Foster	Cincinnati	OF
1976	Joe Morgan	Cincinnati	2B
1975	Joe Morgan	Cincinnati	2B
1974	Steve Garvey	Los Angeles	1B
1973	Pete Rose	Cincinnati	OF
1972	Johnny Bench	Cincinnati	C
1971	Joe Torre	St. Louis	3B
1970	Johnny Bench	Cincinnati	C
1969	Willie McCovey	San Francisco	1B
1968	Bob Gibson	St. Louis	P
1967	Orlando Cepeda	St. Louis	1B
1966	Roberto Clemente	Pittsburgh	OF
1965	Willie Mays	San Francisco	OF
1964	Ken Boyer	St. Louis	3B
1963	Sandy Koufax	Los Angeles	P
1962	Maury Wills	Los Angeles	SS
1961	Frank Robinson	Cincinnati	OF
1960	Dick Groat	Pittsburgh	SS
1959	Ernie Banks	Chicago	SS
1958	Ernie Banks	Chicago	SS
1957	Hank Aaron	Milwaukee	OF
1956	Don Newcombe	Brooklyn	P
1955	Roy Campanella	Brooklyn	C
1954	Willie Mays	New York	OF
1953	Roy Campanella	Brooklyn	C
1952	Hank Sauer	Chicago	OF
1951	Roy Campanella	Brooklyn	C
1950	Jim Konstanty	Philadelphia	P
1949	Jackie Robinson	Brooklyn	2B
1948	Stan Musial	St. Louis	OF
1947	Bob Elliott	Boston	3B
1946	Stan Musial	St. Louis	1B
1945	Phil Cavarretta	Chicago	1B
1944	Marty Marion	St. Louis	SS
1943	Stan Musial	St. Louis	OF
1942	Mort Cooper	St. Louis	P
1941	Dolph Camilli	Brooklyn	1B
1940	Frank McCormick	Cincinnati	1B
1939	Bucky Walters	Cincinnati	P
1938	Ernie Lombardi	Cincinnati	C
1937	Joe Medwick	St. Louis	OF
1936	Carl Hubbell	New York	P
1935	Gabby Hartnett	Chicago	C
1934	Dizzy Dean	St. Louis	P
1933	Carl Hubbell	New York	P
1932	Chuck Klein	Philadelphia	OF
1931	Frankie Frisch	St. Louis	2B

Hall of Famers

The National Baseball Hall of Fame has enshrined 278 members, through 2006. Membership is comprised of 196 retired major league players, 16 managers, 23 executives, 35 former Negro league players, and eight umpires. There are 61 living members.

The Baseball Writers' Association of America has elected 104 retired players. The Hall of Fame Committee on Baseball Veterans has elected 148 members: 92 players, 16 managers, 23 executives, and eight umpires. The defunct Committee on the Negro Leagues elected nine candidates between 1971 and 1977, and a special election held in 2006 elected 17 men and women for their contribution in the Negro leagues or pre-Negro leagues era of black baseball.

Pitchers

Alexander, Grover Cleveland	1938	Grove, Lefty	1947	Plank, Eddie	1946
Bender, Al "Chief"	1953	Haines, Jesse	1970	Radbourn, Charles	1939
Brown, Mordecai	1949	Hoyt, Waite	1969	Rixey, Eppa	1963
Brown, Ray*	2006	Hubbell, Carl	1947	Roberts, Robin	1976
Bunning, Jim	1996	Hunter, Catfish	1987	Rogan, Joe*	1998
Carlton, Steve	1994	Jenkins, Ferguson	1991	Ruffing, Red	1967
Chesbro, Jack	1946	Johnson, Walter	1936	Rusie, Amos	1977
Clarkson, John	1963	Joss, Addie	1978	Ryan, Nolan	1999
Cooper, Andy*	2006	Keefe, Tim	1964	Seaver, Tom	1992
Coveleski, Stan	1969	Koufax, Sandy	1972	Smith, Hilton*	2001
Day, Leon*	1995	Lemon, Bob	1976	Spahn, Warren	1973
Dean, Dizzy	1953	Lyons, Ted	1955	Sutter, Bruce	2006
Dihigo, Martin*	1977	Marichal, Juan	1983	Sutton, Don	1998
Drysdale, Don	984	Marquard, Rube	1971	Vance, Dazzy	1955
Eckersley, Dennis	2004	Mathewson, Christy	1936	Waddell, Rube	1946
Faber, Red	1964	McGinnity, Joe	1946	Walsh, Ed	1946
Feller, Bob	1962	Mendez, Jose*	2006	Welch, Mickey	1973
Fingers, Rollie	1992	Newhouser, Hal	1992	Wilhelm, Hoyt	1985
Ford, Whitey	1974	Nichols, Kid	1949	Williams, Joe*	1999
Foster, Bill*	1996	Niekro, Phil	1997	Willis, Vic	1995
Galvin, Pud	1965	Paige, Satchel*	1971	Wynn, Early	1972
Gibson, Bob	1981	Palmer, Jim	1990	Young, Cy	1937
Gomez, Lefty	1972	Pennock, Herb	1948		
Grimes, Burleigh	1964	Perry, Gaylord	1991		

*Elected on the basis of Negro leagues career.

The inaugural class of the Baseball Hall of Fame at Cooperstown, New York consisted of five baseball immortals: Babe Ruth, Ty Cobb, Christy Mathewson, Honus Wagner, and Walter Johnson.

Left Fielders		Center Fielders		Right Fielders	
Brock, Lou	1985	Ashburn, Richie	1995	Aaron, Hank	1982
Burkett, Jesse	1946	Averill, Earl	1975	Clemente, Roberto	1973
Clarke, Fred	1945	Bell, Cool Papa*	1974	Crawford, Sam	1957
Delahanty, Ed	1945	Brown, Willard*	2006	Cuyler, Kiki	1968
Goslin, Goose	1968	Carey, Max	1961	Flick, Elmer	1963
Hafey, Chick	1971	Charleston, Oscar*	1976	Heilmann, Harry	1952
Irvin, Monte*	1973	Cobb, Ty	1936	Hooper, Harry	1971
Kelley, Joe	1971	Combs, Earle	1970	Jackson, Reggie	1993
Kiner, Ralph	1975	DiMaggio, Joe	1955	Kaline, Al	1980
Manush, Heinie	1964	Doby, Larry	1998	Keeler, Wee Willie	1939
Medwick, Ducky	1968	Duffy, Hugh	1945	Kelly, King	1945
Musial, Stan	1969	Hamilton, Billy	1961	Klein, Chuck	1980
O'Rourke, Jim	1945	Hill, Pete*	2006	McCarthy, Tommy	1946
Simmons, Al	1953	Mantle, Mickey	1974	Ott, Mel	1951
Stargell, Willie	1988	Mays, Willie	1979	Rice, Sam	1963
Wheat, Zack	1959	Puckett, Kirby	2001	Robinson, Frank	1982
Williams, Billy	1987	Roush, Edd	1962	Ruth, Babe	1936
Williams, Ted	1966	Snider, Duke	1980	Slaughter, Enos	1985
Yastrzemski, Carl	1989	Speaker, Tris	1937	Thompson, Sam	1974
		Stearns, Turkey*	2000	Waner, Paul	1952
		Torriente, Cristobal*	2006	Winfield, Dave	2001
		Waner, Lloyd	1967	Youngs, Ross	1972
		Wilson, Hack	1979		

First Basemen

Anson, Cap	1939
Beckley, Jake	1971
Bottomley, Jim	1974
Brouthers, Dan	1945
Cepeda, Orlando	1999
Chance, Frank	1946
Connor, Roger	1976
Foxx, Jimmie	1951
Gehrig, Lou	1939
Greenberg, Hank	1956
Kelly, George	1973
Killebrew, Harmon	1984
Leonard, Buck*	1972
McCovey, Willie	1986
Mize, Johnny	1981
Murray, Eddie	2003
Perez, Tony	2000
Sisler, George	1939
Suttles, Mule*	2006
Taylor, Ben*	2006
Terry, Bill	1954

Second Basemen

Carew, Rod	1991
Collins, Eddie	1939
Doerr, Bobby	1986
Evers, Johnny	1946
Fox, Nellie	1997
Frisch, Frankie	1947
Gehringer, Charlie	1949
Grant, Frank*	2006
Herman, Billy	1975
Hornsby, Rogers	1942
Lajoie, Nap	1937
Lazzeri, Tony	1991
Mazeroski, Bill	2001
McPhee, Bid	2000
Morgan, Joe	1990
Robinson, Jackie	1962
Sandberg, Ryne	2005
Schoendienst, Red	1989

Shortstops

Aparicio, Luis	1984
Appling, Luke	1964
Bancroft, Dave	1971
Banks, Ernie	1977
Boudreau, Lou	1970
Cronin, Joe	1956
Davis, George	1998
Jackson, Travis	1982
Jennings, Hughie	1945
Lloyd, Pop*	1977
Maranville, Rabbit	1954
Reese, Pee Wee	1984
Rizzuto, Phil	1994
Sewell, Joe	1977
Smith, Ozzie	2002
Tinker, Joe	1946
Vaughn, Arky	1985
Wagner, Honus	1936
Wallace, Bobby	1953
Ward, John Montgomery	1964
Wells, Willie*	1997
Yount, Robin	1999

Third Basemen

Baker, Frank	1955
Boggs, Wade	2005
Brett, George	1999
Collins, Jimmy	1945
Dandridge, Ray*	1987
Johnson, Judy*	1975
Kell, George	1983
Lindstrom, Freddy	1976
Mathews, Eddie	1978
Robinson, Brooks	1983
Schmidt, Mike	1995
Traynor, Pie	1948
Wilson, Jud*	2006

Catchers

Bench, Johnny	1989
Berra, Yogi	1972
Bresnahan, Roger	1945
Campanella, Roy	1969
Carter, Gary	2003
Cochrane, Mickey	1947
Dickey, Bill	1954
Ewing, Buck	1939
Ferrell, Rick	1984
Fisk, Carlton	2000
Gibson, Josh*	1972
Hartnett, Gabby	1955
Lombardi, Ernie	1986
Mackey, Biz*	2006
Santop, Louis*	2006
Schalk, Ray	1955

Inducted into the Hall in 1966 as a manager, Casey Stengel also had a long and distinguished career as a player. Playing on several teams between the years 1912 and 1925, Stengel posted a respectable career batting average of .284.

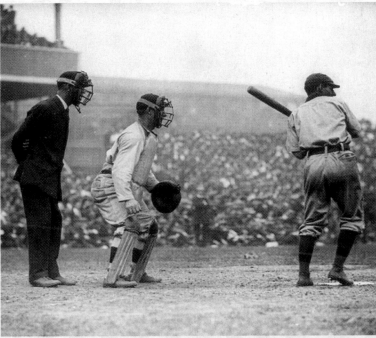

Managers

Alston, Walter	1983
Anderson, Sparky	2000
Durocher, Leo	1994
Hanlon, Ned	1996
Harris, Bucky	1975
Huggins, Miller	1964
Lasorda, Tommy	1997
Lopez, Al	1977
Mack, Connie	1937
McCarthy, Joe	1957
McGraw, John	1937
McKechnie, Bill	1962
Robinson, Wilbert	1945
Selee, Frank	1999
Stengel, Casey	1966
Weaver, Earl	1996

Known as "The Flying Dutchman" because of his blazing speed, Pittsburgh Pirates shortstop Honus Wagner hit over .300 in an incredible 16 straight seasons. Said teammate Tommy Leach: "He wasn't just the greatest shortstop ever. He was the greatest everything ever."

Pioneers and Executives

Barrow, Ed	1953	MacPhail, Lee	1998
Bulkeley, Morgan	1937	Manley, Effa*	2006
Cartwright, Alexander	1938	Pompez, Alex*	2006
Chadwick, Henry	1938	Posey, Cum*	2006
Chandler, Happy	1982	Rickey, Branch	1967
Comiskey, Charles	1939	Spalding, Al	1939
Cummings, Candy	1939	Veeck, Bill	1991
Foster, Rube*	1981	Weiss, George	1971
Frick, Ford	1970	White, Sol*	2006
Giles, Warren	1979	Wilkinson, J.L.*	2006
Griffith, Clark	1946	Wright, George	1937
Harridge, Will	1972	Wright, Harry	1953
Hulbert, William	1995	Yawkey, Tom	1980
Johnson, Ban	1937		
Landis, Kenesaw Mountain	1944		
MacPhail, Larry	1978		

Umpires

Barlick, Al	1989
Chylak, Nestor	1999
Conlan, Jocko	1974
Connolly, Tommy	1953
Evans, Billy	1973
Hubbard, Cal	1976
Klem, Bill	1953
McGowan, Bill	1992

CHAPTER 7

CUSTOMS, RITUALS, AND TRADITIONS

Baseball is a sport of timeworn customs, rituals, and traditions. Moments before the start of each game, the fans and players all rise and remove their caps for the singing of the national anthem. The last line, "and the home of the brave," gets drowned out by the roar of the crowd, the umpire yells "Play Ball!" and the game begins.

For fans, these and a multitude of other familiar traditions are comforting and provide everyone in attendance with a unifying experience. Some stadium traditions, such as the singing of "Take Me Out to the Ball Game," are surprisingly recent developments. Other rituals, however, have far deeper roots. The seventh-inning stretch dates back to 1869, and the practice of having the president of the United States throw out the first pitch of the season began in 1910.

Many common threads make up the fabric of the game. Long before the World Series is contested in October, baseball celebrates its past and present. An All-Star Game is played each year on the second Tuesday in July, and many teams trot out their former heroes and not-quite heroes for fans to cheer once more at the annual Old Timers' Day games.

For young fans in particular, what is old is new again.

Above: Hot dogs at the ballpark have been a tasty tradition since the early 1900s.

Left: The singing of "The Star-Spangled Banner" before baseball games was a common occurrence long before the song became our national anthem in 1931.

Home Stretch

Q: Who started the seventh-inning stretch?

A: No one knows exactly when the seventh-inning stretch became a tradition; however, manager Harry Wright of the Cincinnati Red Stockings noticed fans standing and stretching before the second half of the seventh inning of a game in 1869.

Wright figured the fans were uncomfortable from sitting on hard benches for an hour or so. In a letter to a friend that year, he wrote: "The spectators all arise between halves of the seventh inning, extend their legs and arms and sometimes walk about. In so doing, they enjoy the relief afforded by relaxation from a long posture upon hard benches."

Today, the seventh-inning stretch is practiced at major and minor league ballparks everywhere.

Chicago Cubs broadcaster Harry Caray led the Wrigley Field faithful in the singing of "Take Me Out to the Ball Game" at every home game from 1982 to 1997.

Q: How did the song "Take Me Out to the Ball Game" become the anthem of American baseball?

A: Ever since the Chicago Cubs installed the first ballpark organ at Wrigley Field in 1941, organists have been playing popular songs between innings, including "Camptown Races" and "Take Me Out to the Ball Game." In 1976 Chicago White Sox owner Bill Veeck noticed that Comiskey Park organist Nancy Faust frequently played "Take Me Out to the Ball Game" during the seventh-inning stretch, and he tried to attach the song to the stretch ritual. He gave broadcaster Harry Caray a microphone and told him to sing along with the crowd.

Veeck explained to Caray, "Harry, anybody in the ballpark hearing you sing 'Take Me Out to the Ball Game' knows that he can sing as well as you can. Probably better than you can. So he or she sings along. Heck, if you had a good singing voice you'd intimidate them, and nobody would join in!" Everyone in the ballpark stood up and sang along with Caray, and a tradition was born.

In 1982 Caray moved to the broadcast booth across town to work for the Cubs at Wrigley Field, where the games are televised coast to coast on cable. That's when the custom really caught on, and the ritual singing of "Take Me Out to the Ball Game" with his waving microphone as he leads the crowd in song became a Caray trademark, just like his thick black-framed glasses.

Ironically, the year the song was written, 1908, is the last time the Cubs won a World Series.

Hall of Famer Stan "The Man" Musial awaits the seventh-inning stretch at San Diego's Jack Murphy Stadium in 1996. Musial played "Take Me Out to the Ball Game" on his harmonica during the stretch.

Q: Who wrote "Take Me Out to the Ball Game"?

A: Jack Norworth and Albert Von Tilzer, inspired by a female friend of theirs who loved baseball, wrote "Take Me Out to the Ball Game" in May 1908.

The idea for the song struck Norworth while riding the New York subway. He saw a poster that said, "Baseball Today—Polo Grounds." In 15 minutes he wrote the lyrics to a chorus that would come to define the baseball experience for generations to come. The song, including two verses that are rarely heard, tells the tale of a liberated woman named Katie, who would rather her boyfriend take her to the ballpark than to the theater.

"Take Me Out to the Ball Game" was an instant hit in 1908. Ironically, Norworth and Von Tilzer had never been to a ball game when they had written the song. In fact, Von Tilzer would not see his first game until 1928, and Norworth did not attend his first game until he was honored on Jack Norworth Day at Brooklyn's Ebbets Field, in 1940.

The song has been recorded more than one hundred times, by musicians as diverse as the Andrews Sisters and the Goo Goo Dolls, and it inspired a 1949 movie musical starring Frank Sinatra and Gene Kelly. It is thought to be the third-most commonly played song in America after "The Star-Spangled Banner" and "Happy Birthday to You."

> " Take me out to the ball game, take me out with the crowd.
> Buy me some peanuts and cracker jack. I don't care if I never get back. "
>
> —FROM "TAKE ME OUT TO THE BALL GAME"

Patriotic Fervor

William Howard Taft throwing out the first ball while attending the Washington Senators' home opener in 1912. Taft started this tradition two years earlier.

Q: Which U.S. president was the first to throw out the ceremonial first ball?

A: Opening Day of the baseball season attained ceremonial status on April 14, 1910, when President William Howard Taft, the 27th president of the United States and a former semipro baseball player, threw out the first pitch of a new baseball season, in Washington, D.C. The American president has been throwing out the first ball on Opening Day ever since. The only president who did not was Jimmy Carter, who was in office from 1976 to 1980.

Taft called baseball a "healthy amusement" and would often attend Washington Senators games. On Opening Day in 1910, Senators owner Clark Griffith handed Taft the ball and asked him to throw out the first pitch. Taft tossed the ball to Washington Senators pitcher Walter Johnson, who then pitched a one-hitter in a 3–0 victory against the Philadelphia Athletics.

The presidential first pitch became an annual tradition, a ritual that, as Harold Seymour wrote in his 1971 volume, *Baseball: the Golden Age*, "in effect made [the president] the promoter of organized baseball and gives the appearance of conferring upon it the government stamp of approval." No other American sport can claim this distinction.

When President John F. Kennedy threw out the Opening Day pitch in 1961, the last opener played at Washington's Griffith Stadium, he threw perhaps the hardest pitch ever tossed by a president. A huge sports fan, especially of baseball and his beloved Red Sox, Kennedy had an aide he called his "Undersecretary of Baseball," whose responsibility was to keep him updated with the latest scores.

Other noteworthy presidential pitches:

President Harry Truman was the first left-hander to throw a ceremonial pitch. President Truman was ambidextrous and also used his right arm to toss baseballs out of the presidential box.

After throwing out the game's first pitch, President Gerald Ford witnessed Hall of Famer Hank Aaron's 714th home run, which tied Babe Ruth's legendary record, in the season opener at Riverfront Stadium in Cincinnati, Ohio, on April 4, 1974.

Weeks after the tragic events of September 11, 2001, President George W. Bush, wearing a bulletproof vest, threw out the first pitch before Game Three of the World Series between the Arizona Diamondbacks and the New York Yankees at Yankee Stadium, on October 30, 2001.

Q: When did the custom of playing "The Star-Spangled Banner" begin?

A: The national anthem was performed for the first time at a sporting event on September 5, 1918, in the middle of the seventh inning of Game One of the World Series between the Boston Red Sox and the Chicago Cubs at Comiskey Park. The Cubs chose to play at Comiskey Park (home of the White Sox) instead of their home field, Weeghman Park (now Wrigley Field), because of the greater seating capacity.

During the seventh-inning stretch, a military band played "The Star-

Spangled Banner," which was not yet the national anthem (that did not happen until 1931). Red Sox third baseman Fred Thomas, on leave from the Navy, snapped to attention. People spontaneously began singing. Cubs management ordered the song played again for the next two games. Not to be outdone, when the Series moved to Boston, the Red Sox offered their own military band rendition before the game started. A tradition was born; from then on the song was played at every World Series game.

Eventually, with the introduction of the public address systems and the outbreak of World War II, the singing of the national anthem became the rule before each game, firmly tying baseball to the American spirit.

Violin virtuoso Itzhak Perlman takes a bow after playing the national anthem at New York's Shea Stadium before the start of the Mets home opener in 2001.

Men in Blue

Nicknamed "The Old Arbitrator," umpire Bill Klem had a keen eye when it came to calling balls and strikes. Along with his professionalism behind the plate, Klem also was the first umpire to wear the inside chest protector, which is used by umpires everywhere today.

Q: Who was the first umpire to regularly use hand signals?

A: In 1905 umpire Bill Klem began using hand signals to coincide with verbal calls for all balls and strikes and fair and foul balls. This was a big hit with fans, as it helped them follow the action on the field.

Klem umpired from 1905 to 1940, working exclusively behind the plate for the first 16 years of his career because of his great ability to call balls and strikes. Respected by all in the game, Klem worked a record 18 World Series and is believed by many to be the greatest umpire in baseball history. He was inducted into the Hall of Fame in 1953.

The idea of umpires' signals was suggested long before Klem began umpiring. In a March 1870 letter to the editor published in *The New York Sunday Mercury*, Cincinnati Red Stockings manager Harry Wright wrote: "There is one thing I would like to see the umpire do at [a] big game, and that is, raise his hand when a man is out. You know what noise there is always when a fine play is made on the bases, and it being impossible to hear the umpire, it is always some little time before the player knows whether he is given out or not. It would very often save a great deal of bother and confusion."

Q: Why do major league umpires rub mud on baseballs before a game?

A: Before a big-league umpire yells "Play ball!" he has already dirtied six-dozen baseballs for the game, rubbing them with a special mud mix to soften the leather and get rid of the shininess of a brand-new, right-out-of-the-box baseball. Otherwise, pitchers' fingers would blister and batters would be distracted by the glare.

The mud mix is called Lena Blackburne Rubbing Mud, named for the person who started it all. Blackburne, a former major league infielder and coach, discovered the mud near his home in the Delaware Valley in the 1930s. The special mud removes gloss from new baseballs without discoloring them. It became the exclusive mud of the National and American leagues in 1938, and to this day umpires use this mud to rub on baseballs before games.

Burns Bintliff has been packaging the mud for decades. He inherited the business from his first wife's father, John Haas, a friend of Mr. Blackburne's who took over from him. Bintliff mines the mud and then mixes it with secret ingredients—he will not even tell his second wife what the secret is—and sells the mud in one-pound containers.

"It comes from the ground, and I have a special process that I don't divulge to anybody," said Bintliff. "The man who started it wanted it that way. It was started in 1938, and its come from the same place ever since."

So where does that essential mythic mud originate? Somewhere in New Jersey, although just where it comes from and how it is processed are secrets as closely guarded as nuclear launch codes, or the syrup recipe for Coca-Cola.

Though Bintliff steadfastly refuses to say what makes the mud right for its pur-pose, a 1982 article in the *New York Times* said the mud came from near Pennsauken Creek, a tributary of the Delaware River, in Burlington County. The article reports that an analysis was conducted by a Princeton University professor, who found that 90 percent of the mud was finely ground quartz, probably pulverized by ice that covered New Jersey during the Pleistocene epoch more than ten thousand years ago.

It's a dirty business, but for over 50 years, Jim Bintliff's family has been providing high-quality mud from southern New Jersey to Major League Baseball to get slick, shiny new baseballs ready for play.

Celebrating the Game

Q: How did the All-Star Game originate?

A: The first All-Star Game was staged in 1933 at Chicago's Comiskey Park, in conjunction with the city's "Century of Progress" Exposition. The idea came from Arch Ward, who was sports editor of the *Chicago Tribune*.

Ward persuaded the league owners to agree to a game between stars from the American and National leagues, to build up interest and attendance, which had been slipping. Baseball, like every other commercial enterprise, had felt the aftershocks of the October 1929 stock market crash. With millions of Americans out of work and with so little money, Americans were not spending their few dollars on entertainment. Between 1930 and 1933 major league attendance plummeted by approximately 40 percent. For example, in 1930 the St. Louis Cardinals drew upward of a half-million fans. But by 1933 that number had dropped to about 250,000 spectators.

At the All-Star Game inaugural in 1933, John McGraw, who had recently resigned as manager of the New York Giants, was selected to manage the National League squad. The leader of the American League team was the ageless Connie Mack. Fittingly, it was legendary Babe Ruth—still a force at 38 years old—who left the biggest mark on the inaugural contest. The future Hall of Famer slammed a two-run homer in the third inning off "Wild" Bill Hallahan (the first home run in the game's history) and made a nice running catch in right field to rob the Reds' Chick Hafey of a hit in the eighth. Ruth's exploits helped the Americans capture a 4–2 victory over the Nationals. For the game, American League players wore their individual team

The National League team poses before the first All-Star Game, in Chicago in 1933. National Leaguers wore specially designed league uniforms, while American League players wore their individual team uniforms. The AL won, 4–2.

uniforms, while the National Leaguers wore specially designed league uniforms.

Ward's proposal was for a one-time event, but the All-Star Game proved so popular it has been played every year since—except in 1945, when the game was called off because of travel restrictions during World War II.

In 1983 the Midsummer Classic returned to Comiskey Park, which was the site of the first All-Star Game 50 years earlier. In the third inning, Fred Lynn of the California Angels hit a bases-loaded home run off the Giants' Atlee Hammaker. It was Lynn's fourth All-Star home run and the first grand slam in All-Star history. Lynn's clout punctuated a seven-run inning as the AL coasted to a 13–3 victory and ended its embarrassing 11-game losing streak.

Q: When was the earliest and most significant Old-Timers game?

A: The Yankees held the first official Old-Timers game in 1946, but the earliest and most significant event was held two years later at Yankee Stadium, on June 13, 1948. A throng of 49,641 came out for a ceremony marking the 25th

anniversary of the ballpark in the Bronx and to honor the 1923 squad, the first World Series winners in Yankees history. The Old-Timers game between the 1923 Yankees and other retired Yankees was played prior to the regularly scheduled Yankees-Cleveland Indians game, won by the Yanks, 5-3. The '23 heroes won the two-inning affair, 2-0, when Bob Meusel's short pop-up dropped in for the winning hit.

The day was more significant for the ceremony honoring Babe Ruth. His famed Number 3 was permanently retired and his uniform formally presented to officials from the Baseball Hall of Fame. Using a bat to support his fragile frame, Ruth ambled to a microphone to say good-bye to fans and teammates, speaking in a croaking voice. He was in the late stages of throat cancer and would die two months later, on August 16, 1948.

Babe Ruth, wearing his Number 3 uniform, receives a standing ovation at Yankee Stadium on June 13, 1948, at the ceremony marking the 25th anniversary of the ballpark in the Bronx and the retirement of Ruth's Number 3 for all time.

Haberdashery

Q: Why do baseball managers and coaches wear uniforms?

A: In baseball's early years, when it was common for managers and coaches to also be players, it made sense for them to wear a uniform. As the years passed, the age of the playing manager faded, but the tradition remained. And it is a tradition unique to baseball. In no other sport do the coaches suit up in uniform. Imagine football coach Bill Parcells stalking the sidelines in helmet and shoulder pads. And it would look

also have a practical purpose: The amount of dirt kicked up on a baseball field and the prevalence of saliva and tobacco juice being spit in the dugout is not an atmosphere conducive to wearing one's Sunday best.

Two managers did wear street clothes in the dugout, however. The great Connie Mack wore suits when he managed the Philadelphia Athletics, and Burt Shotton wore a team jacket over a suit and bow tie when he managed the Brooklyn Dodgers from 1947 to 1950.

The darker gray uniforms worn by visiting teams like Melvin Mora's Baltimore Orioles are in sharp contrast to the home team's snow white jerseys.

funny to see basketball coach Pat Riley draw up a play for his team while wearing short pants and a tank top.

Baseball managers and coaches wear uniforms because they are the only coaching staffs in any sport that can legally set foot on the field of play. For this reason, baseball has an unofficial rule, or edict, requiring managers and coaches to be dressed in uniform. It may

Q: Why do visiting teams wear gray uniforms?

A: Visiting teams wear gray uniforms for road games so fans can easily distinguish the visiting team from the home team. This tradition dates back to the late 1800s. Baseball teams began to wear gray, black, or light blue uniforms for road games for logistical purposes, too: teams rarely had an opportunity to launder their uniforms on road trips.

Q: Which team wore the worst uniform?

A: Although the question of "worst uniform" is certainly open to interpretation, it is hard to argue against the 1976 Chicago White Sox "hot weather" uniforms designed by Mary Frances Veeck, the wife of the team's owner, Bill Veeck. These navy blue Bermuda shorts, worn with white nylon pullovers and white kneesocks, looked like Dad's softball outfit, only worse.

When the White Sox took the field against the Kansas City Royals on August 8, 1976, the players made history, but it was because of their knees, not their hitting. The White Sox became the first major league team to wear shorts as part of their uniform.

"You guys are the sweetest team we've seen yet," said Kansas City first baseman John Mayberry.

The cool Sox beat the Royals, 5–2, in the first game of the doubleheader. Not amused to learn they were wearing a publicity stunt, the White Sox players refused to put on the uniforms after just one game. They played the second game wearing pants.

"It was a fiasco," Eric Soderholm told the *Chicago Daily Herald* in 1999. "Players were still talking about them a year later. The guys who had surgery and their knees were all scarred up, well, it wasn't too attractive."

Attractive uniform design was in a slump during the 1970s. This was a decade of weird color combinations like the brown, orange, and yellow San Diego Padres uniforms that Steve Garvey said made him feel like a taco. The decade also gave us the Houston Astros uniforms of 1975 to '86. Designed to evoke the city's first domed stadium and the futurist space center, the red, yellow, and orange rainbows emblazoned across players' chests—and numbers printed on upper thighs—made even Nolan Ryan look, in *Sports Illustrated*'s words, like "a human Popsicle."

Former Chicago White Sox third baseman Eric Soderholm displays his old uniform and a photograph showing him as a member of the 1977 White Sox. Soderholm missed wearing shorts by one season, though he did don the stylish nylon pullover.

CHAPTER 8

THE BUSINESS OF BASEBALL

These days it is almost impossible to talk about baseball without also talking about owner lockouts, arbitration, free agency, and player strikes.

It is a quaint notion now, but until the late 1960s, very few players had agents to negotiate their contracts. Why? Because the owners would not negotiate with agents. There was a players' union then, but it was not very powerful. By the early 1970s players began to see themselves as entertainers who performed for money—and they wanted to cash in. Labor struggles were inevitable as union leaders took a tougher stance in their dealings with team owners, enabling athletes to earn more money under better working conditions.

An average player at the beginning of the 1900s made perhaps $3,000 a year. In 1947 slugger Hank Greenberg became the first player to earn $100,000 in a year. In 1979 Houston's Nolan Ryan became the first $1 million player. Incredibly, more than 60 players currently make over $10 million a year. In December 2000 Alex Rodriguez signed a 10-year, $252 million contract with the Texas Rangers, the most lucrative contract in sports history. Rangers owner Tom Hicks gave Rodriguez $2 million more than he had paid to buy the entire team, including the ballpark, just three years earlier.

Above: The influx of network television dollars resulted in pro baseball franchises becoming very lucrative enterprises, which made players want a bigger slice of the pie.

Left: Alex Rodriguez flashes a multi-million-dollar smile at a news conference in Arlington, Texas, announcing his new contract with the Texas Rangers.

Battle Lines Are Drawn

Q: Who organized the first baseball players' union?

A: John Montgomery Ward, a stellar pitcher and later a shortstop during his playing career in the late 1800s, organized the first players' union.

Ward won 39 games and pitched the second perfect game in National League history, in 1880. His career record stood at 164 wins and 102 losses with a 2.10 earned run average when his pitching career came to an abrupt end in 1884 when his arm gave out. Ward quickly became a standout fielding shortstop, base stealer, and hitter for the New York Giants. He was also the team's manager, winning the 1894 Temple Cup championship, a precursor to the World Series.

Ward's most memorable activities in baseball, however, took place off the field. Since the beginning of the National

League, every player's contract had a clause in it known as the reserve clause. This bound a player to a single team for his entire career. In other words, if a player was dissatisfied with his employer, he was not free to move to another team.

Ward thought the reserve clause was unfair and with other Giants teammates formed the Brotherhood of Professional Base Ball Players—the first players' union —in 1885. Ward, by virtue of his Columbia University law degree, was elected president. He soon began to form chapters among other clubs, and as the Brotherhood grew, the players made known their position against the reserve list.

By the end of the 1887 season, the Brotherhood boasted 100 members. Its mission was to protect and benefit the players collectively and individually, and to promote standards of fair and ethical contract negotiations. When owners

John Montgomery Ward, right, thought the reserve clause in players' contracts was unfair and during his playing days with the New York Giants wrote articles railing against it.

refused to deal with the Brotherhood and imposed salary limits in 1889, Ward organized the Players League to create a rival to the National League and draw away top players.

At the November 1889 press conference announcing the new league, Ward stated: "There was a time when the [National] League stood for integrity and fair dealing. Today it stands for dollars and cents. Once it looked to the elevation of the game as an honest exhibition of the sport. Today its eyes are upon the turnstiles. Men have come into the business for no other motive than to exploit it for every dollar in sight. Measures originally intended for the good of the game have been turned into instruments for wrong . . . Players have been bought and sold and exchanged as though they were sheep instead of American citizens."

Q: How did the Players League affect labor relations?

A: The launching of the Players League in 1890 started another all-out baseball war. Many star players in both the National League and the American Association (including Charles Comiskey and Connie Mack) bolted to the rival new league, in which the players themselves had a stake as part owners.

During the 1890 season the three major leagues competed in many of the same cities. Forging a united front, the AA and NL schemed to schedule their games to conflict with the Players League games. Fans became discouraged because their favorite players were continually moving from one team to another. As a result the fans found it hard to get into a rooting frame of mind. They stayed away from the ballparks, and all three leagues lost money.

Even though the Players League had the best attendance, it was defeated and collapsed after only one year, breaking the Brotherhood. The demise of the Brotherhood allowed owners to harden the reserve clause and institute a salary cap, leaving ballplayers with worse contracts than they had before.

Although his efforts failed, Ward's revolt would be echoed over the next eight decades, until players would finally achieve freedom from the reserve clause.

Connie Mack was a National League catcher who bolted to the Players League in 1890, but he is most remembered as owner and manager of the American League's Philadelphia Athletics.

Salary Wars

Q: **What is the reserve clause and how did it come to be?**

A: National League owners knew that in order to survive through the late 1870s and early 1880s, they needed to hold down player salaries. After all, salaries were a club owner's biggest expense.

A player in those days could sell his services to any team once the season ended. William Hulbert, the NL president and owner of the Chicago White Stockings (today, Major League Baseball would prohibit such a conflict of interest), recognized the danger of such a practice. At an owners' meeting in 1877, Hulbert warned his colleagues: "If we constantly bid against each other for players, salaries will eventually go so high we'll all be ruined.

"It is ridiculous," he added, "to pay ballplayers $2,000 a year, especially when the $800 boys often do just as well."

This was a time of rampant player movement, with player desertion a common occurrence through "contract jumping." In 1879 Hulbert and his fellow owners introduced the most controversial rule baseball has ever known—the reserve clause. The principle was simple: At the end of the season, each team could pick players to put on a reserve list. The owners were pledged not to hire, or attempt to hire, a player on the reserve list of another team, unless the player had been given his outright release. This, Hulbert noted, would assure fans that their favorite teams would have continuity from year to year.

At the outset, the reserve clause was meant for only five players on each team. Owners convinced these players that being reserved meant job security. But soon the reserve clause was applied to everyone. All players were

Washington Senators owner Clark Griffith, right, with his manager Bucky Harris at the 1924 World Series. Griffith called the reserve clause "the backbone of baseball."

source of player-owner conflicts over the next one hundred years—remained in all major league contracts until the 1970s.

Q: How did a Supreme Court ruling affect the business of baseball?

A: The United States Supreme Court weighed in on the national pastime in 1922, ruling that baseball is "sport" and not "commerce" and therefore not subject to federal antitrust laws, which say that all the business owners in an industry can't band together to control the industry. The U.S. Congress had created a special exemption from this antitrust legislation for Major League Baseball.

Justice Oliver Wendell Holmes wrote on behalf of the court in May 1922 that organized baseball cannot be subject to antitrust legislation because "it would not be called commerce in the commonly accepted uses of those words."

The landmark ruling has affected the manner in which Major League Baseball conducts its "sport" ever since. The ruling allows Major League Baseball to make rules for its entire sport from a central office, even though each team is supposedly an independent business. The central office can make decisions for the teams without regard to antitrust laws that govern other businesses in the United States. In essence, the ruling has allowed major league teams to operate as a permanent cartel, with little competition against them. As recently as the 1990s, Congress has reaffirmed this judgment in several decisions and bills.

Oliver Wendell Holmes served nearly 30 years as a U.S. Supreme Court justice and wrote in 1922 that organized baseball cannot be subject to antitrust legislation. The ruling allowed major league teams to operate with little competition against them.

bound to a single team for their entire careers. In the minds of the owners, the reserve clause would bring stability to the game's finances and parity to the playing field. They surmised that placing restrictions on player movement would prevent the richest teams from obtaining the best talent.

Because of Hulbert, the balance of power shifted from the players to the owners. Club owners like Clark Griffith of the Washington Senators called the reserve clause the "backbone of baseball" and pointed out that players were making more money than they would by holding jobs in the outside world. The players, realizing the reserve clause would cap their earnings potential, howled for its removal. The reserve clause—a major

The Revolt

Q: Which player most seriously challenged the reserve clause?

A: Curt Flood was an All-Star center fielder for the St. Louis Cardinals from 1958 to 1969. He batted .300 or better in six seasons and won seven consecutive Gold Glove awards for fielding excellence. Flood was the team captain of the 1967 World Series champion Cardinals.

In the winter of 1969, the Cardinals agreed to a trade with the Philadelphia Phillies that would ship Flood, pitcher Joe Hoerner, outfielder Bryon Browne, and catcher Tim McCarver to Philadelphia in exchange for second baseman Cookie Rojas, pitcher Jerry Johnson, and first baseman Richie Allen. But Flood did not want to play in Philadelphia. He wanted the freedom to choose whom he would play for. Echoing John Montgomery Ward nearly a century earlier, Flood noted that a slave, even one making $90,000 a year, was still a slave.

In December 1969 Flood fired a warning shot across the bow of baseball when he said in a letter to Commissioner Bowie Kuhn that his trade from the Cardinals to the Phillies should be voided and that he should be made a free agent. It read in part, "After twelve years in the major leagues I do not feel I am a piece of property to be bought and sold irrespective of my wishes. I believe that any system which produces that result violates my basic rights as a citizen and is inconsistent with the laws of the United States."

Kuhn's letter of reply reaffirmed baseball's intention to hold Flood to the provisions in his contract, which included the right of the Cardinals to assign Flood's services to whichever team it pleased. Flood declared he would rather retire than report to the Phillies.

In January 1970 Flood decided to file a lawsuit against Major League Baseball, charging baseball with violation of the antitrust laws. Named as defendants were the commissioner of baseball, the presidents of the National and American leagues, and the 24 major league clubs. The lawsuit was a gamble for Flood. Still, he decided the risk was worthwhile and chose to sit out the 1970 season in order to pursue his case.

Flood charged he would suffer irreparable damage if not allowed to play for a team of his choice in 1970. He sought an injunction that would prevent baseball from invoking the reserve clause rules against him, but his request to void the trade was denied. Hall of Famers Jackie Robinson and Hank Greenberg testified for Flood, along with former club owner Bill Veeck and former pitcher and author Jim Brosnan. No active players testified for Flood, nor did any show up to give moral support.

Q: What was the result of the lawsuit?

A: Curt Flood lost his $4 million antitrust lawsuit, in August 1970, but the ruling from Judge Irving Ben Cooper did not address Flood's challenge of the reserve system. The judge's ruling upheld the 1922 Supreme Court decision exempting baseball from antitrust laws because it was sport, not interstate commerce.

As Flood legal team was appealing the case to the U.S. Supreme Court, the Phillies traded Flood to the Washington Senators. When lawyers advised Flood that the tade would not hurt his case, he decided to play for the Senators for the 1971 season. After batting .200 in 13 games, however, Flood left the team and moved to Europe. Meanwhile, his lawsuit continued.

In June 1972 the Supreme Court upheld the lower court by a 5–3 decision against Flood. (Justice Lewis Powell abstained because he was a stockholder in Anheuser-Busch, owner of the Cardinals.) The decision by the country's highest court enabled baseball to remain unaffected by antitrust laws and assert its reserve clause. Nonetheless, the majority opinion called baseball's antitrust exemption an aberration and an anomaly. The narrow 5-3 decision also gave the union hope for a negotiated end to the reserve clause.

Flood's suit had exposed the vulnerability of baseball's legal position. In December 1972, major league owners toned down their hard line stance by agreeing to salary arbitration, in which an impartial arbitrator would work with teams and players on contested contracts.

Although Flood lost his day in court, he helped foster changes in baseball's long-standing reserve clause. Flood stood up for his principles at the expense of his own baseball career. His selfless action is judged by many to be the ground-breaking case of baseball labor relations.

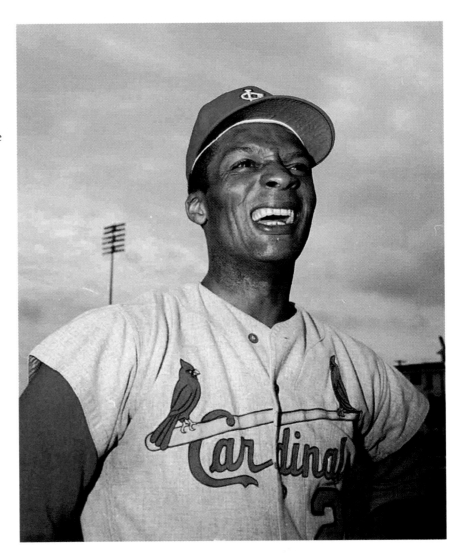

Curt Flood was more than content as a seven-time Gold Glove center fielder. But when he was traded to the Phillies, he sued baseball, arguing he shouldn't be shuttled between teams "like a slave."

Take the Money and Run

Q: **What player's case finally broke the reserve system?**

A: Curt Flood's case reached the U.S. Supreme Court, but the justices refused to invalidate the reserve clause. However, as the Flood case went through the courts, the Major League Baseball Players Association had won the right for an impartial arbitrator to hear grievances against management.

Andy Messersmith, a star pitcher for the Los Angeles Dodgers, set in motion the case that finally broke the reserve system. Messersmith, a 34-game winner over the 1973–74 seasons with the Dodgers, did not sign a contract for the 1975 season. He claimed that after he had played one full year without a contract, he should be a "free agent"—free to play for any team he chose.

Baseball officials objected, but the courts agreed to hear Messersmith's case before labor arbitrator Peter Seitz. On December 23, 1975, Seitz ruled that the reserve clause could not be applied into perpetuity. A player's services could only be reserved for one year at the end of their contracts, after which they became free agents eligible to negotiate with all teams. Messersmith was declared a free agent, and Seitz suggested that a solution on free agency be worked out through the collective bargaining process.

Other stars quickly understood what the ruling could mean for them. More than 20 of them (including Don Gullett, Rollie Fingers, and Sal Bando) refused to sign a contract for 1976, and at the end of the season they became free agents, too.

The owners organized a bidding system for this pool of great talent.

The Seitz decision doomed the reserve clause, realigned the power balance between owner and player, and opened the door for widespread baseball free agency. As a result, the average baseball salary jumped from $45,000 in 1975 to over one million dollars by the 1990s.

Q: **Who signed the first multimillion-dollar contract in baseball history?**

A: On December 31, 1974, Jim "Catfish" Hunter signed with the New York Yankees for $3.75 million over five years—triple any other player's salary at the time.

Labor arbitrator Peter Seitz's decision gave free-agent status to Andy Messersmith in 1975. The ruling allowed any player to become a free agent by playing an entire season without a contract.

Following the 1974 season, after Hunter had helped the Oakland Athletics to their third world championship in a row, a financial dispute with A's owner Charles O. Finley led Hunter to declare himself a free agent—two years before the beginning of official free agency. The dispute stemmed from a contract issue regarding deferred payments. The previous winter Hunter and Finley had agreed on a two-year contract for $100,000 a year, but each year only $50,000 was to be paid to Hunter as straight salary; the remaining $50,000 was to be paid to a life insurance fund. The straight-salary part was paid routinely, but the insurance payments were not made because it would involve unfavorable tax consequences for Finley. Hunter contended Finley did not honor the agreement and therefore voided the contract. Finley said there was no contract violation, just disagreement over interpretation.

Hunter filed for free agency when Finley refused to pay. An arbitrator, Peter Seitz, ruled in Hunter's favor at a hearing on December 13, 1974, and declared Hunter a free agent. The 28-year-old pitcher would be a prized free-agent catch: From 1970 through 1974, Hunter had 106 victories with the A's and was the reigning American League Cy Young award winner.

After an incredible bidding war broke out for his services for the 1975 season, Hunter finally signed with the Yankees on New Year's Eve. The era of the big-contract superstar free agent had officially begun.

Hunter won 23 games for the Yankees in 1975 and was a World Series starter in each of the next three seasons. When he was inducted into the Hall of Fame in 1987, Hunter became the first player born after World War II to gain a spot in Cooperstown. He died of Lou Gehrig's disease in 1999, at the age of 53.

Jim "Catfish" Hunter wearing his Yankees cap for the first time on New Year's Eve 1974. Arm trouble ended his career at age 33, but he still went to Cooperstown. His plaque reads: "The bigger the game, the better he pitched."

> **It all started with a fellow named Catfish Hunter. He showed the world how foolish some owners can be. Catfish went home to Ahoskie, North Carolina, and did nothing but sit there, holding court. The owners came to him with fortunes. This is how the madness began.**
> — *FORMER REDS AND TIGERS MANAGER SPARKY ANDERSON*

Playing Hardball

Q: How did Marvin Miller impact baseball's labor relations?

A: In March 1966 baseball players elected Marvin Miller as the executive director of the Major League Baseball Players Association. The former chief of the tough steelworkers' union brought that steely reserve to baseball labor relations, and his experience totally overmatched the owners, whom he routinely outwitted. Miller changed the fortunes of baseball players and, by extension, all athletes, forever. He did not waste any time getting started. In 1968 Miller obtained an increase in the minimum baseball player's salary from $6,000 a year (it had been $5,000 in 1947) to $10,000.

Miller negotiated five contracts with the owners over the course of his 18-year term as union boss. By the time of his retirement in 1984, Miller saw the average salary skyrocket from $19,000 to $240,000. Today, that figure is well over $2 million. Among Miller's other miracles: an end to the reserve clause, with free movement from team to team through free agency, resulting in much higher salaries; arbitration in labor disputes; the right for veteran players to veto trades; a vastly improved pension plan funded largely through percentages of television revenue; and recognition of the players' union, which led to the right to collective bargaining and the use of agents to negotiate individual player's contracts.

Although he may have been a polarizing figure to fans and owners by organizing

Marvin Miller, executive director of the baseball players' union, at a New York press conference with Joe Torre of the St. Louis Cardinals on April 13, 1972, announcing an end to the first players' strike in the game's history.

two strikes—a 13-day strike before the 1972 season and a 50-day walkout in the summer of 1981—his tough tactics finally got the players a "bigger piece of the pie" in a time of baseball prosperity that saw hundredfold increase in the value of franchises.

Q: Which teammates staged one of baseball's first modern labor disputes?

A: One of baseball's first modern labor disputes began shortly before the start of the 1966 season.

Sandy Koufax and Los Angeles Dodgers teammate Don Drysdale staged a joint holdout, demanding that Dodgers owner Walter O'Malley pay them $1 million over three years, to split evenly between them, or $167,000 each for the next three seasons. They threatened to retire if their demands were not met. They also insisted that the Dodgers deal with their lawyer, not with them. Though common today, dealing with someone who was acting as a player's agent was unheard of then. The two pitchers had led the Dodgers to world champion-

ships in 1963 and 1965 and felt they had a right to be treated as "coequal parties to a contract."

O'Malley refused to negotiate. Eventually, Koufax got $125,000 and Drysdale got $110,000, and the two pitchers became the highest-paid players in the game. Their joint holdout demonstrated the power of collective bargaining.

In 1980, as major league salaries exploded through the stratosphere, Drysdale thought about his holdout and salary agreement of 15 years earlier.

"When we played," said the Hall of Famer, who died in 1993, "World Series checks meant something. Now they just screw up your taxes."

Los Angeles Dodgers pitchers Sandy Koufax and Don Drysdale (53) combined to win 49 of the team's 97 games in 1965, and then staged a joint holdout during spring training the next season.

Another Kind of Baseball Strike

Q: When was the first collective bargaining agreement between owners and players?

A: The Major League Baseball Players Association, the players' labor union, had existed since the 1930s, but its chief function was to collect dues and dole out a paltry pension. By 1965, the

MAJOR LEAGUE BASEBALL
PLAYERS

The negotiating efforts led by acting baseball commissioner Bud Selig and players' union head Donald Fehr could not stave the lockout that canceled the 1994 World Series.

to negotiations toward the first collective bargaining agreement in 1968. The agreement gave the players some much needed leverage at the negotiating table. Team owners had been offering players a "take it or leave it" contract for over 100 years. Now, the union had won the right to file complaints with the National Labor Relations Board whenever a player was thought to be treated unfairly. Players could also now bring grievances to an independent arbitrator for mediation.

The owners did not like the union interference, and especially bristled at players rising up against them.

In 1972 the situation grew volatile. When team owners tried to reduce their payment to the Major League Baseball players pension fund by $500,000, the players decided to fight back: For the first time in baseball history, the players went on strike.

players wanted their fair share of the ever increasing broadcasting revenues, and hired Marvin Miller in the hopes of strengthening their union

When Miller came on board in 1966 and saw what the conditions were, he realized the goal went beyond adding television monies to the players' pension fund. He discovered player salaries to be embarrassingly low compared to other professions. The players were shocked to learn how poorly they were paid. This led

Q: How have labor disputes impacted pennant races?

A: In 1972 major league players walked out at the end of spring training, beginning the first general players' strike in sports history. The walkout lasted until April 13, wiping out 86 of the season's first scheduled games. None of the canceled games were made up—a move that affected the American League East Division when the Detroit Tigers, who played one game more than the Boston Red Sox, finished a half-game ahead of them.

In 1981, after a 50-day strike had wiped out seven weeks of the schedule, baseball owners and players divided the campaign into a split-season format, with the first-half winners (Yankees, A's, Phillies, and Dodgers) facing those from the second half (Brewers, Royals, Expos, and Astros) in an extra round of divisional playoffs. The arrangement was somehow unjust: The Cincinnati Reds had the best overall record, 66–42, but never made the playoffs.

In 1994 a terrible impasse between players and owners forced the owners to lock the players out, on August 11. The dispute centered on the owners' demand to control costs by putting a limit on player payrolls. On September 14, led by Bud Selig, the acting commissioner, the owners voted, 26–2, to cancel the remainder of the regular-season schedule, two rounds of the playoffs, and the World Series. They blamed the players' 34-day strike and what they charged was the union's unwillingness "to respond in any meaningful way" to the clubs' demand for cost containment.

But Donald Fehr, the players' labor leader, countered by saying: "When people think back to what the final image of the 1994 season will be, it may be Bud Selig at a press conference in Milwaukee protesting the pain and gnashing of teeth but nevertheless going ahead and dashing the hopes and dreams of many people. It was their decision to make. They decided their circumstances were more important."

The World Series, which had survived world wars and an earthquake since its inception in 1903, was not played for the first time in 90 years.

The strike became the longest shutdown in the game's history and even extended 18 games into the 1995 season. It was settled in April 1995 when a federal judge forced the owners to return to the rules of the old labor pact.

Onetime Milwaukee Brewers owner Bud Selig was formally appointed commissioner of baseball in 1998.

CHAPTER 9

THE WAR YEARS

Baseball would not be immune to war. During the war years professional baseball suffered from both lack of players and lack of fans. For these were times when America was fighting overseas. As scores of active players changed from flannels to khaki and navy blue, the talent pool would be thinner than ever. During World War I the most famous major league players, like Babe Ruth, were not called to war. They were allowed to continue entertaining American citizens who were working hard at home to support the war effort overseas. Other patriotic athletes, like Ty Cobb and George Sisler, decided to enlist anyway, and they became war heroes. Others, like Christy Mathewson, were not so lucky. In World War II, America's sporting passion inspired President Franklin Roosevelt to say professional games should not be canceled. War left baseball fans with a compendium of what-if statistics. If Bob Feller had not missed nearly four seasons, he might well have won 350 games. Ted Williams missed three full years because of World War II and then most of two more seasons during the Korean War. What if he hadn't missed those five years? He might have 4,000 hits and 650 home runs. Joe DiMaggio, 28 when he went into the army, was never the same player after the war. More than half a century later, fans still wonder: What if?

Above: Thousands of Americans—and several future baseball Hall of Famers—answered the recruiting call from their Uncle Sam and enlisted to fight for the Allied forces during World War I.

Left: Joe DiMaggio joined the army as a sergeant soon after the end of the 1942 season.

Over There!

Q: Who was the first major league player during World War I to enlist in the armed forces?

Hank Gowdy (left) returned from the trenches of World War I to play for manager John McGraw's New York Giants in the 1924 World Series.

A: On June 1, 1917, about two months after the United States formally entered World War I, Boston Braves catcher Hank Gowdy, a hero of the 1914 World Series, joined the Ohio National Guard, becoming the first major leaguer to enlist in the service.

Gowdy missed that season and all of the next while carrying the flag for the famed "Rainbow Division," a nick-name given to the U.S. Army's 42nd Division. One of the original American forces to reach the European theater (in November 1917), the Rainbow Division fought valiantly in six stra-tegically important French campaigns, including the Battle of Champagne and other notable clashes at Verdun and Argonne. The division suffered thousands of casualties by war's end.

After his safe return from the trenches, Gowdy was traded to the New York Giants. As a part-time catcher in 1924, he batted .325 and helped the Giants win the NL pennant. Unfortunately, he was to become the goat of that year's World Series against Washington.

The Senators were batting in the bottom of the 12th inning of the deciding seventh game, and the score was tied 3–3.

With one out and no one on base, Senators' catcher Muddy Ruel popped up behind home plate. While pursuing the foul pop, Gowdy stepped on his discarded mask.

"It held me like a bear trap," he said. The ball dropped safely.

Given a second chance, Ruel slapped a double, and two batters later came around to score the winning run, giving Washington its first and only World Series triumph.

Q: Which legendary pitcher was a casualty of World War I?

A: Christy Mathewson was the National League's dominant pitcher in the early 1900s. He won 373 games from 1900 to 1916 (only the immortal Cy Young and Walter Johnson ever won more), with all but one of those victories coming for the New York Giants.

Mathewson cemented his legend in the 1905 World Series, pitching three complete-game shutouts over six days against the Philadelphia Athletics in what is among the greatest Series pitching performances ever.

In 1916 he was traded to the Cincinnati Reds, where he pitched just one game (a victory) before retiring as a player to become full-time manager. He left the Reds' dugout in midseason 1918 to enlist in the Army's Chemical Warfare Service (now known as the Chemical Corps). The unit—which included four future Baseball Hall of Famers: Commander Branch Rickey, Lieutenant George Sisler, and Captains Ty Cobb and Mathewson—worked to defend U.S. troops from poison gas. While conducting training experiments at Hanlon Field near Chaumont, France, Mathewson mistakenly inhaled a dangerous chlorine gas, permanently scarring his lungs.

"I saw Christy Mathewson doomed to die," Cobb wrote in his autobiography, *My Life in Baseball: The True Record.* "None of us who were with him realized that the rider of the pale horse had passed his way. Nor did Matty, the greatest National League pitcher of them all."

Mathewson returned to baseball in 1919 as a coach for the Giants, but two years later he developed tuberculosis in both lungs, and the illness caused by the gassing would eventually take his life in 1925, at the age of 45.

"Matty" was one of the five players voted into the Hall of Fame in 1936, its first year of inductions.

Christy Mathewson was the preeminent control pitcher of his era, prompting an awed teammate to say he could throw a ball into a tin cup at pitching range. Said Mathewson: "A pitcher's speed is worth nothing if he cannot put the ball where he wants to."

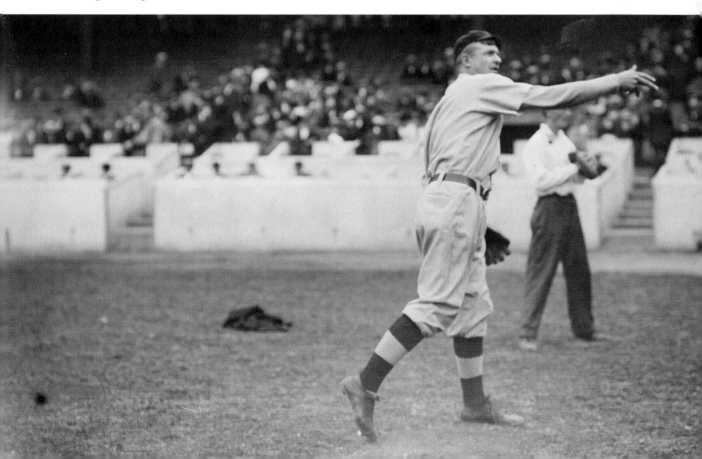

Going to Bat for Your Uncle Sam

Q: How did World War I affect baseball?

A: Baseball was poised to start a new season when the United States formally entered the war, on April 6, 1917. The war exacted a toll on every aspect of American life, including sports. That year a number of major sporting events were canceled. The annual Indianapolis 500 auto race was canceled. In golf, the U.S. Open and the PGA Championship were canceled. Boxing titles were frozen, and college football selected no All-America team. Even so, baseball was able to continue.

By 1918 the war effort had changed Americans' daily life, from the institution of daylight saving time (so there were more hours of daylight for war production work) to a change in the way people watched baseball games. In May government legislators made it legal to play baseball on Sundays. The populations of major cities were increasing with soldiers returning home from the war, and lawmakers wanted to provide these working people with recreation and amusement.

Due to restricted train travel (another war consideration), the 1918 schedule was shortened from 154 games to 125, with the regular season ending

President Woodrow Wilson's right arm kicks off the 1916 baseball season, as he becomes the second chief executive to toss the ceremonial first ball on Opening Day.

on September 2, a month early. President Woodrow Wilson's administration granted baseball approval to stage the World Series, with 10 percent of its revenues donated to war charities. As a result the players received all-time lows in winners' and losers' shares. The winning Red Sox share was a paltry $1,103 per man, and the losing Cubs share was $800 each.

Q: What was the "Green Light Letter"?

A: In January 1942, two months after the United States entered World War II, baseball commissioner Kenesaw Mountain Landis wrote to President Franklin D. Roosevelt and offered to suspend baseball if it suited the needs of the country's war effort.

Landis recalled that President Wilson had halted all "nonessential industries" near the end of World War I, cutting short the 1918 baseball season by one month. Fears that the war would jeopardize baseball again in 1942 were put to rest when Roosevelt wrote back on January 15, 1942, saying that the game should continue because Americans need entertainment—and so baseball went on. The now famous "Green Light Letter" read, in part:

"I honestly feel that it would be best for the country to try to keep baseball going. There will be fewer people unemployed and everybody will work longer hours and harder than ever before. And that means that they ought to have a chance for recreation and for taking their minds off their work even more than before. . . .

"Here is another way of looking at it—if 300 teams use 5,000 or 6,000 players, these players are a definite recreational asset to at least 20,000,000 of their fellow citizens—and that in my judgment is thoroughly worthwhile."

This letter from President Roosevelt to Commissioner Landis gave baseball—and by implication, all major professional and amateur sports—a "green light" to keep playing for the duration of the war. Still, that did not exempt ballplayers from military service.

During World War II President Franklin Roosevelt insisted that the game be given a "green light" to uplift the country's morale. But he did stop visiting the ballpark during the war.

A Call to Arms

Bob Feller, 19, was a pitcher for the Cleveland Indians and only two years out of high school when he won 17 games and led the American League with 240 strikeouts in 1938. The highlight of his season came in October, when he struck out a career-high 18 against Detroit.

Q: **Who was the first player drafted into World War II?**

A: The first regular major league player to get the call was Hugh Mulcahy, a starting pitcher for the Philadelphia Phillies during the late 1930s.

Mulcahy earned the nickname "Losing Pitcher" when, in four consecutive seasons, he compiled a

record of 40–76, leading the league in losses with 20 in 1938 and 22 in 1940. Appropriately, Mulcahy was a National League All-Star that year. The hard-luck right-hander was a victim of poor support. The lowly Phillies never won more than 55 games in a season between 1937 and 1940.

The 27-year-old Mulcahy was inducted into the army on March 8, 1941. When he reported to the 26th Infantry Division for training at Camp Devens, near Cape Cod, Massachusetts, he proudly told *The Sporting News*, "My losing streak is over for the duration. I'm on a winning team now."

In 1944 Mulcahy was shipped overseas, where his unit was stationed in New Guinea and the Philippines. He missed almost five full seasons in the military. After the war, Mulcahy pitched two more seasons for the Phillies and then appeared in two games for the Pittsburgh Pirates in 1947. Overall, he compiled a 45-89 record in nine seasons.

Q: **Who was the first player to volunteer for active duty?**

A: Two days after Japanese planes attacked the United States naval base at Pearl Harbor, on the Hawaiian island of Oahu, 23-year-old Bob Feller, the 25-game winner and league strikeout king for the Cleveland Indians, became the first major league player to volunteer for active duty. Feller's Navy enlistment was broadcast live on the radio, on

December 9, 1941.

While some stars spent the war playing exhibition baseball games to build the troops' morale, Feller served as a chief petty officer aboard the battleship *Alabama* in the Pacific. He won five campaign ribbons and earned eight battle stars for his service.

He returned to the diamond in 1946 and was better than ever. A newly added slider made his fastball and curve even harder to hit than before. He went on to win 26 games that season, including 10 victories by shutout, and whiffed 348 batters, the most by a pitcher in 40 years.

One of the greatest pitchers of his era, Feller lost four of his prime years at the peak of his career to military service, which took away his chance of winning 350 career games. He finished with 266 and still made the Hall of Fame.

When Feller was elected to the Hall in his first year of eligibility, in 1962, he was bothered by his Hall of Fame plaque, which lists his baseball career as spanning "1936 to 1941" and "1945 to 1956" with no explanation for the gap in time. He suggested that the plaque be changed to reflect the facts. When a baseball official said that such a change would be "inconvenient," Feller responded: "Well, it was inconvenient to get shot at."

Q: **Which major leaguer won the Purple Heart for his service in Vietnam?**

A: Roy Gleason, now 64, had a brief stint with the Dodgers in 1963, doubling in his only major league at-bat, before returning to the minors. He did, however, earn a World Series ring for his cameo appearance. During spring training in 1967, he was drafted, and later sent to Vietnam, where he was badly wounded by a mortar round and given the Purple Heart in 1968. When he returned to the states, his ring, which he had brought with him to Vietnam, was missing from his personal effects. Though he never played in the majors again, in 2003 the Dodgers presented their one-hit wonder war hero with a replica of his long-lost ring.

George Washington's profile in courage adorns the Purple Heart that is awarded to soldiers who are wounded in battle.

Hammerin' Hank and Airman Ted

Q: Which player returned from World War II to deliver his team a championship?

A: Hank Greenberg was one of the first professional athletes to sign up for military service during World War II. Coming off a season in which he had led the American League with 41 homers and 150 runs batted in, Greenberg entered the army 19 games into the 1941 season. Sergeant Greenberg, 30, was discharged on December 5 of that same year. Two days later the Japanese bombed Pearl Harbor and the United States officially entered the war. Greenberg turned right around and enlisted in the Army Air Force. He rose to the rank of captain and commanded a B-29 bomber squadron, spending much of the war on active duty in India and China.

"We are in trouble," he said, explaining his reason for enlisting, "and there is only one thing for me to do—return to the service. This doubtless means I am finished with baseball, but all of us are confronted with a terrible task—the defense of our country and the fight for our lives."

Greenberg was wrong about one thing. He did return to baseball, in June 1945, and did so with a bang. He hit a home run at Detroit's Briggs Stadium in his first game back and hit a dramatic ninth-inning grand slam homer on the final day of the season to win the pennant for the Tigers. Then the original Hammerin' Hank slammed two homers and drove in seven runs to lead Detroit to a seven-game World Series victory over the Cubs.

Greenberg played only about nine full seasons because of World War II military service, but he pounded out 331 home runs. If he hadn't missed most of the 1941 through 1945 seasons, he might have had a shot at reaching the lofty 500 home run mark.

Q: Which Hall of Fame player escaped a fiery death during the Korean War?

A: In 1952 the Korean War nearly took the life of Ted Williams, one of America's legendary baseball players.

The "Splendid Splinter," who won seven batting titles and hit

Hank Greenberg of the Detroit Tigers working out at spring training camp in Lakeland, Florida, in February 1940. The next year, he jumped at the chance to serve his country in World War II.

Opposite page: Boston Red Sox star Ted Williams stepped up during the Korean War, flying 37 combat missions as a Marine pilot. He reported for pilot training at Willow Grove Naval Air Station, in Pennsylvania, in May 1952.

an amazing .344 in his 19-year career with the Boston Red Sox, was trained as a pilot in World War II, serving with distinction. He was called up from the reserves in May 1952, and before the Korean War ended in 1953, Williams would fly 37 combat missions as a Marine pilot. His plane was hit by enemy fire several times, including once when he had to land his flaming F-9 Panther jet on its belly. He executed the dangerous maneuver and walked away without serious injury, just moments before the plane exploded.

Williams was awarded many medals for his service, but did suffer hearing loss due to the gunnery noise. He served with John Glenn, who went on to greater fame as an astronaut and U.S. senator.

"Ted flew as my wingman on about half the missions he flew in Korea," says Glenn.

By all accounts Williams was nearly as great a pilot as he was a hitter. In fact, if not for baseball, his first love, Williams may have had a full-time career as a Marine pilot. "I liked flying," Williams said. "It was the second-best thing that ever happened to me."

Williams's career statistics— including 521 home runs and 1,839 runs batted in—are doubly impressive when you consider that he missed nearly five full seasons to war. Since he averaged 32 home runs a year through 1951, it's reasonable to speculate that he lost 150 homers while in the service. And he still came within 346 hits of attaining 3,000.

A League of Their Own

Rose Gacioch played for the Rockford Peaches of the All-American Girls Professional Baseball League from 1945 to 1954. She won 20 games pitching for the Peaches in 1952, with a career-low 1.88 ERA.

Q: **What new league began play during World War II?**

A: As the war effort began to deplete major league rosters, the game suffered from a noticeable lack of talent. Recognizable names were disappearing from lineups by the week, and the game was losing some of its appeal.

Chicago Cubs owner Phillip K. Wrigley feared that the war would shut down baseball and put him out of business. In the spring of 1942, he ordered his top scouts to find the best 200 women softball players in the country.

Wrigley was in many ways a baseball visionary. It was Wrigley who promoted Ladies Day as a way of attracting women to the ballpark by letting female fans in the park for a reduced price. And it was Wrigley, in 1943, who started a new league for women. He called it the All-American Girls Professional Baseball League, and he hoped the girls would fill stadiums until the major leaguers returned from the war.

Wrigley's scouts signed 64 women and divided them into four teams: The Rockford (Illinois) Peaches, the South Bend (Indiana) Blue Sox, the Kenosha (Wisconsin) Comets, and the Racine (Wisconsin) Belles. At first the league used a large ball and pitched it underhand. But it soon changed into true baseball, with knockdown pitches and hard slides into second base. The only difference from the men's game—besides the skirts—was a smaller diamond, with 72 feet between bases instead of 90.

The new league was a surprise hit and successfully expanded to small industrial centers such as Kalamazoo and Battle Creek, Michigan; Fort Wayne, Indiana; and Peoria, Illinois. Attendance grew annually until it peaked in 1948, when the ten-team league drew almost one million fans.

The quality of play was impressive. After watching shortstop Dorothy Schroeder of the South Bend Blue Sox, Chicago Cubs manager Charlie Grimm said, "If she was a boy, I'd give $50,000 for her."

After the war ended, people still came to the women's game, but popularity eventually declined, as fans returned to men's baseball or stayed home to watch the new medium of television. The league lasted 12 years, before finally folding after the 1954 season. It was celebrated in the 1992 film *A League of Their Own.*

Q: What other league was sweeping the nation?

A: In the late 1940s still another baseball league blossomed as Little League baseball increased in popularity. A few years after Carl Stotz, a worker in a sandpaper plant in Williamsport, Pennsylvania, had the idea for an organized children's baseball league, Little League had spread to nearly every state in the nation.

Today, 2.7 million children between the ages of 8 and 12 play Little League baseball in more than 80 countries. They play on fields smaller than a major league diamond (bases are 60 feet apart instead of 90 feet), and with slightly different rules: Games are six innings long (instead of nine) and base stealing is limited.

Each August, Little League holds its world championship in Williamsport, Pennsylvania. Teams travel from around the world to compete in this 10-day tournament. Many of the games are broadcast on television. The international championship game is played at Howard J. Lamade Stadium, which seats 10,000, but 30,000 more watch from the two hillsides just past the outfield fence.

The first Little League World Series was a local affair played in 1947. A crowd of 2,000 watched two Pennsylvania teams play for the crown: The Maynard Midgets of Williamsport defeated Lock Haven, 16–7.

In 1974, following much debate, girls were allowed to play. Two years earlier Maria Pepe had played several games for a team in Hoboken, New Jersey, despite Little League's refusal to lift its ban against girls. The National Organization for Women sued, and a New Jersey court ruled in favor of NOW, and Little League opened to girls as well as boys. Today Little League has more than 100,000 girls playing its game.

Millions of youth baseball players dream of scoring the winning run in the championship game of the Little League World Series, held each year since 1947 in Williamsport, Pennsylvania.

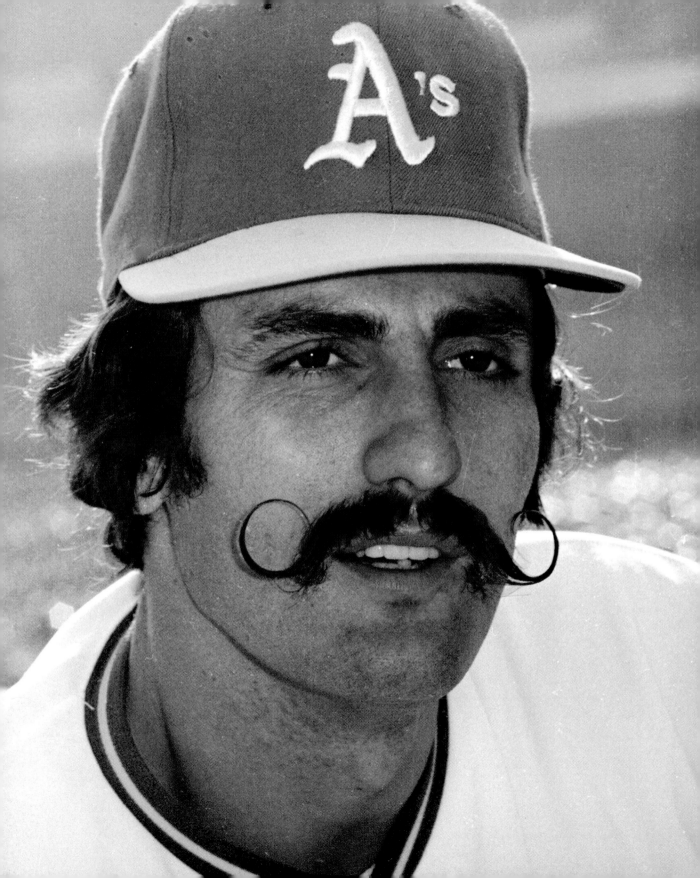

CHAPTER 10

THE CHANGING GAME

Major league baseball has made significant changes since playing by the Knickerbocker rules and it continues to evolve. The growth of the game has spurred new ideas on and off the field. As more and more players became famous, it was important that fans could identify them on the field. Thus, names and numbers on the uniform became standard issue. Fielders' gloves have been used since the 1870s. The earliest gloves were nothing more than flimsy leather that barely fit over the palm of the hand. Modern gloves, made of cowhide, are much larger and cover and protect the entire hand. They come in different sizes and designs to suit the needs of each position player. In the 1950s and 1960s, relief pitchers started playing a more important role during games. Statistics were devised to reflect this evolution, and the entrance of relievers into games is now akin to a gladiator entering the arena. During the following decades, fans' devotion to their heroes was evident in the surging memorabilia business. Baseball card trading, once the hobby of children, is now conducted much like the stock market, with economic cycles and indicators analyzed by experts. Even in arcas such as celebrations and dugout etiquette, the game continues to change.

Above: The earliest baseball gloves could accommodate both left-handed and right-handed fielders.

Left: Rollie Fingers of the Oakland Athletics sported an old-fashioned moustache in 1973, but he was a pioneer in the new era of relief pitchers.

Names and Numbers

Q: Which team was the first to wear numbers on its uniform?

A: On June 26, 1916, the Cleveland Indians, in a 2–0 win against the Chicago White Sox at League Park, wore large numerals pinned to their left sleeves so that fans in the stands could tell who was who on the field, thus becoming the first baseball team to have uniform numbers. At that time a player's number corresponded to his position in the batting order, so the number could change as the batting order changed. The Indians' leadoff batter that day was Jack Graney, who became the first player to bat wearing a number on his uniform. (Graney was also the first batter to face rookie Red Sox pitcher Babe Ruth, and the first former ballplayer to become a broadcaster.)

Cleveland's experiment lasted only a few weeks. The Indians tried again the following year, this time with numbers on the right sleeve, but again abandoned the project after a brief trial.

Q: When did permanent numbers appear on uniforms?

A: The Cleveland Indians and the defending world champion New York Yankees were the first teams to wear permanent numbers sewn onto the backs of their uniforms, in 1929. Starting players were given numbers that matched their usual place in the batting order. That's why Babe Ruth wore Number 3—because he usually batted third.

The numbers and corresponding names were listed in the club's scorecards, and so, perhaps, also marked the first time ballpark vendors called out: "Scorecards, get your scorecards here! You can't tell the players without a scorecard!"

By the mid-1930s, all big league teams were wearing numbers on their home and road uniforms, though it took until 1937 for the final holdout, the Philadelphia Athletics, to follow suit.

Soon players' numbers became a personal statement, of sorts. Bill Voiselle, who played for the Braves and Cubs from 1947

Jack Graney, behind a four-legged friend, was at the center of the Cleveland Indians team photo in 1916. Ray Chapman, who was killed by a pitch in 1920, is fifth from left. Note the stiff cardboard cutout player second from left.

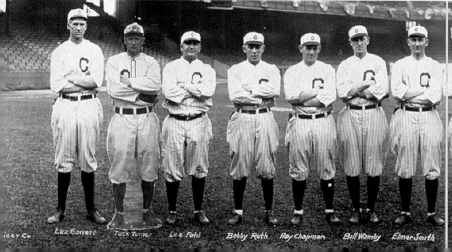
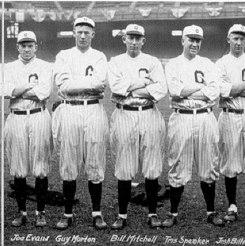

to 1950, wore his beloved home town on his back. Voiselle hailed from Ninety Six, South Carolina.

Carlos May gave folks a constant reminder of his birthday every time they saw the back of his jersey: "May 17."

As a side note, three major league players have worn a numberless uniform since the adoption of uniform numbers. Pitcher Joe Horlen (in 1961) and outfielder Eric Davis (in 1984) each made their major league debut wearing a road jersey with no number because no other uniform was available. In 1999, Detroit center fielder Gabe Kapler wore a numberless uniform to honor Ty Cobb (who never wore a number) in the final game played at Tiger Stadium.

Q: Who had the idea to place players' names on uniforms?

A: Who else? Bill Veeck introduced player names on the back of the uniform jerseys of his Chicago White Sox players for spring training in 1960. Buoyed by baseball's immense popularity on television, the idea was an immediate success. Today, nearly all major league clubs have home and road jerseys adorned with player names. Despite being the first major league club to adopt permanent uniform numbers, the New York Yankees have not adopted the practice, while the the Red Sox and Giants remain nameless on their home uniforms. The Los Angeles Dodgers removed player names from the uniform jersey for the 2006 season, but they will bring them back in 2007.

First baseman Nomar Garciaparra (5) of the Los Angeles Dodgers during the 2006 National League Division Series. The 2007 Dodgers uniforms will include player names.

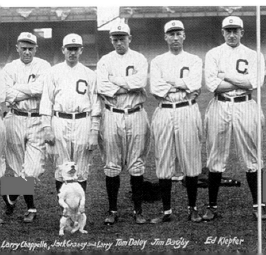

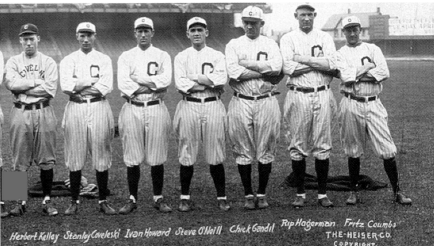

Larry Chappelle, Jack Graney and Larry Tom Daley Jim Bagby Ed Klepfer   Herbert Kelley Stanley Coveleski Ivan Howard Steve O'Neill Chick Gandil   Rip Hagerman Fritz Coombs
THE·HEISER·CO.
COPYRIGHT.

Glove Stories

Q: Who was the first fielder to wear a glove?

A: There is no clear record of who first conceived the notion of fielding with a glove. There are examples of catchers wearing gloves as early as the 1860s. Worn on both hands, these gloves, cut off at the fingers, were thin pads used to protect already sore hands, rather than as a device to improve fielding, as gloves are today.

According to Albert Spalding, the first noncatcher to wear a fielder's glove was Charlie Waitt of the St. Louis Brown Stockings, in 1875. A first baseman, Waitt had injured his fielding hand by catching so many hard throws, and took his position in a game wearing an ordinary flesh-colored leather glove, to protect the palm of his hand. Waitt "confessed that he was a bit ashamed to wear it, but had it on to save his hand," Spalding wrote in 1911. "He also admitted that he had chosen a color as inconspicuous as possible, because he didn't care to attract attention."

Though Waitt's innovation was ridiculed by barehanded teammates and mocked by opponents, Spalding saw a lucrative opportunity in leather. A pitcher and first baseman for the Chicago White Stockings, Spalding had opened a sporting goods manufacturing business in 1877. That season, in hopes of gaining acceptance for this new equipment, Spalding wore a pair of black gloves while in the field. Once considered unmanly, the gloves soon caught on throughout the league, and Spalding was right there to supply equipment to the teams.

Spalding believed that since other players respected him, he avoided any mockery he might have suffered. "I had been playing so long and had become so well known that the innovation seemed rather to evoke sympathy than hilarity," he said.

After Spalding, gloves began to catch on during the 1880s, as players slowly began to understand the benefits of glove wearing, although there were some holdouts.

Q: Who was the last barehanded player?

A: John "Bid" McPhee was a stellar fielding second baseman despite playing barehanded for most of his career with the Cincinnati Reds from 1882 to 1899. McPhee played over 2,000 games in 18 years and remains a career leader in most fielding categories for second basemen. But only in his final four years, long after the glove became standard equipment, did he begin to cover his hand with leather.

By 1895 nearly all players wore gloves on defense. But McPhee continued to play barehanded, soaking his hands in brine to toughen them. "The glove business has gone a little too far," McPhee told the Cincinnati Enquirer in 1890. "True, hot-hit balls do sting a little at the opening of the season, but after you get used to it, there is no trouble on that score."

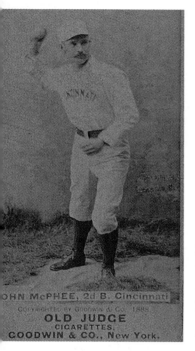

OHN McPHEE, 2d B. Cincinnati

COPYRIGHTED BY GOODWIN & CO. 1888

OLD JUDGE
CIGARETTES.
GOODWIN & CO., New York.

John "Bid" McPhee of the Cincinnati Red Stockings toughened his hands by soaking them in brine.

McPhee transformed the way second basemen play. While others were positioned close to the bag near the middle of the diamond, McPhee roamed far to his left, improving his range. According to the baseball encyclopedia Total Baseball, he handled an average of 6.7 chances per game—second most in history—accounting in the average Cincinnati game for nearly one-quarter of the opponent's outs.

Playing with a glove for the first time to protect a sore finger in 1896, McPhee had a sparkling season defensively, setting a fielding record for second basemen that would remain the benchmark for nearly three decades. He was elected to the Hall of Fame in 2000.

Q: When did players stop leaving their gloves on the field?

A: It seems quaint by today's standards, but players used to leave their gloves on the field when they went up to bat.

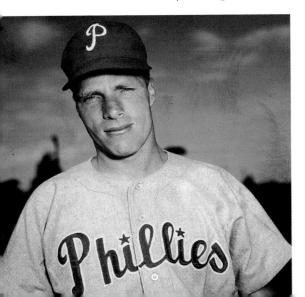

Major League Baseball banned the practice prior to the 1954 season, requiring that "players are to remove their gloves from the field when batting and no equipment is to show on the field at any time."

Richie Ashburn, the Hall of Fame center fielder for the Philadelphia Phillies, complained about not being allowed to leave his glove on the field anymore, saying, "If it's beauty they are striving for in the parks, why don't they plant some flowers?"

In the early days of baseball, players left their gloves on the field in case an opponent needed one. Glove sharing was common among players during the 1910s, when only about two-thirds of all players owned their own glove. By the 1930s nearly all major-league players had a glove of their own, but gloves remained on the field.

The strewn and scattered leather could and did affect play. A glove lying on the field actually helped decide the American League pennant in 1905. It was during the first game of a crucial three-game series between the Philadelphia Athletics and Chicago White Sox in late September. Whichever team won at least two games would be the champion.

The Athletics won the first game, 3–2, as Topsy Hartsel scored from second base with the winning run in the seventh inning. Harry Davis's run-scoring single to short left field hit Hartsel's glove, which the left fielder had dropped in the grass when he came off the field. The A's won again the next day to finish in first place.

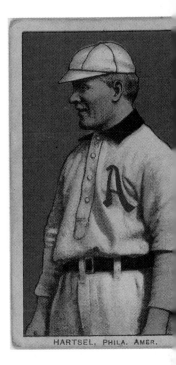

HARTSEL, PHILA. AMER.

Above: An improbable play involving Topsy Hartsel's glove tilted the 1905 AL pennant in favor of the Philadelphia A's.

Left: Philadelphia's Richie Ashburn set records for outfield putouts, assists, and double plays, but he was by no means leather-bound.

Oh, What a Relief It Is

Q: When was the save added as an official statistic?

A: In 1969 the save was added as an official statistic. A relief pitcher is credited with a save if he comes into a game with his team ahead, finishes the game and preserves the win, but is not the winning pitcher.

Chicago Tribune baseball columnist Jerome Holtzman created the statistic to reflect the increasing importance of late-inning relievers. For years starting pitchers and their managers considered it almost unmanly not to complete a ball game. Relievers were seen as pitchers who lacked the talent to start. Today top relievers like New York's Mariano Rivera and San Diego's Trevor Hoffman are among the biggest stars in the game.

Trevor Hoffman of the San Diego Padres became the major league's all-time saves leader, surpassing Lee Smith's mark of 478 during the 2006 season.

One of the first managers to assign a star to the bullpen was Casey Stengel. In 1949 the Yankees manager used fireballer Joe Page in 60 games, and Page responded with 13 wins and a record 27 saves. By contrast the National League leader that season had just nine saves. The following year, 1950, Phillies reliever Jim Konstanty collected 22 saves, 16 wins, and the NL's Most Valuable Player award. In 1990 Bobby Thigpen of the Chicago White Sox set a new record for saves with 57.

Q: Why did relief pitchers stop using golf carts?

A: Like doubleheaders, the bullpen cart has pretty much disappeared from the game, and that's a shame because it was a true slice of Americana.

It was fun to see a reliever, called on to save the day, ride into action in a golf cart topped by a ridiculous, oversized baseball cap. But many bullpens in today's stadiums are located along the foul lines, a short walk from the pitching mound. And in the older parks where the pens are situated beyond the outfield fences, the pitchers have gotten used to jogging to their jobs.

The history of bullpen carts can be traced to 1951 when Hank Greenberg, then general manager of the Cleveland

Indians, thought it would be a great publicity stunt to have pitchers brought in on golf carts. Yankees manager Casey Stengel objected, saying, "Yankee pitchers don't ride in golf carts, they ride in Cadillacs."

The next night, on July 12, 1951, Greenberg had a Cadillac in the bullpen for the Yankees, but New York's Allie Reynolds spoiled the joke by throwing not just a complete game, but also a no-hitter. The automobile was not needed and was gone the next day.

Q: Why is the area where relief pitchers warmup called the bullpen?

A: The term "bullpen" has been widely used since the early 1900s. Several theories exist. One is that early ballparks were built on farms or rural fields that also doubled as rodeo arenas. Relief pitchers would warmup in the pens where the bulls were kept, hence the name.

When the Polo Grounds opened in 1880, the New York Giants relievers warmed up beyond the left-field fence, near a stockyard where bulls milled about in their pens.

Another theory involves tobacco advertising. The outfield fences at minor league ballparks in the South and Midwest were often splashed with advertisements for Bull Durham tobacco. Since relievers warming up beyond the outfield fence were often directly behind the Bull Durham sign, this is how the term might have gotten coined.

Hall of Fame manager Casey Stengel opined that the term came from managers who were fed up with their relief pitchers bothering the rest of the team by shootin' the bull in the dugout during games, so they were exiled to a "bullpen" away from the other players.

Still others conclude that in the earliest days of baseball, fans arriving late to games were herded like cattle to a standing-room-only section known as the bullpen. Later, pitchers warming up would use this area, and the designation stuck.

Pitchers often warm up in a bullpen located beyond the outfield fence. A phone system is used so that managers and bullpen coaches can communicate as to whether a pitcher is ready to enter a game.

Flipping and Trading

Q: When did baseball cards get their start?

A: In the late 19th century, tobacco companies began printing cards and inserting them into packs of cigarettes to advertise their products and attract customers. Subsequently, manufacturers of candy and other products used cards as a gimmick to boost sales.

The modern era of baseball card collecting began in 1933, when the Goudey Gum Company of Boston, Massachusetts, included one baseball card with a slab of pink bubble gum that sold for one penny. This initial set, called "Big League Chewing Gum," consisted of 240 cards. Today that set in mint (perfect) condition is valued at over $50,000.

Soon these sports cards became known as "trading cards" because kids traded them among friends, hoping to replace duplicate cards for ones they needed to complete the set.

The Goudey era of manufacturing sports cards spanned just nine years, yet it opened the door to the lucrative business of collectible trading cards. In the early 1950s Topps Chewing Gum Company of New York took over as the leading issuer of bubble-gum cards, and dominated the field for 30 years.

Today baseball cards issued by a multitude of companies are more popular than ever. The gum, however, has disappeared, because the sticky confection may tarnish the card's resale value.

Q: Which player's card is most valuable?

A: The 1909 Honus Wagner T206 baseball card has developed a mystique that makes it the most highly prized and most valuable of all cards. The multicolored card depicting the great Pittsburgh Pirates shortstop was removed from circulation early in the printing process because Wagner opposed smoking and objected to his name being linked to the cigarettes advertised on the back of the cards.

This highly prized Honus Wagner trading card was included in a package of tobacco in 1909. The cardboard collectible fetched a record sum of more than $1 million in July of 2000.

WAGNER, PITTSBURG

According to legend, Wagner was so upset when he learned of the card's existence that he asked the American Tobacco Company not to sell them. When told that the cards were already printed, Wagner tried to stop the tobacco company from distributing them. He sent the company the amount of money he thought it would have earned if it had issued the cards.

As reported in an article from the October 24, 1912, issue of *The Sporting News,* Wagner wrote a letter to the company saying, "I don't want my picture in any cigarettes, but I also don't want you to lose the ten dollars, so I'm enclosing my check for that sum."

The Wagner cards were pulled off the shelf and destroyed, after fewer than 100 of the cards had been sold. About 50 of the original cards survive today. One was sold at auction for the record price of $1.1 million to a collector from Southern California named Brian Siegel, in July 2000.

Q: How has collecting changed over the past four decades?

A: Only 23,154 fans attended the Yankees' final game of the 1961 season, but many crowded into the right-field stands, hoping to catch the ball if Roger Maris hit home run number 61. A California restaurant owner had offered to pay $5,000 for the ball.

Sal Durante, a 19-year-old truck driver from Brooklyn, New York, was the lucky fan who caught the ball. He received congratulatory pats on the back from the delighted patrons. Contrast that with the legal battle to determine who owned Barry Bonds's record-setting 73rd home run ball. A trial in San Francisco Superior Court involved two men, one who said he caught Bonds's historic homer on October 7, 2001, and had it torn from his hands, and the other who claimed that the ball rolled loose during the melee and he plucked it from the ground. A judge ruled that the two men had to split the proceeds from the ball after it was put up for auction (it fetched $450,000).

Obviously, the zeal of collectors has grown in direct proportion to the skyrocketing value of sports collectibles over those four decades. Proof of just how crazy the market got surfaced in January 1999, when the baseball that Mark McGwire hit for his historic 70th home run in 1998 sold at auction for over $3 million.

A childhood stash of baseball cards hidden in the bedroom closet could be worth a small fortune . . . if Mom hasn't already thrown them away.

Clubhouse Confidential

Q: Who popularized the high five?

A: The high five became popular when a national television audience saw it performed by the Los Angeles Dodgers. The Dodgers may have raised the first high five in baseball, but they do not deserve credit for starting the gesture.

The famous Dodgers high five occurred in 1977, on October 5 (what other day of the month could it have been?) in the second game of the National League playoffs. Left fielder Dusty Baker hit a grand slam home run off Phillies pitcher Jim Lonborg, and when he returned to the dugout he and teammate Glenn Burke raised their arms overhead and slapped hands.

"That was it—the first [baseball] high five," Baker told *Sports Illustrated* in 1981. "But I didn't originate it."

The first high five probably occurred during a volleyball game played on a California beach. In fact, Kathy Gregory, the queen of beach volleyball during the 1960s and 1970s, recalls that high fives and high tens first became common

Japanese-born outfielder Ichiro Suzuki (right) and his high-fiving Seattle teammates use the sporting international handshake to celebrate a Mariners victory.

in her sport as early as the late 1960s, perhaps because players were used to reaching high and hitting hands above the net.

"If a girl hit a ball out or made some other mistake, we just went up and high-slapped her," says Gregory, for 31 years the women's volleyball coach at the University of California at Santa Barbara. "You know, women give so much more support to each other than men do. For every one high five they did, we must have high-fived a million times."

Q: What is the secret to spitting a sunflower seed like a major leaguer?

A: According to Orlando Hudson, second baseman of the Arizona Diamondbacks, who grew up near a sunflower field in Darlington, South Carolina, and is recognized by his peers as one of the best practitioners of this new-age art:

Get a bag of sunflower seeds with the seeds still in their shells. Pour a handful of seeds into the palm of your hand. Shake the seeds in your hand to separate them to pick out imperfections. Remove any seeds with broken shells and seeds with stems.

Put about five seeds into your mouth and use your tongue to push them into your right cheek. Says Hudson: "Pack the seeds like a beaver uses his tail to pack the wood and mud together to build a dam."

Use your tongue to shift one seed over to the left side of your mouth. Crack the shell of the seed using your left-side teeth.

Get the shell to stick to the tip of your tongue and move it to the front of your mouth. Then spit out the shell. But be careful not to hit your teammates with it. "That's nasty," says Hudson.

In the mouth of a major league ballplayer, a handful of sunflower seeds can provide endless (and mindless) entertainment during a game.

CHAPTER 11

TRAILBLAZERS, HEROES, AND ICONS

aseball has been called "America's national pastime" for almost 150 years. Precisely because of its importance in our lives, there are examples of the game as both a progressive agent for change as well as a mirror of the times. Baseball, to be sure, has long been a laboratory for social issues. Consider racial discrimination, for example. Of all the builders who affected baseball in the 20th century, Branch Rickey had the most influence by far. His greatest achievement came in 1947, when he brought Jackie Robinson to the Brooklyn Dodgers, breaking baseball's color barrier. In one bold move Rickey forced integration on the major leagues seven years before the U.S. Supreme Court ordered the integration of public schools. Many of America's success stories took root on the baseball diamond, personified by Hank Greenberg, Sandy Koufax, Roberto Clemente, and many others who succeeded in the face of religious and racial intolerance. The notion that "sport builds character" is better expressed "sport reveals character." We have witnessed too many athletes break the rules of fair play and good conduct, on and off the field. These flaws, however, are the exception, not the rule. The fact remains that ballplayers represent the best and worst of us while also giving us flesh-and-blood examples of courage and bravery.

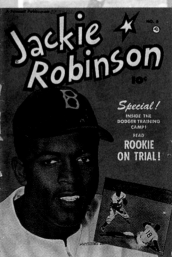

Above: Jackie Robinson, the first black major league ballplayer, gave hope to all minority athletes.

Left: Branch Rickey (right) helped make baseball history in the 1940s by bringing Jackie Robinson to the Brooklyn Dodgers and breaking baseball's color barrier.

You Gotta Believe!

Q: **Which Hall of Fame slugger was cheered for his religious convictions?**

A: During a tight pennant race in 1934, Hank Greenberg faced a dilemma. That year the Detroit Tigers had a chance to reach the World Series for the first time in 25 years. But a crucial game fell on Rosh Hashanah, the Jewish New Year and one of the holiest days on the Jewish calendar. Greenberg wondered whether he should play.

He consulted his rabbi, who suggested that Greenberg attend religious services on the evening of the holiday, which began at sundown, then play the next day, since Rosh Hashanah is a happy occasion. Greenberg followed his rabbi's advice, and he hit two home runs to lead the Tigers to a 2–1 win.

Ten days later, on Yom Kippur, the Day of Atonement and the holiest day of the Jewish year, Greenberg's rabbi suggested he spend the day praying, not playing. Once again, Greenberg followed the guidance of his spiritual leader. He went to synagogue instead of the stadium despite the pennant race. Upon entering the synagogue that day, the worshipers stopped in mid-prayer to salute him with applause. The Tigers lost the game that day but reached the World Series, losing to St. Louis.

Greenberg was the first great Jewish baseball player and much admired for his determination to succeed despite discrimination and prejudice. But he kept his cool and answered the bigots with his bat. In fact, he claimed that the slurs only motivated him to play better.

"I came to feel that if I, as a Jew, hit a home run, I was hitting one against Hitler."

In 1938 Greenberg took aim at Babe Ruth's single-season home run record. He had 58 homers—two shy of Ruth's record—with five games left to play. But Greenberg would not hit another out of the park. Some say anti-Semitic pitchers walked him, but Greenberg and statistics say otherwise. In those five homerless games, Greenberg had five hits in 18 at-bats, with only four walks.

Q: **How did anti-Semitism smear the 1965 World Series?**

A: Sandy Koufax grew up in a mostly Jewish neighborhood in Brooklyn, New York. He was so proud of his heritage that he refused to pitch in games played on the Jewish holidays of Rosh Hashanah and Yom Kippur. In fact, the Dodgers took the Jewish High Holidays into consideration when forming their pitching rotation, so that Koufax could pitch as much as possible during the pennant race in late September and the World Series in early October.

One incident that tested Koufax's relationship to his faith occurred as the Dodgers and Minnesota Twins were playing in the World Series, in October 1965. The opening game fell on Yom Kippur, the holiest day of the Jewish year, and Koufax was not at the ballpark. Don Drysdale pitched poorly in his place, and the Dodgers lost, 8–2.

The next day, the *St. Paul Pioneer Press* published a sports column entitled, "An Open Letter to Sandy Koufax." It contained a number of distasteful jokes and references to Jewish customs. The column ended: "The Twins love matzo balls." (Pitches that are hit for home runs are usually called "meatballs.")

Later, Koufax remarked, "I couldn't believe it. I thought that kind of thing went out with dialect comics."

He pitched the second game later that day and lost. Then the southpaw dominated the Twins by pitching shutouts in Games Five and Seven, and the Dodgers won the World Series, with Koufax gaining MVP honors.

After that, Koufax said, "I clipped the column so that I could send it back with a note that I hoped his words were as easy to eat as my matzo balls. I didn't send it. We were winners."

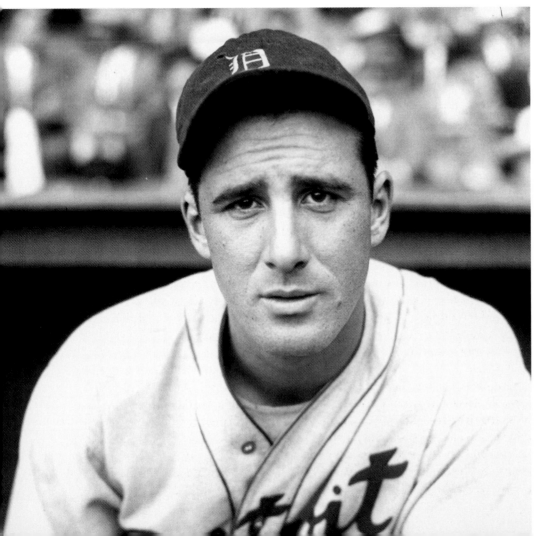

Hank Greenberg, the son of Romanian-born Jewish immigrants, was born and raised in New York City. He was the first great Jewish baseball player and as much a hero in U.S. Jewish communities as Joe DiMaggio was among Italian Americans of the same period.

The Mahatma and the Great Experiment

Q: Who was the mastermind behind baseball's farm system?

A: As general manager of the St. Louis Cardinals in the 1920s, Branch Rickey created a minor league farm system for developing young talent. Rickey was called "the Mahatma," which means "a person of great prestige and wisdom." The title was well deserved. Rickey may have been the sharpest baseball mind ever.

Before Rickey, minor league clubs were all operated independently. Minor league team owners survived by developing and then selling players to the major league clubs. With the backing of St. Louis owner Sam Breadon, Rickey began buying up minor league teams and making them part of the Cardinals organization. This allowed the big club to scout and develop players, grooming them to play for the Cardinals.

Soon the Cardinals had 33 minor league teams—a major league franchise today operates only five or six minor league teams—and more than 600 players in their farm system, nicknamed "Rickey's Plantation." As the organization grew under Rickey's leadership, he fueled it with handpicked scouts, coaches, and managers to give young players major league polish before they played a single game in the big leagues.

Despite the objections of Commissioner Kenesaw Landis— who disliked the system because it decreased the independence of minor league clubs—Rickey's Plantation was a tremendous success. The Cardinals, who had never won a thing, reeled off five pennants from 1926 to 1934, using players developed in their farm system. Within 10 years, every major league club was busy setting up a farm system of its own.

In 1942 Rickey moved on to the Dodgers. He created a spring training complex at Vero Beach, Florida, where hundreds of players could be evaluated and instructed. Under Rickey's guidance the Dodgers organization grew to become one of the finest in baseball, winning seven pennants in 10 years between 1947 and 1956.

Q: How did Branch Rickey help force baseball's expansion?

A: After revolutionizing baseball by developing the farm system, Rickey tried to change the game one more time. He had been pushing baseball owners for years to expand beyond 16 major league teams, but the owners resisted.

In 1959 Rickey announced plans to form a third major league called the Continental League. This league, he explained, would have teams in 20 cities not properly served by the National and American leagues—cities like New York (whose two NL teams had left for California the year before), Atlanta, Houston, and Toronto.

"Twenty great cities cannot be ignored," Rickey said.

Recognizing the threat this plan posed, major league owners moved quickly to prevent Rickey's organization from cutting into their business. They announced expansion of the current leagues into the key cities Rickey had targeted for his new league. The cities were chosen to hurt Rickey's new league before it got off the ground.

Branch Rickey started his major league career as a catcher with the St. Louis Browns and New York Yankees. He went on to manage the Browns and Cardinals, but it was in the front office of the St. Louis Cardinals and Brooklyn Dodgers that Rickey's genius fully showed.

Q: To which cities did baseball spread?

A: In 1961 the major leagues added two new teams to the American League: the Los Angeles Angels (who eventually moved to Anaheim), and the new Washington Senators (who became the Texas Rangers in 1972; the original Senators had already moved to Bloomington, Minnesota, to become the Twins). This marked the first time that new teams had joined the league since the two-league system came into being in 1901. But it was only the beginning of baseball's expansion period.

The following year National League baseball returned to New York with the creation of the Mets, and Houston got a team called the Colt .45s (later renamed the Astros). In 1966 the Braves moved from Milwaukee to Atlanta, and in 1965 the Athletics moved from Kansas City to Oakland, giving the Bay Area one team in each league. Then in 1969 new teams were established in Kansas City (the Royals) and Seattle (Pilots). The team in Seattle lasted only one year before moving to Milwaukee as the Brewers.

The National League set a precedent by awarding one of its expansion teams to Montreal—the first major league team in Canada. The new team was called the Expos and was the only team to have its games broadcast in French. The second NL addition was the San Diego Padres.

Baseball had grown from 16 teams to 24, spread across the country. Facing the 1969 season with 12-team leagues, owners reorganized by dividing each league into two six-team divisions. Division winners would meet in a playoff to determine who would play in the World Series. Thus, after

operating in the same mold for more than six decades, baseball was breaking with the past.

Q: How did Branch Rickey come to choose Jackie Robinson to make civil rights history?

A: Jackie Robinson was chosen by Branch Rickey to break the color barrier because Rickey knew that Robinson had the strength of character, not just the talent, to overcome the taunts that would come.

In 1945 Robinson was playing for the Kansas City Monarchs of the Negro American League. At the same time, in Brooklyn, general manager Branch Rickey of the Dodgers was hatching a plan that few people knew about. Rickey had begun to send scouts all around the country to find the best black ballplayer. Publicly, Rickey said he was scouting talent for a new black professional league he wanted to start. The truth, however, was that he was looking for one special player— a player who had not only great baseball skill but also the

Jackie Robinson of the Negro league's Kansas City Monarchs in 1945. Two years later he wore a Brooklyn Dodgers uniform to make history.

determination and courage to break the color line and become the major league's first African American player.

Rickey's scouts recommended Robinson, 26, the former UCLA football star. Rickey met with Robinson in Rickey's Ebbets Field office in late August 1945. Rickey advised Robinson on how to handle the racism he might face from some players and fans, explaining during the three-hour meeting that he was looking for a man who could take the abuse and insults without incident.

Robinson, a former Army lieutenant, listened intently and then asked, "Mr. Rickey, do you want a ballplayer who's afraid to fight back?"

Rickey replied: "I want a ballplayer with guts enough not to fight back."

Robinson swore he could handle the job, and he was soon playing for the Dodgers' top farm club in Montreal in 1946. He led the International League with a .349 batting average and took the Royals to the minor league title. The time had come for Robinson to join the Brooklyn Dodgers.

Q: How did Robinson's success affect baseball integration?

A: Having signed a contract with the Brooklyn Dodgers, Robinson was in the Dodgers' starting lineup for the team in the season opener against the Boston Braves at Ebbets Field on April 15, 1947. When the crowd of 25,623 saw him take the field with his teammates, Robinson forever changed the game of baseball; some would say he also forever changed America. Although the Brooklyn first baseman that day went hitless in three at-bats against Johnny Sain, the first of Robinson's 1,382 major-league games was a matter of record.

Robinson's first season certainly had its ugly moments of racial intolerance, but it was largely a success. In 1947 he batted .297 and led the National League with 29 stolen bases. He was selected as the first-ever Rookie of the Year (an award that now bears his name) and helped the Dodgers win the NL pennant. Two years later he was the league's Most Valuable Player, hitting .342 with 124 runs batted in and 37 stolen bases.

Still, Robinson's presence did not exactly open the floodgates of integration in Major League Baseball. The Dodgers signed several Negro league stars in the next two years, including Roy Campanella and Don Newcombe, and Cleveland's Larry Doby broke the American League color line in July 1947. But full integration came slowly, and many teams remained all white for years. Most notably, the New York Yankees were not integrated until 1955, when Elston Howard made his debut in pinstripes.

Robinson would help lead the Dodgers to seven pennants in the 10 years he played for them. When he was inducted into the Hall of Fame in 1962, he broke that color barrier as well, becoming the first black man to be inducted. Robinson died at 53 years old, in 1972.

Larry Doby of the Cleveland Indians became the first black player in the American League, three months after Jackie Robinson broke the color line with the Brooklyn Dodgers. Doby became a seven-time All-Star and a Hall of Famer and twice led the league in home runs.

Breaking New Ground

Q: Who was the first black manager?

A: Frank Robinson became the first African American hired to manage a major league team when he took the reins of the Cleveland Indians for the 1975 season.

Actually, the superstar outfielder (he won baseball's Triple Crown in 1966 when he led the American League in batting average, home runs, and runs batted in) and designated hitter had been named the Indians' player-manager back on October 3, 1974, at the conclusion of the previous season. President Gerald Ford described Robinson's appointment as "welcome news for baseball fans across the nation." But his official on-field debut came in the 1975 season opener against the New York Yankees, on April 8.

Robinson the manager penciled himself in as the designated hitter in the lineup that day. Jackie Robinson's widow, Rachel, threw out the cer-emonial first pitch at Municipal Stadium. And in his first at bat in the first inning, Frank Robinson belted a solo home run off New York's Doc Medich for his 575th career home run. Robinson's blast helped the Indians beat the Yankees 5–3 in his debut. Cleveland struggled, however, to a 79–80 record and a fourth-place finish in the American League East by season's end.

Frank Robinson's baseball know-how and fierce competitiveness led to the job of player-manager with the Cleveland Indians in 1975. In 1976 Robbie's Indians had an 81–78 record, their best finish since 1968.

Q: Whose Hall of Fame speech helped champion the forgotten Negro leaguers?

A: Ted Williams was an outspoken figure throughout his playing career. Ever opinionated, frequently contrary, he never shied away from speaking his mind. This was never more evident than on the day in the summer of 1966 when he was inducted into the Hall of Fame. With the whole baseball world watching, Williams chose to bring up the issue of racism in baseball during his induction speech in Cooperstown.

He said: "I hope that someday Satchel Paige and Josh Gibson will be voted into the Hall of Fame as symbols of the great players who are not here only because they were not given the chance." Williams's courageous speech helped start the movement to induct former Negro league players into the Hall. Five years later the newly established Committee on Negro Baseball Leagues began inducting Negro league players into the Baseball Hall of Fame, beginning with Paige in 1971 and Gibson in 1972.

Paige's plaque of recognition was to be hung in a new and different part of the National Baseball Museum, one that would be set aside for the fabled Negro league heroes. Some observers regarded this as a form of segregation, keeping the Negro league stars apart from the other immortals.

"I'm proud wherever they put me in the Hall of Fame," said Paige.

Talk of a separate section would instead give way to a special Negro leagues exhibit, and upon his induction in the summer of 1971, Paige's plaque was placed alongside those of all the other inductees.

Among other black stars later elected to the Hall are James "Cool Papa" Bell, the speedster who played in the Negro, Mexican, and Dominican leagues from 1922 to '48, and Buck Leonard, first baseman and captain of the Homestead Grays from 1934 to '48.

Q: Which team fielded the first all-black starting lineup?

A: In addition to winning games, the Pittsburgh Pirates were breaking new ground as an equal opportunity employer. During their 1971 world championship season, they often fielded a starting lineup with more minority players—including both blacks and Latinos—than whites.

On September 1, 1971, Danny Murtaugh, the Pittsburgh manager, wrote out a lineup card for a game against Philadelphia with the first all-minority lineup in the 100-year history of major league ball: Rennie Stennett, 2b; Gene Clines, cf; Roberto Clemente, rf; Willie Stargell, lf; Manny Sanguillen, c; Dave Cash, 3b; Al Oliver, 1b; Jackie Hernandez, ss; Dock Ellis, p.

In the Pirates' 10–7 victory that day, six players got two hits each, but the lineup did not remain intact for long. Ellis was knocked out after one and one-third innings pitched.

James "Cool Papa" Bell, a star in the Negro leagues, was one of the fastest runners in baseball history. It was said he could turn off the light and be in bed before the room got dark.

Shining Stars

Q: Who blazed a trail for Hispanic players in the major leagues?

A: Puerto Rican native Roberto Clemente broke into the major leagues with the Pittsburgh Pirates in 1955 and made inroads for Latin American players and others from around the world.

Although he hit a modest .255 that season, it quickly became apparent that he possessed remarkable defensive skills and an uncanny ability to hit. He batted .311 in 1956 and won four batting titles in an 18-year career in which he batted .317 in all. He also led the National League in outfield assists four times, and he won 12 consecutive Gold Glove awards.

Clemente's final hit of the 1972 season was the 3,000th of his illustrious career. It also was his last. Tragically, Clemente died in a plane crash that New Year's Eve while helping to bring relief supplies to the victims of a devastating earthquake in Nicaragua.

A short time later the mandatory five-year waiting period for the Baseball Hall of Fame was waived and Clemente was elected on a whopping 93 percent of the ballots.

Clemente not only was the first Latino Hall of Famer, but he also helped to open doors for scores of international players to follow. Today Major League Baseball rosters are dotted with players from all over the world.

Roberto Clemente's clutch home run in the 1971 World Series propelled the Pirates to the championship. Clemente paved the way for young Hispanic players by helping them adjust to life in the big leagues.

Q: When did the Latino talent explosion occur?

A: The Hispanic presence in major league ball had been quietly growing since the 1970s. A small handful of players had appeared before that, most notably Roberto Clemente from Puerto Rico. In the 1990s, however, their numbers multiplied. From 1990 to 2001, according to Northeastern University's Center for the Study of Sport in Society, the number of Hispanic major leaguers swelled to 26 percent from 13 percent.

In fact, in 1998, for the first time, the Most Valuable Players of both leagues were born in Latin American countries: for the National League, Sammy Sosa from the Dominican Republic; for the American League, Puerto Rico native Juan Gonzalez.

Dating to the 1860s, baseball has a long and rich tradition in Cuba, the Dominican Republic, Puerto Rico, and other Latin American lands. Some major league teams used to have spring training camps and play exhibition games in Latin American countries. But not until about the same time Jackie Robinson broke the game's color barrier in 1947 did foreign-born Hispanics catch scouts' eyes. Over the coming decades some would shine as among baseball's best, including Hall of Famers Juan Marichal (Dominican Republic), Rod Carew (Panama), Orlando Cepeda (Puerto Rico), and Tony Perez (Cuba).

Hispanics continued to thrive, if not in numbers, then in stature, into the 1990s. That's when economics led to a tremendous influx of talented Latin players who could be signed for far less money than what U.S. high school and college prospects commanded. By the end of the decade, virtually every major league franchise had opened baseball academies in the Dominican Republic, by far the region's greatest pool of talent. Besides Sosa, the island nation had by then produced such marquee names as Pedro Martinez, Manny Ramirez, and Miguel Tejada.

Hispanics took center stage at the 1998 All-Star Game. The teams included Sosa, Gonzalez, Alex Rodriguez, Ivan Rodriguez, brothers Roberto and Sandy Alomar, Moises Alou, Andres Galarraga, Javier Lopez, and Edgar Renteria. Second baseman Roberto Alomar—on the strength of his home run, walk, stolen base, and superb defensive play—won the All-Star Game Most Valuable Player Award.

Major league players born in Latin America, such as the Dominican Republic's Miguel Tejada, made up nearly 25 percent of major league rosters on Opening Day 2005. The Dominican Republic had 91 players, followed by Venezuela with 46 and Puerto Rico with 34.

The Rescuers

Q: Which National League outfielder became a contemporary hero in 1976?

A: In the midst of the United States' year-long bicentennial celebration, Chicago Cubs center fielder Rick Monday became a modern-day hero when he grabbed an American flag from two men who were trying to set it on fire in the outfield at Dodger Stadium during a game on April 25.

Monday had taken his position in center field for the fourth inning when he noticed the protestors jump out of the stands in possession of the flag. When Monday saw one of the men fumbling with a lighter and he realized what they were trying to do, he sprinted toward them and snatched away the flag before it could be set on fire.

"They couldn't see me coming from behind, but I could see that one had lit a match," Monday said.

Monday safely delivered the flag to the bullpen as security guards arrested the trespassers. The 25,167 fans rewarded him with a standing ovation as the Dodger Stadium message board flashed, "Rick Monday, You Made A Great Play!" Then the crowd burst out singing "God Bless America."

Monday's rescue made national headlines, and he was hailed with praise. The Illinois legislature proclaimed May 4 as "Rick Monday Day" at Wrigley Field, and he received a commendation from President Gerald Ford. He also was named grand marshal of the Flag Day parade in Chicago.

Ironically, the outfielder was traded to the Dodgers the following year and played in Los Angeles for the last eight seasons of his 19-year career. In Game Five of the 1981 National League Championship Series against the Montreal Expos, Monday's dramatic ninth-inning home run off Steve Rogers won the pennant for the Dodgers.

Chicago Cubs outfielder Rick Monday became a national hero of sorts—and received a bicentennial commendation from President Gerald Ford—when he rescued an American flag that two protesters were attempting to burn in center field at Dodger Stadium in Los Angeles in 1976.

Q: **Which American League batting champion rescued two women from Boston Harbor in 2005?**

A: Nomar Garciaparra of the Los Angeles Dodgers rescued two women from Boston Harbor on October 7, 2005.

The former Red Sox shortstop was in his Charlestown, Massachusetts, apartment with his wife and uncle. At about 10:30 PM they heard a splash and a scream. Garciaparra went to the balcony of his apartment and saw that a woman had fallen into the water. He darted out the door and sprinted 100 yards to the marina. During that time, another woman had fallen off the pier as she knelt down to help her friend.

"I didn't know what I would do when I got there," says Garciaparra. "It was instinct that made me run to help."

The shortstop tried to open the marina door, but it was locked. So he climbed over a fence and jumped down into the cold water of Boston Harbor. Garciaparra reached the women, who were struggling to keep afloat. The two-time American League batting champion took both women in his arms and swam to a dock.

"I was holding them and saying, 'Don't let go,'" he says.

Garciaparra's uncle, Victor Campos, had also jumped in the harbor. He held a boat's ladder and helped Garciaparra pull the women out of the water. Garciaparra's wife, former soccer star Mia Hamm, went to a nearby tavern to get help and ask someone there to get the key to open the marina door.

One woman's eye was badly swollen. The other had a big lump on her forehead. But Garciaparra realized the women would be OK when one of them recognized the former Red Sox star. "One of them said, 'Oh, my God, you're Nomar Garciaparra! I can't believe you stuck around [Boston].' And I said, 'Lucky for you I did.'"

CHAPTER 2

THE BALLPARK EXPERIENCE

Whether the ballpark is called a stadium or a field or is named for a vainglorious owner or faceless corporation, just like people, it is what is inside that really counts. Few things in life can match the heightened awareness of senses associated with the stadium experience. The smells of hot dogs and popcorn; the sounds of a vendor's hawking call; that first glimpse of the diamond; the splendor of the green grass and the coffee color of the infield dirt. Talk about love at first sight—one never tires of a baseball field coming into view. On the field, the players provide entertainment not only through their dazzling pitching, hitting, and fielding exploits, but also with an array of colorful quirks and head-scratching superstitions. Baseball flakes are like snowflakes: No two are the same. Baseball traditionalists may yearn for the prehistoric times before mascots roamed the stadium sod (or artificial turf). Back then there were no electronic scoreboards exhorting fans when and what to cheer. Yet the allure of the ballpark experience remains much as it has always been: the eternal hope upon hope of finally, just this once, Dear G-d, perhaps I might catch a foul ball; and the anticipation of seeing something you have never seen before.

Above: Beer here! Get your water! Ice cold soda!

Left: Wrigley Field, home of the Chicago Cubs since 1916. It was called Weeghman Park, after owner Charles Weeghman. In 1926 the park was renamed Wrigley Field, after William Wrigley, the chewing gum magnate, gained controlling interest of the team in 1921.

Turnstiles and Vendors

Q: When did fans first pay admission to games?

A: The first known games that fans paid to watch were held at Fashion Race Course in what is now Corona, Queens, in New York, on July 20, 1858. Admission was 50 cents. The money went toward field maintenance for a three-game series played between all-star teams from New York City and Brooklyn.

The 1,500 fans attending the first game were not disappointed. Brooklyn jumped out to a 7–3 lead, but New York tied the score with four runs in the fifth inning and seven more in the sixth inning on their way to a 22–18 victory. Brooklyn's second baseman Johnny Holder hit the game's only home run, a blast to deep center field "which drew forth thunders of applause," reported the *New York Clipper*.

After paying out the game's expenses, the sponsors donated the $70 surplus to the New York and Brooklyn fire departments. Although the game was held for charity, entrepreneurs realized that fans would pay to see the best players compete, and the amateur game would be transformed forever when, 11 years later, the Cincinnati Red Stockings became the first admittedly all-professional ball club.

Q: Who is considered the grandfather of ballpark concessions?

A: Harry M. Stevens created an empire selling hot dogs, peanuts, soft drinks, and beer at the ballparks.

The London-born Stevens attended his first baseball game near Columbus, Ohio, in 1887. Unable to identify the players, he

The purchase of baseball tickets is now a sophisticated transaction—and much more expensive—than when fans first began lining up for "two behind the plate."

produced and sold the first scorecards. Soon his scorecards were being sold in ballparks throughout the Northeast, and by 1894 he was securing concession rights at these parks, too.

In 1901 he hit the big time by persuading New York Giants owner John T. Brush to permit his army of roving vendors to work the grandstands at the Polo Grounds (the Giants' home park). That spring, after noting that food sales declined in colder weather, he decided to try selling a steamed frankfurter in a bun that would later be named the hot dog. To keep busy in the winter months, Stevens also garnered the concessionaire contract at Madison Square Garden. He prospered as a businessman so much that in 1911, when a fire at the Polo Grounds severely damaged the grandstands, Brush obtained a cash loan from Stevens to rebuild.

The Stevens empire expanded into major league ballparks beyond New York, and then to other sporting venues, notably horse racing. Harry Payne Whitney of Saratoga Race Track once said that Stevens "parlayed a bag of peanuts into a million dollars." That monetary figure, of course, is a lowball estimate. Stevens died in New York in 1934, but his corporation, the Harry M. Stevens Company, continued to thrive, serving baseball fans as a family business until 1994.

Today fans can purchase ballpark regional specialties such as a bratwurst in Milwaukee, garlic fries in San Francisco, crab cakes in Baltimore, Rocky Mountain oysters in Colorado, and sushi in Seattle.

Going, going, gone! Whether you like yours with ketchup and onions, or mustard and sauerkraut, baseball and hot dogs go together like America and apple pie.

Q: What's the most popular ballpark food item?

A: Hot dogs have been a popular snack food item at baseball games for over a century. A trip to the ballpark just would not be complete without one. Fans can get their hot dogs at stands throughout the ballpark or from vendors roaming the seating areas. According to the Aramark Corporation, which provides concession services at 14 major league stadiums, hot dogs are the food item sold most often at ballparks nationwide —followed by peanuts, ice cream, nachos, cotton candy, pretzels, french fries, and pizza. In fact, 52,678 hot dogs, many smothered in mustard and ketchup, were sold at $1 apiece in Philadelphia's Citizens Bank Park during a promotion on April 9, 2006.

Having a Ball

Q: When did fans start keeping baseballs hit into the stands?

A: It was on April 29, 1916, when the Chicago Cubs' new owner, Charles Weeghman, introduced a baseball policy that remains popular today: Fans were allowed to keep baseballs that were hit into the stands at Weeghman Park (later to be renamed Wrigley Field). The decision followed an incident between a fan and park attendants that escalated to a scuffle after the fan refused to give up a foul ball.

Not all clubs went along with Weeghman's new policy. According to a July 14 report in the *Chicago Tribune*, the visiting Philadelphia Phillies requested compensation for eight baseballs hit into the stands and not returned during batting practice.

Since that time, team owners have grown to appreciate the goodwill that results when the average fan catches a foul ball to take home.

Q: On average, how many foul balls are hit in a game?

A: During the average major league game, 50 foul balls are hit into a crowd of about 31,000 people. So the odds of a particular fan catching two foul balls at one game are pretty long. That makes what happened to a fan named Tobey Roland quite astonishing.

In June 2006 at McAfee Coliseum, Roland caught foul balls off the bat of Adam Melhuse on consecutive pitches. Roland was sitting in his seat in Section

A fan's ability to catch a foul ball involves concentration, aggressiveness, timing, athleticism, balance, hand-eye coordination, and lots of luck.

219, Row 5, watching the Oakland Athletics beat the visiting Seattle Mariners. In the bottom of the seventh inning, Melhuse, a left-handed batter, hit two foul pop-ups between home plate and the third-base dugout. Roland, who was wearing a glove, rose to catch the two foul balls over the course of 19 seconds.

Remarkably, this coincidence has happened before. The same fan caught a foul ball on successive pitches on September 3, 2003, at Dodger Stadium. That surreal occurence actually drew recognition in the Bizarre Moment category in that year's MLB.com This Year in Baseball Awards.

In a scarier incident, Philadelphia Phillies star Richie Ashburn fouled off two consecutive pitches that hit the same woman in the stands during an at-bat on August 17, 1957. Alice Roth, the wife of *Philadelphia Bulletin* sports editor Earl Roth, took her grandsons to see the Phillies play the New York Giants at Shibe Park. Ashburn's line drive into the box seats behind third base struck Roth, breaking her nose. After a short delay in which officials tended to the injured Roth, play resumed … and Ashburn fouled off a pitch that struck Roth as she was being carted off on a stretcher.

Another case of "foul play" occurred in the ninth inning of Baltimore's game against Minnesota in September 2006. Jay Gibbons, an Orioles outfielder, fouled a ball straight back over the screen behind the plate—and into his wife Laura's ribs.

"She's a little bruised up. She's going to be OK," said Gibbons.

During the 2005 National League Division Series, the same fan caught two of the biggest home runs in Houston Astros history. Shaun Dean, a 25-year-old comptroller for a construction company, who was sitting in the firm's seats and wearing a glove, snared Lance Berkman's grand slam in the eighth inning of Game 4 against the Atlanta Braves. About three hours later, in the 18th inning, Dean caught Chris Burke's walk-off shot. Dean later gave Burke his home run ball.

"Everyone was congratulating me, patting me on the back," Dean told the *Houston Chronicle*. "I had several people say I should buy a lottery ticket or go to Vegas."

Jay Gibbons of the Baltimore Orioles once fouled off a pitch into the stands, and the ball struck his wife, Laura, in the ribs.

Edifice Complex

Q: Which team played in the first domed stadium?

A: The Houston Astros were the first baseball team to play its home games indoors. The domed stadium, called the Astrodome, was also the first stadium with a field covered in artificial grass known as AstroTurf.

Q: When did old-style ballparks come back in vogue?

A: On April 6, 1992, the Baltimore Orioles took baseball back to the future. At the season's home opener, the team christened its new ballpark, Oriole Park at Camden Yards. Besides generating rave reviews and sold-out crowds, the stadium became the prototype for a new generation of "retro" venues around Major League Baseball.

Camden Yards, constructed on 85 acres at a cost of $110 million, has state-of-the-art scoreboards, grandstands, concessions, clubhouses, and other amenities. Yet it is designed in the style of charming, turn-of-the-20th-century, downtown ballparks that were

Houston's Astrodome, the first domed stadium, was also the first stadium to have a field covered with synthetic turf. The original playing surface actually was a natural grass field, but the grass could not sustain its growth indoors.

The Astrodome, dubbed the Eighth Wonder of the World, opened in April 1965 to 47,876 curious fans (including the president of the United States, Lyndon Johnson), all of whom had come to watch an exhibition game between the Astros and the New York Yankees. Mickey Mantle got the park's first hit and its first home run. As if the dome was not enough, gimmicks included a scoreboard pyrotechnic display after each Astros home run.

integral centers of their communities. Steel, rather than concrete trusses, an arched brick facade, a sunroof over the sloped upper deck, an asymmetrical playing field, and a natural grass field are some of the nostalgic niceties.

Fenway Park (Boston Red Sox), Wrigley Field (Chicago Cubs), Ebbets Field (Brooklyn Dodgers), Crosley Field (Cincinnati Reds), and the Polo Grounds (New York Giants) were retro parks that inspired the designers of Oriole Park. Other retro parks that followed Camden Yards' lead over the next decade included Jacobs Field (Cleveland Indians), Safeco Field (Seattle Mariners), and Great American Ballpark (Cincinnati Reds).

Q: What happens to old stadiums?

A: Every great ballplayer must someday hang up his spikes, and every great stadium must eventually sit empty or yield to the wrecking ball.

Toronto's not-so-great Exhibition Stadium, the Jays' home from 1977 to 1989, has not been razed. It is still used for concerts and other events. Minnesota's Metropolitan Stadium, home of the Twins from 1961 to 1981, was demolished in 1984, and the Mall of America—the world's largest shopping center— has been built in its place.

A number of other storied parks are long gone, too. Ebbets Field in Brooklyn and the Polo Grounds in New York, which were leveled by the same wrecking ball in 1960 and 1964, respectively, are now the home of public housing projects. Connie Mack Stadium in Philadelphia and the first Busch Stadium in St. Louis are vacant lots.

Some old ballparks have been memorialized. The site of Forbes Field is now part of the University of Pittsburgh campus; the centerfield wall still stands, and home plate sits beneath a piece of Lucite set in the floor of the Forbes Quadrangle. Whole sections of Cincinnati's Crosley Field have been moved to a ball field in Blue Ash, Ohio, where charity and commemorative games are sometimes played.

As for Memorial Stadium in Baltimore, it was demolished in April 2001, and the next summer, its broken-up concrete was used to build an oyster reef in Chesapeake Bay.

On his 1973 album *Ol' Blue Eyes Is Back*, Frank Sinatra sings a song by composer Joe Raposo called "There Used to Be a Ballpark," which begins with these lyrics:

And there used to be a ballpark
Where the field was warm and green
And the people played their crazy game
With a joy I'd never seen.

Baltimore's Memorial Stadium gave way to Oriole Park at Camden Yards, which opened in 1992 and became the prototype for a new generation of "retro" venues among Major League Baseball.

Pomp and Circumstance

Q: What was the most outrageous ballpark promotion ever?

A: "Disco Demolition Night" was not a sound idea. Bill Veeck's son, Mike, hated disco music. He had an idea to boost attendance for a doubleheader on July 12, 1979, between the Chicago White Sox and the Detroit Tigers: Use a stick of dynamite to blow up and burn a crate of disco records. Fans bringing a disco record to burn were sold tickets for 98 cents. The game at Comiskey Park was a sellout. Fans brought so many vinyl discs that through-out the game LPs and 45s were flying across the outfield like Frisbees, causing Detroit outfielder Ron LeFlore to wear a batting helmet on defense.

Between games, Steve Dahl, a popular local radio disc jockey, set fire to the disco records on the field as planned. But the promotion went awry as thousands of fans stormed the field, throwing beer and cherry bombs, setting fire to the batting cage, and eventually tearing up the field so badly the umpires had to declare the second game forfeited.

A promotion at Comiskey Park in 1979 went awry when fans set fire to disco records on the field, as planned, between games of a doubleheader against the Detroit Tigers but then refused to return to their seats. The second game had to be forfeited.

Mayhem ensued as fans refused to leave the bonfire and return to their seats. They ran around the field for 45 minutes.

"It was not a riot," Jim Keen, a fan who was there, told the *Chicago Tribune* in 1989. "We were just sliding into bases, running around and acting like the Sox just won the pennant. They had not won one in 20 years, so we figured we'd never get a real chance."

Despite this debacle, Bill Veeck never met a promotion he did not like. Daring and inventive, he brought fun and a hustler's mentality to baseball as owner of the Cleveland Indians (1946–49), St. Louis Browns (1951–53), and Chicago White Sox twice (1959–61, 1976–80). His teams always broke attendance records with door prizes, fan participation, and ingenious promotional schemes.

Veeck introduced to baseball the exploding scoreboard, bat day, and player names on the backs of uniforms. His many memorable innovations included fan participation by letting fans manage his teams for a game, and putting a shower in the bleachers to cool fans off during hot days.

Q: What are some popular stadium rally songs among fans?

A: It has been said that music calms the savage beast. But when combined with the fast-paced, unpredictable tempo of sports, music also excites and invigorates. Professional and minor league baseball teams throughout the country use music to get the crowd fired up to fever pitch.

One foot-stomping tune that resonates in stadiums and ballparks is "Rock and Roll, Part 2" by Gary Glitter. This popular

hit from the 1970s returned to the public consciousness thanks to its heavy play at sporting events.

The song's national coming-out party occurred during the 1991 World Series at the Metrodome in Minnesota. It was played over the public address system when the home team Twins scored a run. It really stoked the crowd by letting them chant "Hey" in unison on every other fourth beat.

It had originally become popular in the Twin Cities earlier that spring when the North Stars reached the Stanley Cup finals. When the Twins reached the American League playoffs, Joe Johnston, then the team's game production manager, decided to play the number.

"It's a crowd-pleaser, a real rally song," Johnston said. "The fans automatically related to the music, and when they yelled 'Hey!' and the homer hankies flew, it was awesome."

Some other fan anthems that have stood the test of time include "We Will Rock You" and "We Are the Champions," both by the pop group Queen, which are sung at a number of stadiums, and "Na Na Hey Hey Kiss Him Goodbye," by the group Steam, a Comiskey Park favorite since 1969.

Homer hankies and a favorite rally song are Minnesota's vaunted home-field advantage. The Twins won all eight World Series games played in 1987 and 1991 in their Metrodome, site of the first Series game ever played indoors.

Mascot Mania

Ted Giannoulas, the Famous Chicken, aka the original San Diego Chicken, may ruffle feathers on and off the field, but the originality of his antics were a giant step for team mascots everywhere.

Q: Who was Major League Baseball's first professional mascot?

A: A college student named Ted Giannoulas, who answered a radio station advertisement for someone to wear a chicken suit at a San Diego Padres game, skittered onto the field at Jack Murphy Stadium on April 9, 1974, becoming the first paid big-league mascot. Despite a public protest by Ray Kroc, the team's owner, the San Diego Chicken became an institution, and the age of major league mascots had dawned.

Soon after Giannoulas began working at Padres games for two dollars an hour while employed for radio station KGB in San Diego, the Chicken grew in popularity. In 1979 he wanted to take his act on the road—in the tradition of ballpark comedians like Max Patkin and Al Schacht—but KGB wanted a share of the profits, and the radio station sued Giannoulas. He won the case, but with the stipulation that he redesign his costume and change the character's name. It is now called the Famous Chicken.

Giannoulas had been barred from performing in San Diego's stadium for two months during the court proceedings, and his return was highly publicized. He was brought into the stadium by an armored truck and was inside a giant papier-mâché egg. The Padres players gently placed him on the infield turf, and then he hatched

from the egg to tremendous applause from the 47,000 fans. Television programming was interrupted in San Diego to bring this event live to local viewers.

By 1982 the Famous Chicken was incorporated and had five people on the payroll, including an office staff in San Diego that was booking him throughout the country. He traveled with a valet who fluffed his tail feathers, and that year he earned a reported $1 million in appearance fees.

Giannoulas had his detractors as well. Once Lou Piniella, the Yankees outfielder, got so angry at his antics—after striking out—that he complained to the umpire and threw his glove at the Chicken.

"He missed," Giannoulas said, "but that's the kind of day Lou was having."

Q: Who is the most recognizable mascot working today?

A: The Phanatic was the brainchild of the team's marketing department after the 1977 season. The name was inspired by the fanatical Phillies fans that visibly unnerved Los Angeles Dodgers pitcher Burt Hooton during the second inning of Game 3 of the 1977 National League Championship Series. The fans' relentless hooting of each Hooton delivery drove Hooton into losing his control and walk-ing in three runs. (He was yanked from the game, but the Dodgers came back to win.)

Wearing bubble-toed size 20 shoes, the Phanatic debuted at Philadelphia's Veterans Stadium on April 25, 1978. Since then he has been riding around on his all-terrain vehicle before each home game and is at his mischievious best during the game.

The Phanatic has been portrayed by two men. Dave Raymond was the original Phanatic for 16 years. Tom Burgoyne has been the Phanatic's alter ego since 1994. Raymond founded the Mascot Hall of Fame in 2005, and the Phanatic was the first enshrined. Raymond's family is no stranger to hallowed hallways. His father, Harold "Tubby" Raymond, former University of Delaware football coach, is a member of the College Football Hall of Fame.

No mascot working today is more entertaining or more recognized than the Phillie Phanatic (left), though Pirate Parrot, Homer the Brave, and Mr. Met are three wild and zany creations.

Creatures of Habit

Q: Which team was considered the most superstitious?

A: During the 1911 season the New York Giants convinced themselves that a good-luck charm would lead them to the World Series.

MCGRAW, N. Y. NAT'L

New York manager John McGraw gave full credit for the Giants' success in the 1911 National League pennant race to a good-luck charm named "Victory" Faust.

The Giants were in St. Louis, Missouri, to play the Cardinals in July, when a man named Charles V. Faust came to see manager John McGraw. Faust said his middle name was Victory and that a fortune-teller had predicted the Giants would win the National League pennant if he were on the team.

The Giants had been playing poorly, and McGraw wanted to shake things up. He invited Faust to sit on the bench during the game, if it was OK with the players. They agreed and, with a wink, handed the 30-year-old, 6-foot 2-inch Faust a batboy's uniform to wear. The newly relaxed Giants won the game, and Faust, their jinx-breaker, was invited back by the players the next day. The Giants won again and convinced McGraw to let Faust continue to travel with them.

The Giants then maintained a winning streak that carried them into first place. The team began paying all of Faust's traveling expenses (though he did not have a contract), and the Giants won the pennant by seven games over the Cubs.

Late in October McGraw let Faust play in two games after the pennant was clinched. He pitched two innings, giving up two hits and one run for a lifetime 4.50 earned run average. Unfortunately, whatever secret powers Faust possessed were lost during the 1911 World Series, as the Giants fell to the Philadelphia Athletics in six games.

Faust failed to persuade McGraw to let him return for the next season, and for two years tried in vain to be reinstated with the Giants. In December 1914 he was admitted to a mental hospital in Washington, where he died six months later of pulmonary tuberculosis.

In his autobiography, McGraw wrote, "Wherever Charles Faust is today, I want him to know that I give him full credit for winning the National League pennant for the Giants in 1911."

Q: Who is the most superstitious player in the Hall of Fame?

A: Wade Boggs, who collected 3,010 hits during an 18-year career with the Boston Red Sox, New York Yankees, and Tampa Bay Devil Rays, was quite superstitious. A left-handed hitter with a stroke as steady as a metronome, Boggs won five batting titles during the 1980s and set an American League record by rattling off seven consecutive seasons in which he collected at least 200 hits. He posted a lofty .328 lifetime batting average.

Boggs' superstitions nearly overshadowed his hitting prowess. He was called "Chicken Man" by Boston teammate Jim Rice because he ate chicken before every game, and though he is not Jewish, he scratched a Hebrew word "Chai," meaning "life," in the dirt of the batters' box with his cleat before each at-bat.

He busied himself with more than 80 different pregame and postgame rituals, from leaving his house to come to the ballpark at exactly the same time each day (1:47 PM for a 7:05 night game), to the precise number of ground balls

he fielded in warm-ups (150), to his after-game meal (two hot dogs, a bag of barbecue potato chips, and a glass of iced tea).

His daily idiosyncrasies were mind-boggling. For night games he would never take the field until the stadium clock struck 4:17 PM; he took batting practice at 5:17 PM and ran wind sprints at 6:17. These peculiarities were carried out in a seemingly unconscious manner.

Due to his passion for poultry, Boggs's wife, Debbie, developed over 40 chicken recipes, even publishing a cookbook called *Fowl Tips*.

On August 7, 1999, he became the only player to hit a home run for his 3,000th career hit. He retired after that season and was elected to the Hall of Fame in 2005, in his first year of eligibility.

Wade Boggs belts a home run in the 1989 All-Star game. Boggs, who posted a lofty .328 lifetime batting average, was known for his superstitions as much as his hitting.

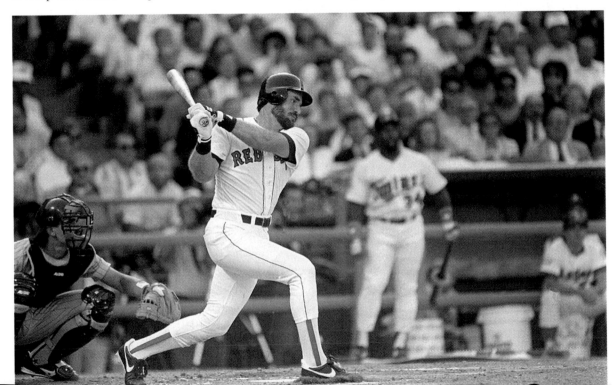

Laughing Matters

Q: Whose wardrobe gaffe made for one of baseball's most embarrassing moments?

A: During his major league baseball career as a utility infielder, Steve Lyons did not play much. But when he did, you knew it by his dirt-encrusted, grass-stained uniform.

In a 1990 game against Detroit, Lyons was making a rare start at first base for the Chicago White Sox. At bat, he attempted to hit safely by dragging a bunt. The ball trickled perfectly between the pitcher's mound and first base. Realizing that the play would be close, Lyons dived headlong into first, creating a massive dirt cloud.

"Safe!" barked the umpire, setting off an argument with Tigers players. While the dust cleared, Lyons was feeling uncomfortable because dirt was falling down the inside of his uniform bottoms. So he matter-of-factly pulled his pants down and brushed off the dirt. Lyons soon realized he had dropped his drawers on national television! He immediately hitched up his britches, suitably embarrassed.

Some teammates wondered if Steve, who is known as "Psycho" for his down-and-dirty attitude, had not pulled an intentional prank. "I may be off the wall, but I'm not stupid," he insists.

Luckily, Steve heeded his mother's advice and, at the time, was wearing clean shorts under his uniform pants. "She's the one who always told me to wear clean underwear in case something happened and I had to show them to strangers."

Former player turned broadcaster Steve "Psycho" Lyons (center) became the butt of jokes in 1990. Before Lyons, said a writer, "no one had ever dropped his drawers on the field. Not Wally Moon. Not Blue Moon Odom. Not even Heinie Manush."

Q: Who pulled off the wildest "hidden ball" trick ever?

A: There were three games left in the 1987 season, and the Williamsport (Pa.) Bills were in seventh place in the Class AA Eastern League, 28 games out of first place. Catcher Dave Bresnahan was bored and wanted to stir things up. So he peeled a potato before a game against Reading and kept it in a spare catcher's mitt in the dugout.

In the fifth inning, with a runner on third base, Bresnahan told the home plate umpire he needed to change mitts. When he came back he had the potato hidden in his glove. As the pitch came in, he switched the potato to his throwing hand, caught the ball, and then threw the potato wildly over the head of the third baseman.

When the Reading runner saw what he thought was the ball rolling into left field, he came jogging home, but was tagged out at the plate by Bresnahan. Because baseball rules state that you cannot fool a runner, the umpire called the runner safe. Dave's team was so mad at the stunt that he was released the next day. Surprised, Bresnahan said he was "just trying to put some fun into the game. I mean, it's not like it was the seventh game of the World Series."

Glossary

AMERICAN LEAGUE CHAMPIONSHIP SERIES (ALCS): A second-round playoff series between the two winning AL Division Series teams. The winner is said to capture the league flag, or pennant, and goes on to the World Series.

AMERICAN LEAGUE DIVISION SERIES (ALDS): A first-round playoff series between the three AL division winners and the wild-card winner (the second-place team with the best record). The two winning teams go on to the American League Championship Series.

ASSIST: Statistic credited to fielders when they throw runners out.

BACKSTOP: A high fence behind home plate that protects spectators and keeps batted or thrown balls within the field of play. Also a slang term for the catcher.

BALK: A variety of potential illegal actions by a pitcher while his foot is on the pitcher's rubber, the umpire will call a balk; all runners advance one base.

BALL: Any pitch outside the strike zone at which a batter does not swing.

BASELINES: Lines extending out from home plate denoting fair and foul territory.

BASE RUNNER: Any player who safely reaches base.

BATTER: An offensive player who comes up to home plate to try to get on base.

BATTER'S BOX: The 6' by 4' rectangle on each side of home plate in which batters must stand when they are hitting.

BATTING AVERAGE: The number of hits divided by the number of at-bats; example: A batter with 7 hits in 21 at-bats has a .333 batting average; this is calculated as 7 (hits) divided by 21 (at-bats).

BOX SCORE: A detailed summary of statistics from a particular game in box form.

BRUSHBACK: A pitch thrown dangerously close to a batter. Also called a duster, close shave, buzz saw, chin music.

BULLPEN: The area where pitchers warm up before and during games, usually located behind the outfield wall.

BUNT: A soft hit resulting from the batter holding the bat out and letting the ball hit it instead of swinging the bat. Also called a dribbler, bleeder, nubber, squib, roller, topper, or trickler.

CATCHER: A defensive player who plays behind home plate and receives pitches from the pitcher.

CENTER FIELDER: A defensive player who is positioned in the center of the outfield.

CHANGE-UP: A slow pitch that is usually thrown after several fast ones to throw off the timing of a batter's swing. A pitcher who throws a successful change-up is said to "pull the string."

CLEANUP: The fourth batter in a lineup is called the cleanup hitter because there are often runners on base for him to drive in and, in that way, "clean up" the bases.

COMPLETE GAME: A game in which a pitcher pitches every inning until the end of the game.

CURVEBALL: A pitch that curves as it reaches the plate. It is thrown by snapping the wrist sharply away from the body as the pitch is released, so the ball spins rapidly and veers down and to the left (if thrown with the right hand) or right (if thrown left-handed). Also in slang known as a breaking ball, hook, bender, biter, crook, downer, yacker, and Uncle Charlie. Dwight Gooden of the Mets had a curve so good players called it Lord Charles.

CUTOFF MAN: An infielder who intercepts a throw from an outfielder when runners are on base. The cutoff man then chooses to throw the ball home, to a base, or hold it.

CYCLE: When a player hits a single, double, triple, and home run in one game.

DIAMOND: Another word for the infield.

DOUBLE: A hit on which the batter reaches second base safely. Also known as a two-bagger.

DOUBLEHEADER: When the same two teams play two games on the same date. Also called a twin bill.

DOUBLE PLAY: When two outs are made by the defense during one play. Known by the offense as a "twin killing" and by the defense as the "pitcher's best friend."

DOUBLE STEAL: A play in which two runners attempt to steal separate bases at the same time.

EARNED RUN: A run scored because of a hit or walk that is charged to a pitcher's earned run average. Runs that score because of errors are unearned.

EARNED RUN AVERAGE (ERA): The average number of earned runs a pitcher allows in a nine-inning game. Calculated as the earned runs multiplied by nine and then divided by the number of innings pitched; example: A pitcher who allows 10 earned runs in 30 innings pitched has an ERA of 3.00; this is calculated as 10 (earned runs) x 9 (innings per game), which equals 90, divided by 30 (innings pitched).

ERROR: A misplay by a fielder that allows a runner to reach base safely or score. Also called a bobble or muff.

FAIR TERRITORY: Any part of the playing field within the baselines.

FASTBALL: A pitch that is thrown with great speed and power. A fastball pitcher with a great "heater" is said to be "throwing smoke." Also called "cheese."

FIRST BASEMAN: A defensive player who is positioned on the right side of the infield near first base. Also called the first sacker.

FLY BALL: A ball hit high in the air, usually to the outfield.

FORCE PLAY: A play in which the runner must advance to the next base.

FORKBALL: A pitch thrown by holding the ball with the first and second fingers spread apart on top and the thumb on the bottom. Forkballs sink sharply because they have little spin on them. Also called a sinker or split-fingered pitch.

FOUL TERRITORY: Any part of the playing field outside the baselines.

GRAND SLAM: A home run with the bases loaded. In slang also called grand salami.

GROUNDBALL: A ball hit on the ground; also called a grounder.

GROUND RULE DOUBLE: When a batter is awarded two bases on a hit that lands in fair territory and bounces over the fence or is interfered with by fans.

HOME PLATE: A rubber slab at which the batter stands to receive pitches; a batter must start and end a trip around the bases at home plate. In slang also called the dish.

HOME RUN: A four-base hit. Balls traveling over the fence are also called a four-bagger, round-tripper, and dinger, among other things.

INFIELD: The part of the field close to home plate that contains the bases; also called a diamond.

INFIELD FLY RULE: If a batter hits a catchable fly ball above the infield while runners are on first and second or on all three bases with fewer than two outs, the batter is automatically out.

INNING: A segment of a baseball game in which each team has a turn at bat; major league games are nine innings, while most youth baseball games are six innings.

KNUCKLEBALL: A slow pitch that is thrown by gripping the ball with the knuckles or fingertips. The ball barely spins after it is released, so breezes and air currents cause it to flutter and jump in unpredictable ways.

LEFT FIELDER: A defensive player who is positioned on the left side of the outfield.

LINE DRIVE: A ball hit in the air straight out from the bat. In slang, a hard-hit line drive is called a frozen rope, pea, bullet, or laser.

MITT: Another term for a catcher's glove.

NATIONAL LEAGUE CHAMPIONSHIP SERIES (NLCS): A second-round playoff series between the two winning NL Division Series teams. The winner is said to capture the league flag, or pennant, and goes on to the World Series.

NATIONAL LEAGUE DIVISION SERIES (NLDS): A first-round playoff series between the three NL division winners and the wild-card winner (the second-place team with the best record). The two winning teams go on to the National League Championship Series.

NO-HITTER: When a pitcher or pitchers on the same team do not allow a base hit during a game. In slang also "no-no."

ON-BASE PERCENTAGE: A batter's number of hits plus walks plus times hit by a pitch divided by the number of at-bats plus walks plus times hit by a pitch.

OUTFIELD: Usually a large, grassy area beyond the infield.

PASSED BALL: When a catcher fails to stop a pitch he could have caught, allowing a base runner to advance. If a passed ball comes on a third strike, the batter can run to first.

PEPPER: A pregame exercise in which one player bunts brisk grounders and line drives to a group of fielders who are standing about 20 feet away. The fielders try to catch the ball and throw it back as quickly as possible. The batter hits the return throw.

PERFECT GAME: A game in which a pitcher pitches every inning and does not let a single batter reach base. In slang also "perfecto."

PITCH: A throw by the pitcher issued to a batter.

PITCHER: A defensive player whose job is to throw the baseball across home plate within the strike zone in an attempt to get the batter out.

PUTOUT: A fielder is credited with a putout for catching a fly ball, pop-up, line drive, or throw that gets an opposing player out. A catcher receives a putout for catching a strikeout.

RIGHT FIELDER: A defensive player who is positioned on the right side of the outfield.

RUNDOWN: A base runner trapped by the defense while between two bases, being chased back and forth, before either being put out or reaching a base safely. A runner caught in this unenviable position is said to be "in a pickle."

SACRIFICE: A bunt or fly ball that allows a runner to score or advance to another base at the expense of the batter, who is out.

SAVE: A pitcher gets credit for a save by finishing a close game while protecting his team's lead. If his team has a big lead, he can get a save by pitching the last three innings.

SCREWBALL: A pitch that usually curves in the opposite direction of a regular curveball. A pitcher throws it by snapping his wrist in the direction towards his body.

SECOND BASEMAN: A defensive player who is positioned on the right side of the infield near second base.

SHORTSTOP: A defensive player who is positioned on the left side of the infield near second base.

SHUTOUT: When a team loses a game without scoring.

SINGLE: A one-base hit. Also called a base knock or bingle.

SLIDER: A pitch thrown with the same motion as a fastball, but the off-center grip applies pressure to the outer half of the ball, creating a natural spin. It looks like a fastball but breaks sharply just as it reaches the plate.

SLUGGING AVERAGE: This is calculated by dividing the total number of bases a player has reached on singles, doubles, triples, and home runs by his number of times at bat.

SPITBALL: An illegal pitch thrown with saliva, sweat, or any slippery substance on the ball that makes it break more sharply.

SQUEEZE PLAY: When a batter attempts to score a runner from third base by bunting the ball. The play is called a suicide squeeze if the runner takes off before the ball is bunted, because if the batter misses the pitch, the runner will most likely be tagged out.

STOLEN BASE: A base gained by advancing when a batter does not hit a pitch.

STRIKE: Any pitch that passes through the strike zone, at which a batter swings and misses, or is so called by the umpire, or is hit into foul territory.

STRIKEOUT: An out recorded when a pitcher delivers three strikes to a batter during one at-bat.

STRIKE ZONE: The area over the plate from the batter's knees up to his armpits. If a pitch passes through this area and the batter doesn't swing, the umpire calls a strike.

TAG: To touch a player with the ball for an out.

TAGGING UP: On a fly ball, waiting until the ball has been caught before leaving a base to advance to the next open base or score a run.

TEXAS LEAGUER: A fly ball that falls just beyond the reach of an infielder and in front of an outfielder for a base hit. Also called a blooper, flare, dying quail, tweener, clunker, or plunker.

THIRD BASEMAN: A defensive player who is positioned on the left side of the infield near third base.

TRIPLE: A three-base hit. Also three-bagger.

WALK: A free trip to first base for a batter after a pitcher has issued four balls during one at-bat. Written as BB in scoring for base on balls. Also called a free pass.

WILD PITCH: An erratic, uncatchable pitch that allows a base runner to advance or score. If a wild pitch occurs on a swinging third strike, the batter can run to first base.

WORLD SERIES: Played each October between the National and American League champions to decide the championship of Major League Baseball.

Further Reading

Books

Adair, Robert K. *The Physics of Baseball, 2nd ed.* New York: Harper Collins, 1994..

Dickson, Paul. *The New Dickson Baseball Dictionary.* New York: Harcourt, 1999.

Falkner, David. *Nine Sides of the Diamond.* New York: Times Books, 1990.

Fimrite, Ron. *The World Series.* New York: Time Inc., 1993.

Fischer, David, and William Taaffe. *Sports of the Times.* New York: St. Martin's Press, 2003.

Gershman, Michael. *Diamonds.* Boston: Houghton Mifflin, 1993.

Hickok, Ralph. *The Encyclopedia of North American Sports History.* New York: Facts on File, 1992.

Honig, Donald. *Baseball When the Grass Was Real.* New York: Coward, McCann & Geoghegan, 1975.

Light, Jonathan Fraser. *The Cultural Encyclopedia of Baseball.* North Carolina: McFarland & Co., 1997.

McCambridge, Michael. *ESPN SportsCentury.* New York: Hyperion, 1999.

Okkonen, Marc. *Baseball Uniforms of the 20th Century.* New York: Sterling Publishing Co., 1991.

Paige, Satchel, and David Lipman. *Maybe I'll Pitch Forever.* New York: Grove Press, 1961.

Pietrusza, David, Matthew Silverman, and Michael Gershman. *Baseball: The Biographical Encyclopedia.* New York: Total Sports, 2000.

Slater, Robert. *Great Jews in Sports, rev. ed.* New York: Jonathan David Publishers, 2000.

Smith, Ron. *The Sporting News' This Day in Sports.* New York: Macmillan, 1994.

Ritter, Lawrence S. *The Glory of Their Times.* New York: Macmillan, 1966.

Thorn, John, Pete Palmer, and Michael Gershman. *Total Baseball, 7th ed.* New York: Total Sports, 2001.

Internet Sites

All-American Girls Professional Baseball League
www.aagpbl.org

Baseball Almanac
www.baseball-almanac.com

Baseball Library
www.baseballlibrary.com

Baseball Reference
www.baseball-reference.com

Little League
www.littleleague.org

Major League Baseball
www.mlb.com

Major League Baseball Players Association
www.mlbplayers.com

The National Baseball Hall of Fame
www.baseballhalloffame.org

The New York Times Article Archive
www.nytimes.com/ref/membercenter/nytarchive.html

The Sporting News Vault
www.sportingnews.com/archives

At the Smithsonian

The Smithsonian Institution in Washington, D.C., boasts an impressive collection of baseball memorabilia and artifacts, such as vintage uniforms, game-used equipment, and photographs. While many items have been donated to the museum at the behest of major league officials, much of the Smithsonian's archived collection comes from private donors and hobbyists.

Located primarily in the American History Museum, the Archive Center is home to many privately donated photographs, sound recordings, films, and texts that are deemed important to the cultural history of America. The archives house various game programs, baseball card collections, ticket stubs, and other baseball-related collectibles. These items serve as invaluable research tools for Smithsonian historians and can often be found on display in one of the institution's many exhibitions.

You don't need to travel to our nation's capital to appreciate the relics of America's national pastime, however. For over 50 years, the Smithsonian Institution Traveling Exhibition Service (SITES) has been committed to bringing the work of the Smithsonian to the country at large. One of the Smithsonian's four outreach programs, SITES uses items from the Smithsonian archives, as well as audio-visual teaching tools, to take entertaining and informative exhibitions to libraries and museums all over the country. Currently, there are two SITES exhibitions that explore both the history of baseball and the sport's impact on our society.

"Beyond Baseball: The Life of Roberto Clemente" is a bilingual exhibition that celebrates the life of the former Pittsburgh Pirates star. Through the display of short essays, photographs, memorabilia, and video clips, "Beyond Baseball" explores how the Puerto Rican–born Clemente became not only one of the most celebrated athletes in the major leagues, but also a symbol of heroism and courage the world over. This exhibition can also be viewed online at http://www.robertoclemente.si.edu.

Important baseball artifacts can also be found on display as part of "Sports: Breaking Records, Breaking Barriers," an exhibit devoted to outstanding athletic feats, as well as to the issues of race and gender that have been at the forefront of sports—and society at large. Items on display in this exhibit include baseballs signed by legendary players such as Babe Ruth, as well as powerhouse teams such as the 1952 Brooklyn Dodgers. This exhibit, which has been on display since October 2004, will conclude its seven-city tour in 2008. To learn more about SITES tours, visit http://www.sites.si.edu or call (202) 633-3168.

There is even more baseball memorabilia on display at the Smithsonian's National Museum of American History. These items, including the bat Stan Musial used to collect his 3,000th hit, as well a ball autographed by the major leagues' first African American player, Jackie Robinson, are part of the "Sports and Lesiure" collection. This collection is home to roughly 6,000 objects that reflect the importance of all sports, not just baseball, in our national history. The non-baseball objects in this gallery represent a cross-section of the many sports, teams, and figures that have captivated the American public. These items include a pair of Muhammad Ali's boxing gloves, a handball used by President Abraham Lincoln, and early conceptions of the in-line roller skate, among others.

Including its sports collections, the National Museum of American History houses more than 3 million artifacts, among them Abraham Lincoln's top hat and the original Star-Spangled Banner. As with all other Smithsonian museums, admission is free. The normal operating hours are 10 AM to 5:30 PM daily. E-mail info@si.edu or phone (202) 633-1000 for more information.

The Smithsonian's National Museum of American History is located on the Mall in Washington, D.C. The museum's collections and scholarship are dedicated to inspiring a broader understanding of the United States and its many peoples. The baseball memorabilia contained in the museum also reflects this diversity.

Index

A

Aaron, Hank, 46, 52, 53, 76, 84, 108, 116, 129
Adair, Robert K., 63
Adcock, Joe, 76, 77
Addy, Bob, 10
Alexander, Grover Cleveland, 24, 69
All-American Girls Professional Baseball League, 160
Allen, Richie, 142
Alomar, Roberto, 70, 185
Alomar, Sandy, 70
Alomar, Sandy Jr., 185
Alou, Moises, 185
American Association, 15, 65, 139
American League, 15, 16, 17, 20, 21, 24, 26, 28, 30, 33, 34, 35, 44, 46, 47, 51, 52, 54, 68, 75, 79, 82, 83, 86, 102, 103, 106, 108, 111, 113, 114, 116, 132, 139, 145, 149, 156, 158, 167, 178, 180, 181, 182, 185, 187, 197, 201
Anderson, Sparky, 145
Arlin, Harold, 36
Ashburn, Richie, 167, 193
Astor, William Waldorf, 31
Astrodome, 194
Atlanta Braves, 15, 74, 90, 95, 108, 116, 117, 180, 193
Atlanta Falcons, 95

B

Bagby, Jim, 84
Bailey, Ed, 108
Baines, Harold, 96, 97
Baker, Dusty, 172
Baker, Frank "Home Run," 24, 34
Baker Field, 37
Ball, Philip, 21
Baltimore Orioles, 16, 71, 76, 82, 83, 87, 115, 116, 134, 193, 194
Baltimore Terrapins, 20, 21
Bando, Sal, 144
Banks, Willie, 87
Barber, Steve, 76
Barnes, Jesse, 96
Barnes, Ross, 14
Barrett, Red, 73
Barrow, Ed, 31, 105
Baseball Writers' Association of America, 120
Baylor, Don, 58
Beck, Erve, 17
Bell, Gus, 108
Bell, James "Cool Papa," 183
Beltran, Carlos, 87
Bender, Charles "Chief," 34
Bennett Park, 18, 19
Berkman, Lance, 193
Biggio, Craig, 58
Bintliff, Burns, 131
Black Sox Scandal, 26, 28, 30
Blomberg, Ron, 54
Blyleven, Bert, 69
Bochte, Bruce, 56
Boggs, Wade, 94, 200, 201
Bonds, Barry, 111, 117, 171
Boone, Bret, 65
Borden, Joe, 14, 114

Boston Bees, 72
Boston Braves, 1, 14, 34, 41, 45, 68, 73, 89, 92, 93, 96, 97, 115, 117, 152, 164, 181
Boston Pilgrims, 16, 114
Boston Red Sox, 17, 18, 19, 23, 31, 32, 33, 41, 46, 47, 52, 54, 66, 68, 75, 76, 79, 91, 92, 99, 106, 107, 110, 111, 114, 116, 117, 128, 129, 149, 155, 158, 159, 164, 165, 187, 194, 200
Boston Red Stockings, 13, 14, 114
Boudreau, Lou, 46, 66, 84
Boyer, Clete, 53, 108
Bradley, George, 14
Bragan, Bobby, 54
Branca, Ralph, 48, 49
Braves Field, 96
Breadon, Sam, 178
Bresnahan, Dave, 202
Brett, George, 112
Briggs Stadium, 158
Brinkman, Joe, 112
Brooklyn Dodgers, 33, 37, 38, 45, 48, 49, 50, 64, 72, 74, 86, 89, 96, 97, 101, 114, 115, 134, 175, 176, 178, 179, 180, 181, 194
Brooklyn Excelsiors, 9, 62
Brooklyn Stars, 9
Brooklyn Tip-Tops, 21
Brosnan, Jim, 142
Brotherhood of Professional Base Ball Players, 138
Brown, Mordecai "Three-Finger," 18, 19, 20
Browne, Byron, 142
Bruce, J.E., 16, 56
Brush, John T., 191
Buckner, Bill, 107
Buffalo Feds, 20
Bunning, Jim, 74, 75, 76
Burdette, Lew, 76
Burke, Chris, 193
Busch Stadium, 195
Bush, "Bullet" Joe, 34
Bush, George W., 129

C

Cadore, Leon, 97
Cain, Bob, 44
California Angels, 56, 57, 71, 82, 108, 112, 133
Callahan, Jim, 17
Camilli, Dolph, 37
Campanella, Roy, 181
Candlestick Park, 73, 108
Canseco, Jose, 117
Caray, Harry, 126
Carew, Rod, 185
Carlton, Steve, 43, 91
Carter, Jimmy, 128
Cartwright, Alexander Joy, 6, 7, 12, 114
Carty, Rico, 108
Cash, Dave, 183
Cepeda, Orlando, 185
Chadwick, Henry, 2, 8, 9
Chamberlain, Elton, 65
Chance, Frank, 18, 19
Chapman, Ray, 25, 58, 59, 164
Chase, Hal, 84

Chicago Cubs, 18, 19, 20, 21, 33, 34, 39, 41, 43, 64, 74, 78, 86, 87, 100, 101, 114, 115, 116, 117, 126, 129, 155, 158, 160, 161, 164, 186, 189, 192, 194, 200
Chicago White Sox, 13, 14, 15, 16, 17, 18, 26, 27, 28, 29, 66, 74, 76, 84, 96, 102, 114, 126, 129, 135, 140, 164, 165, 166, 167, 168, 196, 197, 202
Cicotte, Eddie, 26, 27, 29
Cincinnati Buckeyes, 12
Cincinnati Reds, 12, 13, 15, 26, 27, 37, 38, 43, 57, 64, 65, 70, 72, 73, 74, 76, 84, 88, 90, 92, 93, 108, 114, 116, 117, 126, 130, 132, 145, 149, 152, 153, 166, 190, 194, 195
Citizens Bank Park, 191
Clemens, Roger, 70, 91, 116
Clemente, Roberto, 175, 183
Cleveland Blues, 17
Cleveland Forest Citys, 13
Cleveland Indians, 17, 25, 33, 46, 58, 61, 66, 68, 74, 76, 84, 102, 115, 133, 156, 164, 168, 181, 182, 195, 197
Cleveland Naps, 17, 114
Cleveland Spiders, 16, 68
Clines, Gene, 183
Cobb, Ty, 23, 24, 25, 35, 102, 103, 115, 116, 151, 153
Colavito, Rocky, 108
College Football Hall of Fame, 199
Colorado Rockies, 58
Comiskey, Charles, 26, 27, 28, 139, 196
Comiskey Park, 32, 66, 74, 126, 129, 132, 133, 196, 197
Committee for Statistical Accuracy, 76
Connie Mack Stadium, 195
Connor, Roger, 14, 102
Continental League, 178
Coolidge, Calvin, 20
Coombs, Jack, 34
Cooper, Gary, 104
Cooper, Irving Ben, 142
Coors Field, 99, 113
Corriden, John "Red," 102
Crone, Ray, 86
Cronin, Joe, 54, 72
Crosley Field, 38, 73, 194, 195
Culbertson, Leon, 107
Cummings, Candy, 62
Curtis, Cliff, 89
Cuthbert, Eddie, 10

D
Dahl, Steve, 196
Dallas Cowboys, 95
Davis, Eric, 165
Davis, George "Iron," 92
Davis, Harry, 167
Davis, Jim, 86
Dean, Dizzy, 66, 116, 193
DeBerry, Hank, 45
Delsing, Jim, 44
Dent, Bucky, 107
Detroit Tigers, 16, 18, 19, 24, 44, 61, 75, 76, 79, 91, 102, 108, 114, 116, 145, 149, 158, 176, 196, 202
Dickey, Bill, 72, 101
DiMaggio, Joe, 66, 81, 84, 85, 107, 151, 177
Dinneen, Bill, 114
"Disco Demolition Night," 196
Doby, Larry, 181
Dodger Stadium, 186, 193
Doubleday, Abner, 8
Dressen, Charlie, 48
Drysdale, Don, 79, 91, 147, 176

Durante, Sal, 171
Durocher, Leo, 1, 48, 72

E
Ebbets Field, 37, 38, 48, 72, 115, 127, 181, 194, 195
Ehmke, Howard, 31
Ellis, Dock, 183
Elysian Fields, 6, 7
Erickson, Scott, 87
Erskine, Carl, 86
Evers, Johnny, 18, 19, 100
Exhibition Stadium, 195

F
Face, Roy, 89
Fashion Race Course, 190
Faust, Charles V., 200
Faust, Nancy, 126
Federal League, 20, 21, 28
Feeney, Chub, 54, 116
Fehr, Donald, 148, 149
Feller, Bob, 74, 151, 156, 157
Felsch, Hap, 27, 29
Fenway Park, 1, 18, 19, 41, 46, 47, 54, 93, 117, 194
Ferrell, Rick, 101
Fewster, Chick, 45
Fingers, Rollie, 144, 163
Finley, Charles O., 66, 145
Flood, Curt, 142, 143, 144
Florida Marlins, 89
Flowers, Ben, 86
Floyd, Cliff, 87
Forbes Field, 36, 86, 195
Ford, Gerald, 129, 182, 186
Forsch, Bob, 74
Forsch, Ken, 74
Fort Wayne (Indiana) Kekiongas, 13
Fosse, Ray, 108, 109
Fox, Nellie, 76
Foxx, Jimmie, 72
Franco, Julio, 51
Frazee, Harry, 32, 106
Frick, Ford C., 108, 111

G
Gacioch, Rose, 160
Gaedel, Eddie, 44, 45
Galarraga, Andres, 185
Gallico, Paul, 105
Gandil, Chick, 27, 29
Garagiola, Joe, 107
Garciaparra, Nomar, 165, 187
Gehrig, Lou, 2, 52, 72, 82, 83, 104, 105, 117, 145
Giannoulas, Ted, 198, 199
Gibbons, Jay, 193
Gibson, Bob, 79, 183
Glavine, Tom, 51
Gleason, Roy, 157
Gleason, William "Kid," 27
Glenn, John, 159
Glitter, Gary, 197
Goldsmith, Fred, 62
Gomez, Lefty, 72
Gonzalez, Juan, 185
Gooden, Dwight "Doc," 73
Gossage, Rich "Goose," 112

Gowdy, Hank, 152
Graney, Jack, 164
Great American Ballpark, 195
Green, Dallas, 89
Greenberg, Hank, 137, 142, 158, 168, 169, 175, 176, 177
Greene, Khalil, 42
Gregory, Kathy, 172, 173
Griffey, Ken Jr., 56, 57, 81, 86, 87
Griffey, Ken Sr., 56, 57
Griffith, Clark, 128, 140, 141
Griffith Stadium, 20, 50, 128
Grimes, Burleigh "Old Stubblebeard," 64, 114
Grimm, Charlie, 161
Grove, Lefty, 68
Gullett, Don, 144
Guzman, Jose, 86

H

Haddix, Harvey, 76, 77
Hafey, Chick, 132
Halladay, Roy, 61
Hallahan, Bill, 132
Hall of Fame, 8, 18, 23, 28, 29, 33, 43, 62, 66, 68, 72, 78, 83, 85, 89, 91, 101, 105, 115, 120, 130, 133, 145, 153, 157, 158, 167, 169, 176, 181, 183, 184, 200, 201
Hamm, Mia, 187
Hammaker, Atlee, 133
Harding, Warren, 36
Harridge, William, 45
Harris, Bucky, 50, 93, 140
Harris, Greg, 65
Hartsel, Topsy, 167
Harwell, Ernie, 83
Hawkins, Andy, 76
Hearst, William Randolph, 11
Herman, Floyd, 45
Hernandez, Jackie, 183
Herrmann, August, 16
Hershiser, Orel, 81, 90, 91
Hicks, Tom, 137
Hoak, Don, 108
Hodges, Russ, 49
Hoerner, Joe, 142
Hofferth, Stew, 73
Hoffman, Tevor, 168
Holder, Johnny, 190
Holmes, Oliver Wendell, 21, 141
Holtzman, Jerome, 168
Homer the Brave, 199
Homestead Gray, 183
Hooton, Burt, 199
Hoover, Herbert, 33
Hopper, DeWolfe, 11
Horlen, Joe, 165
Hornsby, Rogers, 35, 84
Houston Astros, 58, 69, 71, 74, 76, 87, 90, 113, 116, 135, 137, 149, 180, 193, 194
Houston Colt .45s, 76, 180
Howard, Elston, 181
Howard J. Lamade Stadium, 161
Howser, Dick, 112
Hubbell, Carl, 72, 73, 81, 88, 89
Hudson, Orlando, 173
Huggins, Miller, 59, 105
Hulbert, William A., 14, 15, 140, 141
Hunt, Ron, 58
Hunter, Jim "Catfish," 144, 145

Hurley, Ed, 44
Huston, Tillinghast, 31

I

Indianapolis Hoosiers, 20

J

Jackson, "Shoeless" Joe, 24, 27, 29
Jackson, Bo, 81, 94, 95
Jackson, Reggie, 2, 91
Jack Murphy Stadium, 127, 198
Jacobs Field, 195
James, Bill, 92, 93
Jenkins, Ferguson, 43
Johnson, Alex, 108
Johnson, Ban, 15, 16, 26, 28, 102, 103
Johnson, Jerry, 142
Johnson, Ken, 76
Johnson, Lyndon, 194
Johnson, Walter, 20, 23, 24, 28, 33, 75, 79, 114, 115, 128, 152
Johnston, Joe, 197
Jones, Davy, 24

K

Kaline, Al, 108
Kansas City Athletics, 66, 115, 180
Kansas City Monarchs, 66, 180
Kansas City Royals, 57, 94, 95, 112, 135, 180
Kapler, Gabe, 165
Kauff, Benny, 20
Keeler, William "Wee Willie," 17, 84
Keen, Jim, 197
Kelly, Gene, 127
Kelly, Mike "King," 10, 11
Keltner, Ken, 84
Kennedy, John F., 128
Kenosha (Wisconsin) Comets, 160
Kile, Darryl, 113
Kilgus, Paul, 86
Kim, Byung-Hyun, 58
King, Stephen, 107
Kingdome, 87, 116
Klem, Bill, 130
Knickerbocker Base Ball Club of New York, 6, 7, 12
Konstanty, Jim, 168
Korakuen Stadium, 53
Koufax, Sandy, 68, 70, 78, 147, 175, 176, 177
Koy, Ernie, 72
Krakauskas, Joe, 84
Kroc, Ray, 198
Kuhn, Bowie, 54, 108, 142

L

Labine, Clem, 48, 115
Lajoie, Napoleon, 17, 102, 103
Landes, Stan, 108, 109
Landis, Kenesaw Mountain, 21, 25, 28, 29, 114, 155, 178
Lannin, Joe, 92
Lardner, Ring, 27, 36
League of Their Own, A, 161
League Park, 164
LeFlore, Ron, 196
Lena Blackburne Rubbing Mud, 131
Leonard, Buck, 183
Lewis, Duffy, 19
Linebrink, Scott, 51

Little League World Series, 161
Lockman, Whitney, 48
Lonborg, Jim, 172
Long, Dale, 81, 86, 114
Lopez, Javier, 185
Los Angeles Angels, 111, 180
Los Angeles Dodgers, 73, 78, 79, 81, 87, 90, 91, 111, 115, 117, 144, 147, 149, 157, 165, 172, 187, 199
Los Angeles Raiders, 94, 95
Louisville Grays, 15
Lynn, Fred, 133
Lyons, Steve, 202

M

Mack, Connie, 16, 25, 34, 132, 134, 139, 195
MacPhail, Larry, 38, 113
Madison Square Garden, 191
Major League Baseball Players Association, 144, 146, 148
Mantle, Mickey, 1, 50, 194
Maranville, Walter J. "Rabbit," 92
Marichal, Juan, 185
Maris, Roger, 30, 110, 111, 171
Marquard, Rube, 88
Martin, Billy, 112
Martinez, Pedro, 185
Mathewson, Christy, 23, 34, 115, 151, 152, 153
Mattingly, Don, 81, 86
May, Carlos, 165
Mayberry, John, 135
Mays, Carl, 58, 59
Mays, Willie, 1, 48, 108, 115, 116
McAfee Coliseum, 192
McCarthy, Joe, 105
McCarver, Tim, 142
McCaskill, Kirk, 57
McClelland, Tim, 112
McCormick, Frank, 73
McCormick, Harry "Moose," 100
McDaniel, Lindy, 86
McFarland, Herm, 17
McGowen, Roscoe, 37
McGraw, John, 16, 34, 93, 132, 152, 200
McGwire, Mark, 111, 171
McLain, Denny, 61, 79, 116
McMillan, Roy, 108
McMullin, Fred, 27, 29
McPhee, John "Bid," 166, 167
Meadows, Lee, 96
Medich, George "Doc," 182
Melhuse, Adam, 192
Memorial Stadium, 195
Mendoza, Mario, 56
Merkle, Fred, 100, 101
Messersmith, Andy, 144
Metrodome, 197
Meusel, Bob, 133
Miller, Marvin, 146, 148
Miller, Ray, 83
Miller, Stu, 76, 108, 109
Mills Commission, 8
Milnar, Al, 84
Milwaukee Braves, 15, 34, 45, 68, 72, 73, 74, 76, 77, 86, 89, 90, 92, 93, 95, 96, 152, 164, 180, 181, 193
Milwaukee Brewers, 16, 87, 96, 116, 149, 180
Minnesota North Stars, 197

Minnesota Twins, 69, 86, 87, 117, 176, 177, 180, 193, 195, 197
Minor, Ryan, 83
Mr. Met, 199
Monday, Rick, 115, 186
Montreal Expos, 43, 58, 65, 87, 90, 116, 149, 180, 186
Morris, Hal, 65, 117
Most Valuable Player, 118
Mulcahy, Hugh, 156
Mullane, Tony, 64, 65
Municipal Stadium, 84, 182
Murray, Eddie, 89
Murtaugh, Danny, 183
Musial, Stan, 108, 127

N

"Na Na Hey Hey Kiss Him Goodbye," 197
National Association, 62
National Association of Base Ball Players (NABBP), 7, 13
National Association of Professional Base Ball Players, 13
National Commission, 16, 27, 28
National Football League, 95
National League, 9, 14, 15, 16, 17, 18, 20, 21, 25, 34, 35, 48, 54, 63, 64, 68, 70, 75, 78, 84, 88, 90, 91, 92, 93, 96, 100, 101, 108, 109, 114, 116, 132, 138, 139, 140, 152, 153, 165, 168, 172, 178, 180, 181, 184, 185, 186, 193, 199, 200
Negro leagues, 66, 180, 181, 183
Newark Peps, 20
Newcombe, Don, 48, 181
New York Base Ball Club, 7
New York Giants, 18, 30, 34, 48, 64, 73, 74, 88, 92, 93, 96, 100, 101, 114, 115, 132, 138, 152, 169, 191, 193, 194, 200
New York Highlanders, 17, 18, 19, 84, 115
New York Mets, 39, 43, 51, 71, 73, 74, 75, 87, 89, 91, 115, 129, 180
New York Mutuals, 13, 15, 62
New York Yankees, 1, 2, 17, 18, 23, 30, 31, 32, 33, 34, 35, 50, 52, 54, 58, 59, 64, 69, 74, 76, 83, 84, 85, 86, 95, 101, 104, 105, 106, 110, 111, 112, 114, 115, 129, 133, 144, 145, 149, 164, 165, 168, 169, 171, 179, 181, 182, 194, 199, 200
Norworth, Jack, 127
Nuxhall, Joe, 70

O

O'Brien, Buck, 19
O'Connor, Jack, 102
O'Malley, Walter, 147
O'Rourke, Jim, 14, 114
Oakland Athletics, 91, 116, 117, 145, 149, 163, 180, 193
Oeschger, Joe, 97, 114
Oglivie, Ben, 96
Oh, Sadaharu, 52, 53
Oliver, Al, 183
Oriole Park at Camden Yards, 83, 194, 195
Ott, Mel, 88
Overall, Orval, 18
Owens, Jesse, 72
Owens, Mickey, 115

P

Pacific Bell Park, 111
Paciorek, Tom, 56
Paige, Leroy "Satchel," 66, 183
Parcells, Bill, 134
Park, Chan Ho, 87
Patkin, Max, 198

Patterson, Red, 50
Patterson, Roy, 17
Pepe, Maria, 161
Perez, Tony, 185
Perlman, Itzhak, 129
Pesky, Johnny, 107
Petco Park, 51
Pfiester, John, 18
Philadelphia Athletics, 13, 14, 15, 16, 17, 25, 34, 46, 51, 93, 114, 128, 134, 139, 152, 164, 167, 200
Philadelphia Keystones, 10
Philadelphia Phillies, 17, 36, 38, 39, 43, 56, 63, 65, 68, 74, 75, 76, 96, 114, 142, 149, 156, 167, 183, 192, 193
Phillie Phanatic, 199
Piniella, Lou, 199
Pipp, Wally, 104
Pirate Parrot, 199
Pittsburgh Alleghenys, 87
Pittsburgh Crawfords, 66
Pittsburgh Pirates, 1, 18, 25, 36, 56, 65, 76, 77, 86, 89, 93, 114, 115, 116, 123, 156, 170, 183, 184
Plank, Eddie, 34
Players League, 139
Polo Grounds, 15, 30, 31, 48, 59, 72, 74, 89, 93, 96, 100, 127, 169, 191, 194, 195
Porter, Chuck, 96
Post, Wally, 108
Powell, Lewis, 143
Pulliam, Harry, 16, 100

Q

Queen, 197
Quinn, Jack, 51

R

"Rock and Roll, Part 2," 197
Racine (Wisconsin) Belles, 160
Ramirez, Manny, 52, 185
Raposo, Joe, 195
Raymond, Dave, 199
Raymond, Harold "Tubby," 199
Ready, Randy, 65
Renteria, Edgar, 185
Reulbach, Ed, 18
Reuschel, Rick, 94
Reynolds, Allie, 169
Rice, Grantland, 36
Rice, Jim, 201
Richmond, John, 14
Rickey, Branch, 9, 153, 175, 178, 179, 180, 181
Riley, Pat, 134
Ripken, Cal Jr., 2, 81, 82, 83, 104, 117
Risberg, Swede, 27, 29
Riverfront Stadium, 108, 129
Roberts, Robin, 68, 69
Robinson, Frank, 108, 116, 182
Robinson, Jackie, 142, 175, 180, 181, 185
Robinson, Rachel, 182
Rockford (Illinois) Forest Citys, 10, 13
Rockford (Illinois) Peaches, 160
Rodriguez, Alex, 117, 137, 185
Rogers, Steve, 186
Rojas, Cookie, 142
Roland, Toby, 192
Roosevelt, Franklin D., 38, 151, 155
Rose, Pete, 76, 84, 108, 109, 116, 117
Roth, Alice, 193

Royals, 57, 94, 95, 112, 113, 135, 149, 180, 181
Rudolph, Dick, 92, 93
Ruppert, Jacob, 31, 105
Rusie, Amos, 114
Ruth, Babe, 2, 23, 30, 31, 32, 33, 35, 46, 52, 72, 84, 105, 106, 110, 111, 114, 115, 116, 129, 132, 133, 151, 164, 176
Ryan, Nolan, 2, 70, 71, 74, 78, 94, 135, 137

S

Safeco Field, 195
Sain, Johnny, 181
Sanders, Deion, 81, 95
Sanders, Reggie, 65
Sanguillen, Manny, 183
San Diego Chicken, 198
San Diego Padres, 42, 91, 116, 135, 168, 180, 198
San Francisco 49ers, 95
San Francisco Giants, 43, 90, 111, 116, 117, 165
Saucier, Frank, 44
Sawyer, Eddie, 63
Schacht, Al, 198
Schroeder, Dorothy, 161
Seattle Mariners, 56, 57, 86, 87, 91, 95, 116, 117, 193, 195
Seattle Pilots, 180
Seaver, Tom, 68, 81, 91, 96
Seitz, Peter, 144, 145
Selig, Bud, 54, 148, 149
Seymour, Harold, 128
Shaughnessy, Dan, 107
Shawkey, Bob, 31, 34
Shea Stadium, 75, 89, 91, 129
Shibe Park, 46, 193
Shotton, Burt, 134
Siegel, Brian, 171
Simmons, Al, 72, 86
Sinatra, Frank, 195
Sisler, George, 35, 84, 151, 153
Slaughter, Enos, 107
Smith, Al, 84
Smith, Lee, 168
Smith, Red, 49
Smith, Sherry, 33
Smithson, Mike, 86
Soderholm, Eric, 135
Soriano, Alfonso, 117
Sosa, Sammy, 185
South Bend (Indiana) Blue Sox, 160
South End Grounds, 93
Spahn, Warren, 86
Spalding, Albert Goodwill, 14, 15, 166
Speaker, Tris, 18, 19
Sportsman's Park, 35, 44
Springer, Dennis, 111
St. Louis Browns, 14, 16, 21, 26, 35, 44, 51, 66, 84, 102, 166, 179, 197
St. Louis Cardinals, 35, 37, 42, 64, 68, 70, 73, 79, 81, 86, 87, 91, 99, 107, 111, 116, 117, 132, 142, 143, 146, 178, 179, 200
St. Louis Terriers, 21
Stallard, Tracey, 110, 111
Stallings, George, 92
Stargell, Willie, 183
Steam, 197
Stengel, Casey, 168, 169
Stennett, Rennie, 183
Stevens, Harry M., 190
Stobbs, Chuck, 50

Stotz, Carl, 161
Sunday, Art, 56, 130
Super Bowl, 95
Suzuki, Ichiro, 35, 172
Suzuki, Yasumiro, 52

T

"Take Me Out to the Ball Game," 125, 126, 127
Taft, William Howard, 128
Tampa Bay Buccaneers, 95
Tampa Bay Devil Rays, 200
Tatis, Fernando, 81, 87
Taylor, Zach, 44
Tejada, Miguel, 185
Temple, Johnny, 108
Temple Cup championship, 138
Texas Rangers, 56, 71, 86, 111, 137, 180
Thayer, Ernest Lawrence, 11
Thayer, Frederick, 114
"There Used to Be a Ballpark," 195
"The Shot Heard Round the World," 48
"The Star-Spangled Banner," 125, 127
Thomas, Fred, 129
Thompson, Ryan, 89
Thomson, Bobby, 2, 48, 49
Thorpe, Jim, 74
Tiant, Luis, 54
Tinker, Joe, 18, 19, 20
Tokyo Giants, 53
Toney, Fred, 74
Toronto Blue Jays, 61, 82, 117, 195
Torre, Joe, 146
Trojans, Troy, 14
Troy (New York) Haymakers, 13
Truman, Harry, 128
Twain, Mark, 17
Tyler, Lefty, 92, 93

V

Valenzuela, Fernando, 73
Vance, Dazzy, 45
Vander Meer, Johnny, 38, 72
Van Slyke, Andy, 65
Vaughn, Hippo, 33, 74
Veeck, Bill, 44, 66, 126, 135, 142, 165, 196, 197
Veeck, Mary Francis, 135
Veeck, Mike, 196
Veterans Stadium, 199
Vincent, Fay, 111
Voiselle, Bill, 164
Von Tilzer, Albert, 127

W

"We Are the Champions," 197
"We Will Rock You," 197
Wagner, Honus, 1, 23, 24, 25, 115, 123, 170, 171
Waitt, Charlie, 166
Walters, Bucky, 37
Ward, Arch, 132, 133, 138, 139, 142
Warhop, Jack, 23
Washington (D.C.) Olympics, 13
Washington Nationals, 13, 87, 90, 117
Washington Park, 21
Washington Senators, 16, 20, 30, 31, 34, 50, 66, 81, 84, 93, 105, 111, 114, 128, 140, 141, 143, 152, 180
Weaver, Buck, 27, 29

Weeghman, Charles, 21, 74, 129, 189, 192
Wehmeier, Herman, 86
Whitney, Harry Payne, 191
Williams, Claude "Lefty," 27, 29
Williams, Ken, 35
Williams, Ted, 41, 46, 47, 151, 158, 159, 183
Williamsport Bills, 202
Wilson, Hack, 41, 66
Wilson, Jimmy, 38, 39
Wilson, Woodrow, 154, 155
Worcester Ruby Legs, 14
World Series, 1905, 152
World Series, 1906, 18
World Series, 1907, 18
World Series, 1908, 126
World Series, 1910, 34
World Series, 1911, 34, 200
World Series, 1913, 34
World Series, 1914, 34, 152
World Series, 1916, 33
World Series, 1918, 33, 155
World Series, 1919, 26, 27, 28, 29
World Series, 1924, 93, 152
World Series, 1926, 35
World Series, 1931, 64
World Series, 1934, 176
World Series, 1945, 158
World Series, 1946, 106, 107
World Series, 1950, 69
World Series, 1953, 50
World Series, 1965, 176, 177
World Series, 1967, 79, 142
World Series, 1968, 79
World Series, 1969, 71
World Series, 1971, 184
World Series, 1976, 57
World Series, 1985, 37
World Series, 1986, 107
World Series, 1987, 197
World Series, 1988, 91
World Series, 1991, 197
World Series, 1992, 95
World Series, 1994, 82, 149
World Series, 2001, 129
World Series, 2004, 99
Wright, Harry, 12, 13, 126, 130
Wrigley, P.K., 39, 160
Wrigley, William, 189
Wrigley Field, 2, 39, 43, 114, 115, 116, 126, 129, 186, 189, 192, 194
Wynn, Early, 68

Y

Yakult Swallows, 52
Yankee Stadium, 23, 30, 31, 86, 104, 105, 110, 111, 112, 113, 115, 129, 133
Yastrzemski, Carl, 79, 116
Yomiuri Giants, 52, 53
Young, Anthony, 81, 89
Young, Denton "Cy," 17, 24, 61, 68, 114, 152
Young, Matt, 76
Youngblood, Joel, 43

Z

Zachary, Tom, 31

Acknowledgments & Picture Credits

This book would not have been possible without the creativity, sound judgment and tireless work of my collaborators at Hydra Publishing. The scope of the book was greatly enhanced by the imagination of Ward Calhoun, senior editor at Hydra Publishing. Many thanks to Russell Wolinsky, Rachael Lanicci, and Glenn Novak, for keeping me honest. Thanks also to James Buckley Jr. and Molly Morrison for bringing me onboard. Naturally, this project would have been difficult to complete without the understanding and support of my wife, Carolyn, and my children, Rachel and Jack. Finally, to Robert L. Fischer, for knowing the answers to all of my baseball questions. Many others contributed ideas, time, advice and encouragement. They include William Taaffe, Michael Teitelbaum, Elliott Kalb, Nick Friedman, Alan Schwarz, John Rolfe, Richard Klein and Bob Woods. To all of them, and to numerous other friends and associates who shared my vision, my deep and abiding thanks.

The author and publisher also offer thanks to those closely involved in the creation of this volume: consultant Russell Wolinsky at the National Baseball Hall of Fame and Museum; Ellen Nanney, Senior Brand Manager and Katie Mann, with Smithsonian Business Ventures; Collins Reference executive editor Donna Sanzone, editor Lisa Hacken, and editorial assistant Stephanie Meyers; Hydra Publishing president Sean Moore, publishing director Karen Prince, editorial director Aaron Murray, art director Brian MacMullen, designers Erika Lubowicki, Ken Crossland, Eunho Lee, Pleum Chenaphun, La Tricia Watford, editors Lisa Purcell, Amber Rose, Mike Smith, Rachael Lanicci, Kristin Maffei, copyeditor Suzanne Lander, picture researcher Ben Dewalt, and proofreader Glenn Novak.

The following abbreviations are used: SI—Smithsonian Institution; LoC—Library of Congress; PR— Photo Researchers; AP—Associated Press; Wi— Wikimedia; SXC Stock Exchng; IS—Istockphoto, SS—Shutterstock

(t=top; b=bottom; l=left; r=right; c=center)

Cover
LOC; SS/ Suzanne Tucker; SS/ Pierre E. Debbas

Introduction
IVt SS/Aun-Juli Riddle IVb SS/Scott Lomenzo IV-Vbgt SS/ Dragan Trifunovic IV-Vbg SS/Steve Degenhardt V SS/Bobby Deal; RealDealPhoto VI-1 SS/Joy Brown 1 SS/Robert Pernell 2 SS/Elias H. Debbas II 3 CA

Chapter 1: Baseball's Early Days
4 SS/Suzanne Tucker 5bg Jl 5r LOC 6 AP 7 LOC/Currier & Ives 8 LOC/Matthew B. Brady 9 LOC 10 LOC/Sarony, Major, & Knapp Lith/Otto Boetticher 11 LOC/B.M. Clineddinst 12 LOC 13 LOC/Tucharber, Walkley, & Moellman 14 LOC 15 LOC 16bl LOC 16tr LOC 17 LOC/American Tobacco Co. 18 LOC/ American Tobacco Co. 19tl LOC/Geo. R. Lawrence Co. 19br LOC/American Tobacco Co. 20 LOC 21 LOC/W.O. Breckon Studios; Federal League Baseball Club of Brooklyn

Chapter 2: Babe Ruth and the Golden Age
22 LOC/The Peale Museum 23 LOC/J242488 U.S. Copyright Office 24 LOC 25 LOC 25 LOC 26 LOC/D. Buchner & Co. 27tl LOC 27br LOC 28 LOC/H101640 U.S. Copyright Office 29 AP 30 AP 31 LOC 32 LOC/American Memory/ Chicago Daily News 33 LOC 34 LOC/Honest Long Cut and Miners Extra brands 35 AP 36 LOC 37 LOC 38 AP 39 AP/Beth A. Keiser

Chapter 3: The Hitters
40 AP 41 WI 42 SS/JustASC 43 AP 44 AP 45 LOC/American Memory/Chicago Daily News 47 AP/Ted Sande 48 AP 49 AP/Marty Lederhandler 50 AP 51 AP/Lenny Ignelzi 52 AP 53 AP 55 AP/Harry Harris 56 AP/Kathy Willens 57 AP/Al Behrman 58 AP/David J. Phillip 59 LOC

Chapter 4: The Pitchers
60 AP 61 SS/Eugene Buchko 62 AP/AP National Baseball Hall of Fame 63 AP 64 AP 65 LOC 67 AP 68 LOC 69 AP 70 AP 71 AP/Jch 72 AP 73 AP 74 AP 75 AP 77 AP 78 AP/Harry Hall 79 AP

Chapter 5: Streaks and Feats
80 AP 81 AP/Tom Gannam 82 AP/Fred Jewell 83 AP/ Roberto Borea 85 AP/Tom Sande 86 AP/Mike Albans 87 AP/Gary Stewart 88 AP 89 AP/Kathy Willens 90 AP/Paul Sukumas 91 AP/Ray Stubblebine 92 LOC 93 LOC 94 AP/Diana Smith 95 AP/Bob Galbraith 96 LOC 97 AP/John Swart

Chapter 6: Legends, Myths, and Lore
98 AP/Sue Ogrocki 99 SS/Richard Fitzer 100 LOC/American Tobacco Co. 101 AP 102 LOC 103 LOC 104 AP/Murray Becker 105 AP 106 CA 107 AP 109 AP 110 AP 111 AP/Julie Jacobson 112 AP/Kevork Djansezian 113 AP/David Zalubowski

Ready Reference
114-15bg SS/Mike Liu 115 CA 116 SS/Richard Coencas 117 SS/ Jason Figert 121 WI 122 LOC 123 LOC

Chapter 7: Customs, Rituals, and Traditions
124 SS/Scott Lomenzo 125 SS/Lisa Vivona 126 AP 127 AP/Joel Zwink 128 AP 129 AP/Kathy Willens 130 LOC 131 AP/Coke Whitworth 132 AP 133 AP/Harry Harris 134 SS/ Eugene Buchko 135 AP/Ted S. Warren

Chapter 8: The Business of Baseball
136 AP/Donna McWilliam 137 SS/Mike Aunger 138 LOC 139 LOC/Goodwin & Co. 140 AP 141 AP 143 AP 144 AP 145 AP/ Ray Stubblebine 146 AP 147 AP/Dfs, Staff 148 AP/Stephen J. Carrera 149 AP/Michael S. Greene

Chapter 9: The War Years
150 AP 151 LOC/Leslie-Judge Co, NY 152 LOC 153 LOC 154 LOC 155 AP 156 AP 157 SS/Tony Campbell 158 AP 159 AP 160 AP 161 SS/Terry Poche

Chapter 10: The Changing Game
162 AP 163 SS/Chris Silvey 164-5 LOC 166 SS/Mike Liu 167bl AP 167tr LOC/American Tobacco Co. 168 AP/Denis Poroy 169 AP/Jeff Robertson 170 AP/Kathy Willens 171 SS/Jason Figert 172 SS/Alan C. Heison 173 SS/Graca Victoria

Chapter 11: Trailblazers, Heroes, and Icons
174 AP 175 LOC 177 AP 179 AP 180 LOC/Kansas City Call Newspaper 181 AP 182 AP/Cleveland Plain Dealer/Dorkse 183 AP/HMB 184 AP 185 SS/Elias H. Debbas 186-7 AP/ James Roark, Los Angeles Herald Examiner

Chapter 12: The Ballpark Experience
188 SS/Jenny Solomon 189 SS/Joy Brown 190 AP/Julie Jacobson 191 AP/Ed Betz 192 AP/Morry Gash 193 AP/James A. Finley 194 AP 195 SS/Heath Oldham 196 AP/Fred Jewell 197 AP/Jim Mone 198 AP/Denis Poroy 199 AP/Nanine Hartzenbusch 200 LOC/American Tobacco Company 201 AP/Leonard Ignelzi 202-3 AP/Mark Humphrey

At the Smithsonian
211 SI/Eric Long

Cover
SS/Aun-Juli Riddle LOC SS/Suzanne Tucker SS/Pierre E. Debbas LOC